D1798012

Public Emotions

Also by the editors

Perri 6
MANAGING NETWORKS OF TWENTY FIRST CENTURY ORGANISATIONS
(*co-author*)

BEYOND 'DELIVERY': POLICY IMPLEMENTATION AS SENSE-MAKING AND
SETTLEMENT
(*co-author*)

E-GOVERNANCE: STYLES OF POLITICAL JUDGMENT IN THE INFORMATION
AGE POLITY

TOWARDS HOLISTIC GOVERNANCE: THE NEW REFORM AGENDA
(*co-author*)

Susannah Radstone
SWEET DREAMS (*editor*)

MEMORY AND METHODOLOGY (*editor*)

REGIMES OF MEMORY (*co-editor*)

CONTESTED PASTS: THE POLITICS OF MEMORY (*co-editor*)

CULTURE AND THE UNCONSCIOUS (*co-editor*)

ON MEMORY AND CONFESSION: THE SEXUAL POLITICS OF TIME

Corinne Squire
CULTURE IN PSYCHOLOGY (*editor*)

MORALITY USA (*co-author*)

HIV IN SOUTH AFRICA

LINES OF NARRATIVE (*co-editor*)

Amal Treacher
THE DYNAMICS OF ADOPTION (*co-editor*)

LINES OF NARRATIVE (*co-editor*)

Public Emotions

Edited by

Perri 6
Nottingham Trent University
Susannah Radstone
University of East London
Corinne Squire
University of East London
Amal Treacher
University of Nottingham

Selection and editorial matter © Perri 6, Susannah Radstone, Corinne Squire and Amal Treacher 2007
Individual chapters © their authors 2007

All rights reserved. No reproduction, copy or transmission of this publication may be made without written permission.

No paragraph of this publication may be reproduced, copied or transmitted save with written permission or in accordance with the provisions of the Copyright, Designs and Patents Act 1988, or under the terms of any licence permitting limited copying issued by the Copyright Licensing Agency, 90 Tottenham Court Road, London W1T 4LP.

Any person who does any unauthorized act in relation to this publication may be liable to criminal prosecution and civil claims for damages.

The authors have asserted their rights to be identified as the authors of this work in accordance with the Copyright, Designs and Patents Act 1988.

First published 2007 by
PALGRAVE MACMILLAN
Houndmills, Basingstoke, Hampshire RG21 6XS and
175 Fifth Avenue, New York, N. Y. 10010
Companies and representatives throughout the world

PALGRAVE MACMILLAN is the global academic imprint of the Palgrave Macmillan division of St. Martin's Press, LLC and of Palgrave Macmillan Ltd. Macmillan® is a registered trademark in the United States, United Kingdom and other countries. Palgrave is a registered trademark in the European Union and other countries.

ISBN-13: 978–0–230–00719–2   hardback
ISBN-10: 0–230–00719–8   hardback

This book is printed on paper suitable for recycling and made from fully managed and sustained forest sources.

A catalogue record for this book is available from the British Library.

Library of Congress Cataloging-in-Publication Data
Public emotions / edited by Perri 6 ... [et al.]
       p. cm.
    Includes bibliographical references and index.
    ISBN-13: 978–0–230–00719–2 (cloth)
    ISBN-10: 0–230–00719–8 (cloth)
    1. Emotions. I. 6, Perri, 1960-

BF531.P83 2007
152.4–dc22   2006049862

10   9   8   7   6   5   4   3   2   1
16 15 14 13 12 11 10 09 08 07

Printed and bound in Great Britain by
Antony Rowe Ltd, Chippenham and Eastbourne

Contents

List of Figures and Pictures

Chapter 1

Chapter 9

Acknowledgements

The editors would like to thank, first, all contributors to this volume, for their creative engagement with the book's theme, and their painstaking work in readying their chapters for publication. We also owe a great debt to our editor Jill Lake and her assistant Melanie Blair at Palgrave, who have been unfailingly supportive and helpful about this endeavour.

We are extremely grateful to the participants in the *Matters of Feeling* seminar series, out of which this book grew, and to *Economy and Society* for funding meetings of this study group. Participants in the earlier *Affect, Ethics and Citizenship* seminar series also had a powerful influence on this book's concerns. In particular, we would like to acknowledge the thought-provoking, insightful and generous contributions of the late Ian Craib, who was involved with this project at its beginning.

Notes on the Contributors

Perri 6 is Professor of Social Policy at Nottingham Trent University. He is author or co-author of more than 20 books and numerous articles. He is well-known for his contribution to the development of the neo-Durkheimian institutional theory. His recent books include *Managing networks of twenty first century organisations* (with N Goodwin, E Peck and F Freeman, 2006), *Beyond 'delivery': policy implementation as sensemaking and settlement* (with E Peck, 2006), *E-governance: styles of political judgment in the information age polity* (2004), and *Towards holistic governance: the new reform agenda* (with D Leat, K Seltzer and G Stoker, 2002), and he is currently working on another book to be published in 2007 with Christine Bellamy and Charles Raab on the tensions between joined-up government and confidentiality.

Andrew Cooper is Professor of Social Work at the University of East London and the Tavistock Clinic. He is also a practising psychoanalytic psychotherapist who has always taken an interest in the application of psychoanalytic thinking within the public sphere, and in the development of cross-disciplinary theoretical models of psycho-social phenomena.

Stephan Feuchtwang is a professorial research associate of the Department of Anthropology, London School of Economics. His current research interest is an anthropology of history, which he is currently pursuing by enquiry into the transmission of grievous loss and which in turn will lead him to joint projects of research on self-realisation, its hopes and ambivalence, its frustration, and its substantiation at the expense of 'others'. His main area of research has been China and Taiwan, but now it includes Germany.

Stephen Frosh is Pro-Vice-Master, Professor of Psychology and Director of the Centre for Psychosocial Studies at Birkbeck College, University of London. He was previously Consultant Clinical Psychologist and Vice Dean in the Child and Family Department at the Tavistock Clinic. His most recent books are *The Politics of Psychoanalysis* (1999), *Young Masculinities* (with Ann Phoenix and Rob Pattman, 2002), *After Words* (2002), *Key Concepts in Psychoanalysis* (2002), *Critical Narrative Analysis in Psychology* (with Peter Emerson, 2004), *Hate and the 'Jewish Science':*

Anti-Semitism, Nazism and Psychoanalysis (2005) and the second edition of *For and Against Psychoanalysis* (2006).

Hélène Joffe is a social and health psychologist in the department of psychology, University College London. She has written extensively on the emotional and symbolic aspects of the human response to risk. She wrote the book *Risk and 'the Other'* (1999) and her most recent papers include H Joffe and C Staerkle (2007) 'The centrality of the self-control ethos in western aspersions regarding outgroups: a social representational analysis of stereotype content' in *Culture & Psycholology* and P Washer and H Joffe (2006) The 'hospital superbug': Social representations of MRSA in *Social Science & Medicine*.

Susannah Radstone is Reader in Cultural Studies at the University of East London. She writes on cultural theory, particularly psychoanalysis and memory, and on contemporary film and literature. She is a member of the Memory and Narrative editorial group (Transaction Books) and of the Raphael Samuel History Centre, and co-organises the Cultural Memory seminar (Institute of Romance Studies/Raphael Samuel History Centre) and the annual international Culture and the Unconscious Conference (UEL/Tavistock Clinic). Recent publications include *Contested Pasts: The Politics of Memory* and *Regimes of Memory* (both ed., with Katharine Hodgkin, 2003); *Memory and Methodology* (ed. 2000); 'Trauma Dossier' *Screen*, 42.2, Summer 2001. Forthcoming co-edited collections include *Culture and the Unconscious*. She is currently completing, *On Memory and Confession: The Sexual Politics of Time*, and *Mapping Memory* (co-edited with Bill Schwarz).

Paul Richards is an anthropologist with many years of research experience in West Africa. He currently holds the chair of Technology and Agrarian Development at Wageningen University, The Netherlands and is Professor of Anthropology at University College London. His current research focuses on the association between unemployment and insurgency, and on terrorism as ritual. He also carries out research on food security issues and the right to food. He recently edited the collection *No peace, no war: an anthropology of contemporary armed conflicts* (2005).

Michael Rustin is a Professor of Sociology at the University of East London, where he was for ten years Dean of the Faculty of Social Sciences, and is a Visiting Professor at the Tavistock Clinic. He has written widely on psychoanalysis and its social and cultural applications, as well as on politics and social theory. His books include *The Good*

Society and the Inner World (1991), *Reason and Unreason: Psychoanalysis, Science and Politics* (2001), and with Margaret Rustin, *Narratives of Love and Loss: Studies in Modern Children's Fiction* (1989/2001) and *Mirror to Nature: Drama Psychoanalysis and Society* (2002). He is currently writing a book on the methods and philosophy of psychoanalytic research. He is a founding editor of *Soundings*.

Corinne Squire is Reader in Social Sciences and Co-director of the Centre for Narrative Research at the University of East London. She is the author of *HIV in South Africa: Talking about the big thing* (2007), and *Morality USA* (with Ellen Friedman, 1998), and editor of *Culture in Psychology* (2000), and *The Uses of Narrative* (with Molly Andrews, Shelley Sclater and Amal Treacher, 2004).

Amal Treacher is Associate Professor in Psychosocial Studies at Nottingham University. She was a co-ordinator for the longstanding conference *Psychoanalysis and the Public Sphere;* this conference concentrated on issues, and understandings, of affect in public life. Since completing her PhD, Amal Treacher has concentrated on developing Psychosocial Studies as a theoretical discipline. Her research has concentrated on issues of children's identity, ethnicity – especially mixed-heritage identity and adoption. She is a co-editor (with Ilan Katz) of *Dynamics of Adoption* (2000).

Introduction

Perri 6, Corinne Squire, Amal Treacher and Susannah Radstone

The place of public emotions

Public life is full of emotions. Understanding better how this emotionality works is an urgent challenge for the sciences and the humanities. Without such understanding, there is limited scope for comprehending patterns of public speech and action generally, or for limiting conflict. This book presents new thinking from several disciplines and traditions, to contribute to a conversation on how best to develop our understanding of public emotions.

According to Cicero, the Roman republican revolutionary, Gaius Gracchus, hired a slave to play notes on a flute, in order to guide his emotional pitch during his speeches, since his extravagant tears, appeals and rage sometimes became too much even for Roman sensibilities. Gracchus was not manipulating his own or his audience's emotions insincerely. Rather, he was trying to rein in his own emotional performance to conform to Roman conceptions of public life, which themselves allowed more demonstrative emotion in public speech than do ours (Connors, 1997).

Much more recently, the Iraq conflict has demonstrated a specific and highly necessary emotional lexicon. Exhibitions of public sympathy in Britain for the plight of Ken Bigley, the hostage taken in Iraq, ranging from those of different family members and fellow-Liverpudlians, to fellow citizens such as members of the Muslim Council of Great Britain, have been as definitive of the politics of inter-continental confrontation as have the highly staged emotional performances of the late Mr al-Zarqawi's group, filming themselves beheading their captives for a worldwide audience. Indeed, no account of the conflict exclusively in terms of oil interests, radical Islamic revolt, American aggrandisement or

1

media power can be adequate, if it does not also show the emotions implicated with these forces.

Public discussions of contested issues are now heavily imbricated with emotion, even within superficially emotionless areas such as technology and law. In much of the developed world, issues of technological, food and environmental risk have become the occasions for public fear. In such conflicts as those over the MMR vaccine, genetically modified crops, mobile phones and power lines, governments must try to manage fear in the process of making policy. Public fears about crime have been both responded to and reinforced by political discourses that link crime with fear, and by many governments' fear-driven policies on longer sentencing and larger prison populations. Politics are also now at times grief-saturated: in one well-known example, British Prime Minister Blair presented himself as empathising strongly with public grief on the occasion of the death of Diana, Princess of Wales. Politicians, though, rarely confess their own emotional state if they fear this vulnerability might expose them to ridicule. Yet in 1998 then Norwegian Prime Minister, Kjell Magne Bondevik, received much public praise for his openness and candour about taking time off work for stress and depression, and in the UK too political figures now reflect commonly, if retrospectively, on their emotional travails. Perhaps these events betoken a more general change in political sensibility. In law, too, emotionality seems on the rise: damages may now be awarded for emotional distress; emotional crimes such as hate speech have been defined; popular discussions of justice are highly emotionalised (Friedman and Squire, 1998); victims may now make emotional appeals before convicted persons are sentenced; some commentators have gone so far as to speak of an 'emotionalisation of law' (Karstedt, 2002).

Beyond politics and law, more everyday aspects of life in public are also defined by emotion. The street corner society of the 1950s and 1960s (Anderson, 1978; Whyte, 1955) and the worlds of rave (Redhead, 1993; St. John, 2003) and rap (Quinn, 2004) are indices of the ways in which rage, frustration, bitterness, release, oblivion and exhilaration structure what people count as their interests, their social networks, their informal institutions – indeed all those factors that are conventionally invoked to explain behaviour. Even the most instrumental and interest-driven activities of investment are partly driven by the emotions that define our risk preferences and our responses to losses and gains in normal times, let alone in the great herd movements of booms, bubbles and busts (Barbalet, 1998; Pixley, 2002a). The very boundary between the public and private is marked in our own and many societies by informal rules about just what emotional performances are permitted in each zone. Indeed, these rules are sanctioned in the breach by emotions of shame, embarrassment and revulsion at either excess or insufficiency or inappropriate public emotion. Norbert Elias' (1994) social theory is largely built around this point. Eighteenth-century European culture was riven by conflicts over the extent to which the new manners should corset emotional display and channel public emotion or else allow free rein to 'sensibility' (Porter, 2000, pp276–94). This protracted debate over manners and sensibility, representing negotiation over public life through negotiation of emotions, is replicated today in the proliferating arguments about appropriate emotional organisation and behaviour, that range from denunciations of the banality of overemotialised societies (Furedi, 2004; Meštrović, 1996) to calls for new, emotionalised versions of intelligence and literacy (Goleman, 1996; Orbach, 1999).

There continues to be little convergence between disciplines in their understanding of just how and with what consequences fear, sadness, rage, happiness, disgust and surprise; more complicated emotions like fury, elation, shame, guilt, grief, nostalgia, hope, *Schadenfreude, Weltschmerz, amour propre*, sympathy and still subtler and more ambiguous hybrid feelings, shape our public life. Still less has academic inquiry achieved a shared understanding of what might be emotionally astute ways in which to conduct that public life. There is even a continuing history of debate about whether emotions are extraneous to the public sphere (Habermas, 1989) or essential to it (Thompson and Hoggett, 2001), or whether the expression of many of them is simply undesirable in public life (Arendt, 1963, p85ff; see Kateb, 1984 and Tamborino, 1999, p188). There is, too, a cacophony of claims in the fields of therapy, education and management, particularly for what is now called emotional intelligence (Goleman, 1996) or emotional literacy (Orbach, 1999). Intellectual understandings of the emotions in public life thus remain compartmentalised or in conflict over emotions' definition, ideology and significance. Psychological, social-scientific and humanities-based approaches hardly converse, reducing our chances of understanding a foundational aspect of public life, and preventing us from developing some potentially more productive approaches to conflict.

This collection presents important new work that addresses these omissions, by exploring the consequences of emotions for public life.[1] It offers a conversation between several disciplines and approaches. In particular, the book presents recent developments in Durkheimian, psychoanalytic, Foucaultian and poststructuralist understandings of the role of emotion in public life.

As far as possible, the contributions avoid the now set-piece debates about the relative place of nature and nurture in the genesis of emotions, and about the definition and value of particular emotional repertoires. We have not sought to represent, even critically, those traditions that have developed straitjacketed models of emotional order and disorder, such as rational choice, conventional cognitive psychology, neuroscience or mainstream economics, and that have less to contribute to this volume's concerns. The writers in this volume generally avoid heavily value-laden judgements of specific emotions. At the same time, they make a strong case that emotions matter, by investigating their relation to the formation and experience of social and political events, to the construction and negotiation of political and other discourses, and to the making and breaking of solidarities and divisions. None of the approaches promote emotional expression nor its supposed libratory possibilities, nor emotional repression or control. No separation is made, either, between so-called 'positive' and 'negative' emotions, for such crude dichotomies take insufficient account of the complex and contradictory nature of emotions in public life.

In this Introduction, we first define the scope of the book and offer a survey of ways in which emotions in public life have been understood. Focusing on five themes or dimensions, we explore the impact of emotions on public life – these are conflict, collectivity, categorisation, historical time, and authority and power. Next, the main traditions of thought about the consequences of emotions are contrasted. We show that social thought refracts understandings of the effects of affect, through debates about the tension between reason and emotion. Some developments in social science and humanities research are reviewed, in order to situate the chapters. We show how these research developments enrich understanding of the five dimensions of public life mentioned above, and add nuance to the existing rival traditions. Finally, we explore the novel contribution to the literature that the chapters in this book make to understanding the consequences of emotion for public life, and indicate what they show about conflict, collectivity, categorisation, historical time, and power and authority.

Describing public emotions

It is important to define some key terms, in order to make clear the scope of this book.

The terms 'emotion', 'feeling' and 'affect' have similar but not identical meanings. Writers have largely despaired of producing agreed definitions of these terms as if they denoted natural kinds (for instance, Ben-Ze'ev, 2000; Elster, 1999; Evans, 2002; de Sousa, 1994). Some philosophers define emotions as affective states entered into in response to propositions (see Greenspan, 1988; Matravers, 1998), an approach that can obscure distinctions between the three terms. In this account, a feeling may neither be objectively observable by others nor easily categorised by the self. Commonly however, a 'feeling' is distinguished as the phenomenological aspect of an emotion, or a syndrome of several, that is most palpable to immediate consciousness, something that is experienced privately or internally (Music, 2001). Elster (1999), though, defines one sense of 'emotion' as just this phenomenological aspect. He gives a broader, behavioural account of emotions in general, which therefore permits the special case in which the phenomenological process is suppressed. Things regarded as emotions tend to be specific and observable: 'anger' or 'joy' are emotions that are often understood to have observable effects on bodies and behaviour. Some psychologists assimilate feelings to emotions by stressing the hedonic intensity of emotions as their defining characteristics (Carbanac, 2002). Others contrast feelings with emotions, regarding emotions as behavioural processes evincing motivation (Evans, 2001). In this vein, Damasio (2003) argues that feelings should be understood as the sensible reflections and indeed perceptions of emotions, which are bodily processes of motivational response to circumstance. Others (for instance, Sturdy, 2003) prefer simply to list affect, motivation, phenomenology, behaviour, language, social structure and so on as 'dimensions' of emotionality. There may also be good reasons for distinguishing the terms, 'emotion', 'sentiment' and 'passion'. Some (for instance Hall, 2005; Rorty, 1980) regard passions as fiercer and sentiments as milder subtypes of each emotion. Others argue that the concept of an emotion is a recent one, which has confused matters by replacing subtler and more exact terms perhaps no longer available for historical and structural reasons (Dixon, 2003).

'Affect' is a term deployed within three theoretical domains. Its most common usage is found in psychoanalytic theory. In British object-relations psychoanalysis (Rustin, this volume) it may be used to designate that which common parlance terms the emotions or feelings. In continental post-Freudian psychoanalysis 'affect' refers strictly, however, only to that which derives from and has its roots in the sexual and aggressive drives (Green, 1999; Radstone, this volume) and not to the broad range of feelings or emotions that may derive from affect but which are not affect itself. Elsewhere, though, informed by the writings of Spinoza (2000, 1989[1677]), Bergson (1988), Deleuze (1990), Deleuze and Guttari (1987), 'affect' is now deployed in new materialist and anti-psychoanalytic theories of culture, that reject theories of representation in favour of an approach to culture that foregrounds the impact of, for instance, the fluctuations of sound and light that constitute film at a proto-subjective and affective level (Kennedy, 2000; Shaviro, 1993). Finally, in neurological approaches, 'affects' are regarded as perceptions of the utility of external or mental objects (Panksepp, 2003), which would assimilate them to Damasio's (2003) 'feelings'.

The contributors to this volume use the terms 'feelings', 'emotions' and 'affect' as they see fit. Given their different theoretical approaches, we have not sought to impose standard usage on them. In our view, the question of the reach and purchase of each of these terms remains open to future debate. For the remainder of this Introduction, we shall use the term 'emotion' to include phenomenological, unconscious and behavioural aspects.

By 'public life', we mean to encompass at once the formal public sphere of political life; the wider sphere of shared participation in state institutions and civil society; the world of everyday cultures lived in the public spaces of outdoor streets, parks and squares and indoor places of more or less open gathering (Sennett, 1974); and contemporary public representations and discourses that themselves describe and constitute different aspects of public life (Moscovici, 2000; Rose, 1996).

For the purposes of this Introduction, we shall focus on five themes representing important dimensions of public life, which have been at stake in much recent research on the emotions, and which enable us to explore the significant contributions made by the chapters in this book. These are the themes of *conflict* and its management, negotiation, limitation or containment; *collectivity* and its construction; *categories*, and shifts in them; social time, or both collective *memory* and the sense of a *future*, change and continuity; and *power* and *authority*. The five themes are closely related and often interdependent. Conflict involves challenges to authority and power, for instance, but also a very particular formation of categories within which people and events are placed, as well as historical reconstructions of – and breaks with – memories of past grievances and future-directed responses to them. Collectivities also require the use of shared categories; authority and power need both to maintain and question those categories; and the construction, forgetting and rupture of historical memories and the futures they dictate are conflict-laden processes of power and of making collectivities. Together, while by no means providing a full description of the emotional fabric of public life, the five themes afford us an integrated heuristic framework within which the contributions of different disciplines and traditions can be examined and compared.

Emotion, reason and consequences

Debates in the social sciences and in the humanities about the consequences for public life of the emotions are very closely related to the disagreements about the relationship between emotions and reason. In this section, we argue that there are four rival theses about how emotions affect public life, each defined by a distinct view of the relationship between reason and emotion.

One common view is that emotions are not deeply consequential in public life. In many conventional rational choice explanations, and in interest-driven accounts of political economy or corporate behaviour which identify the instrumental with the rational, emotions are at worst noisy deviations from, and at best marginal, decorative additions to, the processes by which outcomes are achieved (for instance Coleman, 1990). Collins (1986, pp145–66), for example, shows that emotions of political support for states are instrumentally stirred by leaders for geopolitical ends. If, like Weber in one strand of his work (1958, 1976) or Habermas (1984), one laments this situation, then it is seen as an iron cage or as the colonisation of the 'lifeworld' by instrumental reason, but this regret adds little more to one's account of consequentiality than a romantic poignancy. On this view, emotions are a-rational, but not greatly consequential in their own right. Basic constituents of public life, such as conflict and collectivity, categories, historical continuity and change, and power and authority, are not themselves emotional.

A second view holds that emotions are both necessary and functional for reason. When Hume famously wrote that reason is and must be the slave of the passions (1969 [1739], p462), he drew together two distinct claims that continue to inspire ideas about the consequentiality of emotion. The first is that the goals that we rationally and instrumentally pursue appeal to us, in many cases, not because they are necessities for survival, but because of the emotional achievements that we can find for ourselves in them. The rational cultivation of the goals of the collector, the theatregoer, the politician, the newshound and the *flâneur* reflects the emotional satisfactions and challenges available to them in these pursuits. Secondly, Hume implied – and many others since have developed this thought – that the ability rationally to pursue a goal beyond bare survival, depends on our ability to sustain the emotions which will support that pursuit. The theatre-goer may pursue in the tragedies she prefers the emotional sensibilities that can be gained by close attention to the tragic. In addition, the commitment to become and remain a theatre-goer depends on the emotions that are required to see oneself as a member of a theatre-going group of the public. When sociologists analyse the functional role of appropriate emotional capacity and performance at weddings, funerals, cocktail parties, academic seminars and town meetings, they exemplify Hume's second thesis, that emotions are reasonable precisely to the extent that they serve our goals, which themselves are also of value for their emotional yield.

Some in the broadly Weberian tradition such as Barbalet (1998) have come to adopt a view along these lines. The righteous fury of the rebellious, for example, may both sustain their ability to rebel and follow from their goal of the just correction of institutions. A more longstanding example is the tradition of research on the small rituals of speech and action that define life in public places, associated with Goffman (1967). These rituals serve the goals of maintaining social order precisely by performing emotions of shame, deference and civil inattention, on a basis appropriate to the order to be maintained. In the process, these performances also enable the emotions to give meaning to the goals. Ricoeur's (1981) work on metaphor gives emotions a similarly enabling place. What Ricoeur calls 'feelings' (saving the term 'emotion' for a narrower category) are part of the imaginative grasping for knowledge that happens within metaphor. In dialogue with the more straightforward 'feelings' attached to rational, scientific, explanatory discourse, these feelings are essential for developing the understanding that guarantees and is, indeed, the purpose of, public life. Emotions, in this second view, could hardly be more consequential, for they sustain both our goals and our abilities to pursue them, but they do so best and are most sustained when they are reasonable and orderly enough to be functional. On this view, emotions can contribute as much to collectivity and the containment of conflict as to conflict generation, and they are unlikely to make or break categories in ways that fundamentally undermine rationality and functionality.

A third view is that the more genuinely 'emotional' a feeling is, the more independent of, and even undermining of, rationality it is. In one strand of his thought, this appears to be a view taken by Weber, when he contrasts 'affectual' action with instrumentally rational action, and suggests that a process of historical rationalisation is decreasing the importance of affectual action. In the same vein, he stresses the role of emotion in pietistic religion and in charismatic authority, and in both cases, emphasises their lack of resilience against instrumental rationality. However, Weber's account of the role of emotion in Calvinism suggests that at the very least, affectual action may be an important historical route toward capitalist rationalisation. Moreover, his lectures on science and politics as vocations certainly recognise the role of emotional commitment in sustaining a variety of forms of rule and indeed rational inquiry itself, at least when passion is cultivated within an ethic of responsibility, so greatly nuancing the account in some of his writings of emotions as associated principally with irrationality (see Barbalet, 1998).

Many readings of Freud (1963 [1930]), too, for example, would suggest that human subjects are rooted in unconscious fantasy and drives, the creatures of hardly-controlled impulses and the products of ill-assimilated infantile frustrations. In this account, any attempt at rational goal formation is threatened by our limited capacity to think or act maturely. This irrational emotionality has immense consequences for public life: as humans, we continually have to live with our limited abilities rationally to inhabit the environment, interact with others and understand ourselves (Freud, 1963). The 'discontent' in Freud's title indicated disappointment, disaffection and upheaval – the emotions aroused by struggling to live with the reality principle and its social injunctions. Sociologists such as Elias (1994), who learned much from Freud, suggest that only with the rational containment of dangerous emotions, by the civilising discipline of manners and, perhaps, psychotherapy, can reason and a functioning social order be maintained. In this account, emotions are a source of conflict and of overweening collectivities; they erode social categories; and they render power relations, authority, and historical memory and imagination too labile to sustain a public realm. Emotions, then, are consequential precisely to the degree that they are dysfunctional and not merely a-rational but irrational.

Standing outside these categories of the emotions as reasonable or unreasonable, weighty or inconsequential, is work that examines these categories themselves in the light of their public functioning, and the emotional investments that may sustain them. In *Elementary Forms of Religious Life* (1995 [1912]), Durkheim put forward the thesis that the very classifications we use – including, he implied, the categories of rationality and consequentiality – are sustained and fixed only to the extent that they have some more or less legible relationship with shared emotions (Rawls, 1996). For Durkheim and his tradition, emotions are consequential because the particular forms that anger, bitterness, *Schadenfreude*, nostalgia, envy, enthusiasm and commitment take in any organisation or group or society, *define* what will be counted as consequential, and, indeed, as moral – for Durkheim, like Hume and Freud, thinks emotions are essential for defining morality. That emotions will sometimes be functional and sometimes dysfunctional, sometimes reinforcing and sometimes undermining of individual and collective capacities for the rational pursuit of goals, follows from the rest of Durkheim's theory that every form of social organisation and its set of attendant emotional sensibilities and capabilities will, sooner or later, 'overshoot' and begin to disorganise itself by exaggerating the very commitments that at first sustain it.

A stance rather similar in its independence of the debate about rationality, but distinct in its lack of interest in emotions' essential driving capacity, is that of Foucault (1978). The management of ineluctable orders of feeling and public life, and relations between them, is not discussed in Foucault's writing. Instead, he is interested in tracing the ties between certain structures of feeling – for instance, emotions related to selfhood and sexuality – and specific formations of the public sphere – for instance, those placing the individual subject at the centre of citizenship. By tracing these ties, hidden in full view, we may loosen them or perhaps make others possible, as well as destabilising the categories they link and their apparent ahistoricity. This process involves both analysing and resisting the power relations in which emotions inhere. Relations of power and authority are for Foucault exerted, experienced, resisted and reproduced emotionally; power and emotions travel along the same lines. Such analyses, standing slightly outside traditional debates about emotion, reason and consequences, are typical of poststructuralist work on emotionality, which is often, inaccurately, assumed not to care about emotions (Terada, 2001). Work such as that of Burkitt (2005) and Ahmed (2004), for instance, attempts to write the generation of meaning and power across significatory and economic structures, alongside the generation of emotional flows. In both these cases, the emotionality of racialisation, war and 'terror' are primary examples.

Disciplinary approaches to the emotions

Emotions were, until recently, strangely absent from postwar western social thought. However they have a sustained history in earlier western social philosophy. Aristotle devoted most of the *Rhetoric*, several books of the *Politics* and three books of the *Nichomachean Ethics* to understanding how emotion shaped civic life, mobilising through emotional rhetoric, threatening civil strife (*stasis*), or sustaining civil friendship between citizens (Kalimtzis, 2000). He saw many emotions as consequential and collectively irrational, but others as amenable to rational persuasion (Rorty, 1996). Roman and Greek Stoics produced extended reflections on the extent to which emotional political participation threatened or was necessary to varying conceptions of a desirable civic life (Erskine, 1990). These reflections continued within a counter-Reformation movement in Catholic Europe which developed a distinctive and highly expressive style of relations between emotions and public life, discernable in the literature of the day, the architecture of baroque churches, and high mannerist painting intended to impart an emotionalised religious tenor to public life as well as private piety. The Romantic movement was much preoccupied with the role of emotional expression in public life as a kind of political programme (Schenk, 1966). Rousseau (1973 [1755]) specifically argued that societies that encouraged emotional expression were both freer and more desirable, precisely because expression would enable people to cultivate more responsible emotions rather than ruinous passions. The early Frankfurt School was greatly concerned with the issue, especially in Adorno and colleagues' *Authoritarian Personality* (Adorno *et al.*, 1950). Marcuse's (1974) later work is also profoundly occupied with the issue of emotions and political life, from a partly psychoanalytic perspective.

On the other hand, until recently, emotions have been marginalised within many academic disciplines, conceived of either as irrelevant, or as needing to be jettisoned so that reason can prevail. Now, however, emotions are being placed on the theoretical maps of all the social sciences broadly conceived – for example, they figure in various degrees in current work in political science, cultural studies, sociology and anthropology. In these disciplines, the focus tends to fall on raising the profile of emotions in areas of study where they were previously neglected, as in organisational behaviour; on developing accounts of their social or cultural construction, or their biological functionality; or on promoting the social and political benefits of emotional intelligence and literacy

(Goleman, 1996; Orbach, 1999). This last tradition has a sociological parallel that begins with Giddens' (1992) *The Transformation of Intimacy*, which heralded the benefits of the emotionalisation of public life and acted as a springboard for other work of this persuasion (for instance, Brown and Richards, 2000; Richards, 1999).

Understanding the emotions has become increasingly central in sociology since the 1970s (Bendelow and Williams, 1998); has moved to the centre of organisational studies during the 1990s (Fineman, 2000); became less prominent during the 1990s in anthropology, though in the 1970s and 1980s the challenge of mapping and explaining the variation between societies in the menu of emotions available was important (Shweder and LeVine, 1984); remains marginalised in political science and has been addressed scantily in cultural and media studies (Harding and Pribram, 2002).

Recent sociological and anthropological work on the emotions can be divided into several clusters (6, 2003). There are historicist accounts, which propose that patterns of emotions change markedly between periods; the plethora of studies using Foucault's (1978, 1980, 1986) and Elias' (1994) theories are the best known. Richards' (1999) thesis of the recent, therapeutic 'emotionalisation' of society, Giddens' (1992) benign view of a transformation of intimacy, Meštrović's (1996) of a malign and compassion-fatigued 'postemotional society' with ubiquitous *ersatz* emotion, and Scherer's (2001) account of changing emotional repertoires in response to declining social control, mass media manipulation and new technologies, are rival historicist theories, arguing that emotions have become either consequential and functional or steadily less consequential and dysfunctional. Their fundamental logic of 'different times and places, different feelings' is consonant with a kind of anthropological theory that holds that emotional structures have developed differently in different, geographically or socially separated societies (Shweder and LeVine, 1984). However, this historicist cluster of accounts adopts different positions, from agnostic, through rejection, to strong acceptance and endorsement, on emotions' consequences or correlations within the public realm; on emotions' enabling or disabling relations to rationality; and on the stability and usefulness of the categories of 'emotion' and 'reason'.

While rational choice accounts would once have treated emotions as 'irrational' forces that erupt to block rationality or else are quelled by it, recent work in these traditions seeks, as we have mentioned above, to accommodate emotions within the operations of rationality itself. Elster's work (for example, Elster, 1999) proposes that emotions should be seen as more or less intelligent solutions to individually experienced cognitive problems, subject presumably to some neuropsychological constraints on the solutions available. Luhmann (1986) presents 'love' as an 'interpersonal interpenetration' of communication systems, explaining inexplicable passion by deciphering its social codes. Barbalet (1998) argues that macro-social structures and processes use a restricted subset of emotions – pride, fear, resentment, shame – in order to further more or less rational, if private, collective interests that are in conflict and to handle responses to status inequality. In a similar vein, Pixley (2002b, 2005) argues that large financial organisations rely on emotions of euphoria and fear in order to set expectations and to adopt rules about trust and distrust in their decision making; it is not only when trust and expectations break down that emotions enter into the content of financial rationality but in 'normal' periods too.

Another cluster of sociological accounts, often linked to the historically-oriented tradition, could be described as socially constructivist. These accounts propose that both the emotions available to be felt and the consequences of emotional performance are best understood as the products of particular social structures and their biases. One strand of this, particularly influential in Britain and well able to make common cause with Tavistock Centre left-psychoanalytic concerns about social processes, has been work emphasising the emotional injuries of class subordination (for example Hoggett, 2000, 2001). Another strand concentrates on the gendered intersection between unconscious and culturally specified 'feelings' (Chodorow, 1999). Drawing on Marx's concepts of exchange and use value, Hochschild's (1983) work, bringing class and gender together, has inspired a large literature on emotional labour as the current form of alienation and labour exploitation. Capacities for emotional performance toward clients in service industries are required from ever more people in their work lives, Hochschild argues, with damaging consequences for integrity, reduced capacity for 'real' emotion and increased burn-out. In this literature, emotions appear again as highly consequential: functional for a particular mode of production, but dysfunctional for individuals. Deborah Lupton's (1998) work offers a similar diagram of emotional construction while widening the sphere of emotions' individual effects. Similarly adopting a broader view of emotions' political functioning, Jeff Goodwin *et al.* (2001) and their contributors map a set of emotional constructions – shame, anger, disgust, fear and love – that work to support and propel individual and political resistance, in movements from animal rights to HIV activism.

Whereas older anthropological theories rooted emotional structures in organisational patterns and presumed that the range of emotions would be limited by the fundamental unity of humankind, postmodern versions allow an indefinite variety of emotions to be 'socially constructed', and tend to the idealist view that it is ideology or worldview rather than institutions that carry out the constructions (for instance, Harré, 1986; Lutz and Abu-Lughod, 1990). The more particular work of, for instance, Lupton (1998) and Goodwin *et al.* (2001), modifies such idealism.

Finally, the Durkheimian tradition in sociology and anthropology recognises social construction but denies the postmodern thesis of indefinite variety and insists upon a basis in institutions rather than ideas (6, 2003). Its core argument is that emotions are necessary for elementary classification and cognitive thought, and they are sustained through ritual (Collins, 2004; Alexander, 1988). The strength of these recent post-Durkheimian anthropological studies of emotion lies in the serious attention that they pay to the cultural and social meanings of emotions and their roles in categorisation and collective memory as well as in their attention to the constitutive role of emotions in the formation and breaking of social solidarities, an issue often neglected by social constructionists and postmodernists. However, as Nancy Chodorow has recently argued, some Durkheimian-inspired studies of emotion risk postulating the meanings of emotions *only* in terms of their understanding of social structure. Those anthropological studies of 'self and feeling' which attempt to go further than this, by looking at the intersection of personal and public meanings of emotions, have also been criticised for lacking adequate theoretical tools (Chodorow, 1999, pp129–71).

In mainstream political science and political theory, the study of emotion has remained subterranean. In political psychology, individualistic cognitive models remain dominant, and emotions tend to be attached in fairly simple and binary ways to expressions of political attitudes in survey research or laboratory experiments using political examples (Marcus *et al.*, 2000). Marcus (2002) has built upon this approach to argue that the emotional condition of anxiety is an important causal pre-condition of deliberative political attitudes and openness to consideration of points of view to which one is initially hostile, whereas anger is the reverse, a view that some political theorists of anger such as Lyman (2004) would want significantly to nuance (compare Hoggett and Thompson's [2002] psychoanalytic argument for designing group dynamics to limit and contain paranoia as a precondition for such deliberativeness). Slightly richer accounts can be found in some of the 'symbolic politics' tradition, but here emotions tend to be seen as the object of more or less conscious manipulation by already powerful interests (Edelman, 1985 [1967], 1988), rather than as (in some sociological views) playing a role in the constitution of interests and power. Normative political philosophy and theory, especially in the liberal traditions, has tended to neglect the role of the emotions (Hall, 2002; Walzer, 2002). In the postwar years, an association of emotions in political theory with fascist or at least authoritarian thought and collective action (see Schmitt, 1996) even led political theorists to turn away from concerns with emotions. Rawls' (1970) and Nozick's (1974) treatises addressed the tension between distributive justice and property rights rather than the passions at stake there. Arendt (1992, 1969, 1963) focused political thought on power and judgment with public emotions constrained. Indeed, emotions were eclipsed for a generation. There has been some resurgence of interest with writers such as Walzer (2002) and Hampshire (1999), but emotions are still marginal to the discipline. The broad consensus remains that emotions are irrational and dysfunctional in politics. Following sociology, any interest in the emotions that has developed has tended to focus around conflict rather than categorisation or collectivity. What is more surprising is that political science and theory have little that is distinctive (rather than borrowed from other disciplines) to say – save by way of analysis of reported attitudes – about the role of emotions in *reproducing* authority and power, instead focusing on the role of emotions such as anger in *undermining* authority and power (Berezin, 2002).

Despite emotions seeming to the lay imagination to be self-evidently part of psychology's field, this discipline has also found them difficult to address. Psychological analyses of emotions provide, however, for emotional consequences that fall within all the themes we shall be considering in this book: shifts in attention and categorisation, social inclusion and social division – though usually without being explicit about these explanatory consequences.

Most psychological accounts trace their lineage to a biological text – Darwin's (1890) *The Expression of the Emotions in Man and Animals*. This genealogical endeavour also, however, leaves open several possible modes for understanding emotions' effects in the public arena. The genealogy is often a way of emphasising emotions' biological, evolved nature, as in the recent school of evolutionary psychology, closely connected to 1980s socio-biology, which sees emotions as functionally specialised programmes that have evolved to solve specific problems of adaptation (for instance, Cosmides and Tooby, 2000: for a similar approach, integrating sociological and evolutionary models, see Turner, 2000).[2] The evolutionary grounding of psychological emotional theorising need not, however, preclude considering emotions also as social-cognitive states. In James' (1955 [1890]) work for instance emotions arise from bodily sensations and have unique, evolved psychologies, but the cultural and individual experiencing of them has an importance that cannot be explained fully in these terms (see also Barbalet, 2004; Damasio, 2003). Evolution is also part of the mainstream dualist psychological account of 'primary' or universal emotions of sadness, happiness, fear, disgust, anger and surprise – internal emotional states, with more or less general physiological correlates in the autonomic nervous system, brain and facial expressions, though with some variation in display rules (Ekman, 1980) and cognitive appraisal – and 'secondary', more culturally variable emotions, more highly dependent on cognitive appraisal, with much more variable display rules, which appear in specific social and cognitive contexts (Smith and Ellsworth, 1985). This still-hegemonic account within the discipline implicitly allows 'emotions' to promote social inclusion through their human generality; to generate felt cultural specificities, misunderstandings and conflicts and also to foreground different forms and categorisations of emotion as the pattern of secondary emotional phenomena varies.

There is a strong strand of work within psychology that focuses on emotions that result from the cognitive appraisal of perceived internal states and external situations (Lazarus, 1999). The premise here is that many emotions arise from cognitive processing patterns that are biologically founded but are also responsive to variable social rules. This approach allows for a complex, contextualised view of emotions as broadly consequential and rational, that has also been taken up within philosophy (Nussbaum, 2001; see also Evans and Cruse, 2004). In this account human beings notice and remember events that evoke emotions of joy, sorrow, pleasure and pain. Thus, 'emotions provide the principal currency in human relationships as well as the motivational force for what is best and worst in human behaviour' (Dolan, 2002). Dolan argues for further research on emotions, because they 'are less encapsulated than other psychological states as is evident in their global effects on virtually all aspects of cognition' (Dolan, 2002, p1191) – although studies of 'emotional intelligence' have in fact found rather weak relationships between it and positive outcomes in the fields of education, organisations and mental health (Rhodes *et al.*, 2004). Within this cognitively-grounded account, emotions can have diverse social consequences, and a degree of ambiguity is to be expected. For example, a recent article in *Psychological Science* explores the relationship between fear and risk following the attack of 9/11; the chapter reveals gendered emotional responses to policy – men were less pessimistic about risk than women (Lerner *et al.*, 2003). Other studies find that male anger and fear is more closely linked with preferences for punitive action (Gault and Sabini, 2000).

The founding place of evolution is also central in Freudian and subsequent psychoanalytic addresses to emotions, although again not in a wholly determining way, since emotions crystallise in these accounts around idiosyncratic unconscious memory traces. Emotions are therefore allowed a similar ambiguity in the psychoanalytic as in the psychological accounts, operating at a level of human generality, and – in this case – individual, rather than cultural, specificity, but ultimately coded at a biological level (Damasio, 2003; LeDoux, 1996; Panksepp, 2003). In some psychoanalytic accounts, social formations may, by their analogical relation to individual experiences, variously trigger fairly general but unconscious emotions that change the public map of emotions (Kristeva, 1982; Cooper, this volume), draw lines through it or leave holes in it (Lacan, 1977; Frosh, this volume), or help create a shared emotional territory (Honneth, 1996; Rustin, this volume). Again, these possibilities take in emotions' compatibility with, antithesis to and irrelevance to rationality, and allow them to have a range of strengths and types of social effectiveness.

Cultural studies emphasises everyday life, home, family and media, perhaps leading one to expect a well-developed investigation of emotions. As Grossberg (1984) points out, affect is a constitutive part of popular culture – and, we would add, all culture – and cultural forms and activities cannot be adequately understood solely by considering them as cognitive, rational or ideological practices (quoted in Harding and Pribram, 2002). Cultural studies claims to take 'experience' seriously, and to analyse the complex relations between the micro-worlds of everyday life and the macro-world of governance, power and resistance. However, the scope to think about the everyday life of the emotions and its relations with those macro worlds seems limited by lack of adequate theories and methods, and by the limits the discipline has so far set on the range of emotions to be studied.

In the 1980s, a focus on the pleasures made available by, for instance, the cinema, or fashion, countered the denigration of popular or mass culture by Marxist critical theory in general and the Frankfurt School in particular (Adorno and Horkheimer, 1997 [1955]). This new emphasis on popular pleasures posited a relation between the pleasures offered by popular culture, and the politics suggested by these pleasures (Jameson *et al.*, 1983). Thus, though cultural studies of pleasure took emotion seriously, they did so in order to posit a relation between the pleasures of popular culture, and the political consciousness, alliances or resistances that such pleasures might represent or foster. The study of pleasure was directed, that is, at the question of its political meanings. Until recently, a similar tendency has prevailed in film studies, where one of the most influential approaches to mainstream cinema's popular pleasures was disseminated by the journal *Screen*. In the 1970s, the analysis of mainstream film developed by '*Screen* theory' incorporated Lacanian psychoanalysis and Althusserian Marxism to produce an account of mainstream cinema's role in sustaining the illusory coherence of 'bourgeois' subjectivity (Althusser, 1971; Lacan, 1977). The pleasures of continuity editing and cinematic identification systems were aligned, here, with mainstream cinema's role in the production of a politically dubious illusion of reality (Heath, 1981). In Mulvey's (1975) seminal paper 'Visual pleasure and narrative cinema', the pleasures of mainstream film are also deemed complicit with the sustenance of phallocentric, patriarchal culture. More recently, however, and due to the impact of cultural studies on film studies, the pleasures of mainstream film have begun to be approached less negatively. Musicals, for instance, have been associated with utopian desires for abundance (Dyer, 1985). Meanwhile, psychoanalytic mobilisations of 'fantasy' by studies of the cinema and culture have now developed beyond the wholly negative alignment of mainstream culture with the sustenance of the late capitalist, patriarchal order to stress the unconscious aspects of mainstream culture as wayward, excessive, and resistant to surface meanings (Burgin *et al.*, 1986; Wide Angle, 1988).

The repertoire of emotions addressed by cultural, film and media studies remains somewhat limited. Alongside pleasure, the most extensive literature in the discipline focuses on panic and fear. A strong tradition influenced by Cohen's influential (2002 [1972]) work on moral panics has analysed the orchestration of public emotions of panic to serve the interests of the dominant culture. Much of the work undertaken in the US and Britain focusing on popular pleasures and mass panic has been influenced, in part at least, by the Gramscian tradition that was developed by Stuart Hall and the Birmingham Centre for Cultural Studies (for instance, Hall and Jefferson, 1976). Here, the influence falls on the orchestration of and struggles within cultural and political hegemony, rather than on the imposition from above of a political and cultural order. Recently, the Gramscian concept of 'hegemony' has been extended into the field of cultural studies of the emotions. Yet though this work promises to progress cultural research on the emotions, its address still places the power and meanings of the emotions within a Foucaultian framework that limits the scope for investigating the relations between the personal and the public, to that of the exercise of micro power-politics. A more nuanced analysis of the ways in which emotions cross between the domains of the personal and the public is still to be achieved (Harding and Pribram, 2002; Jagger, 1989).

Harding and Pribram's work on emotional hegemony, though located within cultural studies, borrows from work in feminist epistemology. Feminist-informed cultural studies and political philosophy promises to allow theoretical space to analyse how emotions are gendered, classed and ethnicised, and to place emotions carefully on the agenda in what may seem a contradictory fashion – both problematically and unashamedly. The question of the relation between politics and emotions persists in the work of feminists such as Jacqueline Rose, Judith Butler, Wendy Brown and Sara Ahmed. From their diverse perspectives these scholars are concerned with the theorisation of the political and cultural spheres, bearing in mind how emotions bind (Ahmed, 2004); matters of power within psychic life (Butler, 1997, 2004); the endurance of emotional and political attachments and the limits of liberal theory and practice (Brown, 1995); and for Rose (1998), fantasy's workings in the political field. In *States of Fantasy*, Rose argues that fantasy should be at the heart of our political vocabulary for '[L]ike blood, fantasy is thicker than water, all too solid – *contra* another of fantasy's more familiar glosses as ungrounded supposition, lacking in foundation, not solid *enough*' (Rose, 1998, p5, emphasis in original). In a similar vein, Žižek, has argued that fantasy is material, and its matter has effects. The issue for Rose and for Žižek is not just recognising fantasy, but trying to grasp how fantasy fuels politics, and of course how politics fuel fantasy. For Žižek, drawing upon Lacanian accounts, unconscious emotional structures are always those of excess, and can never be accounted for entirely by material realities. War, for instance, is 'always a *war of fantasies*' (quoted in Frosh, 2002, p154, emphasis in original). In these accounts, emotions are irrational and consequential, not capable of being fully coopted for rational ends, but not necessarily spelling the complete undoing of rationality either.

Finally, it is important to consider the contribution of clinical psychotherapeutic and psychoanalytic practice to understandings of public emotions, even though their literatures are rather diffuse and of a quite different nature from that of the academic social sciences and humanities. Given the UK backgrounds of the clinical contributors to this book, we shall concentrate here on practice within Britain.

A number of clinical therapists took part in the seminar series that led to this book. At the risk of oversimplification, clinicians tend to see emotions as expressive primarily of an individual's state of mind. Emotions are regarded as layered, with the experience and expression of one emotion screening the self from an encounter with a potentially more troubling emotion. In this account, unconscious emotions are always intertwined with conscious feelings and thoughts, producing a complex state of mind in which nothing is as it seems. As Green points out, Freud 'conceives of affect above all as a disorganising factor in the psychic apparatus' (Green, 1986, p177). Increasingly, however, in UK psychoanalysis influenced by Klein (1975, 1988) and Bion (1967) the focus is on the relationship between thought and emotion. It is the capacity to think and reflect on emotions and states of mind that is now thought to mark out maturity. Influenced by the American analyst Thomas Ogden (1992) and the British object relations analyst Ronald Britton (1998), emphasis is now placed on opening out a space to reflect, termed by Britton the 'third space', and on the capacity to think about raw and indigestible experience as elaborated by Ogden. This version of psychoanalysis and the cognitive psychology of emotions have much in common; in both, also, emotions are conceptualised as bodily sensations.

The issue of representation and affect haunted Freud, and this vexed matter persists both within contemporary psychoanalytic theorisations, and within cultural studies. In the British psychoanalytic tradition, the most important processes of affect are conversion, displacement, and other transpositions of anxiety. There are two primary issues for the psychoanalytic tradition described above. First, how can we promote sustained thinking about emotions and unconscious life? Second, following Winnicott (1964), how can we promote a 'good enough' environment that allows emotions to be nurtured, encountered and shared? Music asserts that 'psychoanalytic thinking aims to enable us to tolerate a broader range of emotional experience, both positive and negative, and consequently to enhance our capacity to accept ourselves and relate to others'. However, the aim of clinical practice is to enable the individual to 'mentalise' (2001, p72). There is a difference between how academics and clinicians understand 'mentalisation'. In the therapeutic setting, mentalisation involves gaining insight into one's emotional landscapes so that a greater range of emotions can be identified and tolerated. Given the conspicuous failure of many attempts to 'psycho-analyse societies', it continues to be a major challenge for clinical practice to extend the conception of mentalisation from the case of the distressed individual to understanding the role of such processes in public life. Rustin's (1991) *The Good Society and the Inner World* is an exemplar of an application of Kleinian thinking to various cultural and social phenomena which argues that psychic development can in this historical moment be seen as an increasingly universal demand, and sets out a model of psychic and social ambiguity tolerance that can contain contemporary conflicts.

Themes in public life: the contribution of chapters in this volume

From this review of disciplinary contributions to understanding emotions in public life, it is clear that there remain major lacunae in our appreciation of how emotions can play a role in the containment of conflict, the building of collectivities, the governance of collective memories and futures, the fixing and shifting of categories, and the formation, exercise and resistance of forms of authority and power. To bring out more clearly the contributions to the literatures that the chapters in the book make, we focus here on these five key themes.

The first chapter, by Perri 6, is one of an initial three in the first section, entitled 'Emotions, conflict and settlement: a new Durkheimian approach.' It draws on Durkheimian concepts to understand emotions' route to and functioning within the public realm. 6 provides us with a theoretical overview of this field. He applies the systems-theoretic concepts of requisite variety to ritual forms. He suggests that such variety can provide the necessary basis for a negative feedback within and between social structures, which will avoid conflict escalation. This account fills out the Durkheimian insight that public life is sustained emotionally through ritual. By recasting Durkheim's own taxonomy of ritual forms in relation to feedback across differently remembered time and anticipated futures, 6 presents a novel account of the relation of ritual containments of conflict to time, as key to the containment of conflict more generally. In doing so, he reworks Durkheim's account of conflict containment as occurring through ritual but collective moral education (1951, 1957).

The second chapter, by Paul Richards, applies the Durkheimian perspective of the previous chapter to understanding the emotionalisation, and the failure to contain it, of a particular conflict, the Sierra Leonean civil war, a recent and extremely violent conflict that is still a focus of intense public grief, reflection and incomprehension. Richards draws on the contemporary rapprochement between Durkheimian and systems theories to show that positive feedback dynamics, or self-reinforcement processes in polarising conflict are not only necessarily emotional in character, but take the form of a very particular ritual order. Taking Durkheim's (1995 [1912]) concept of the piacular rite as one in which fixed categories come to have the highly emotionalised status of religious authority, Richards shows how a ritual order of positive feedback reinforces a strongly bounded and intensely bonded world of sect and sodality, and works to brutalise conflicts – an argument with large potential implications for other conflict situations. Richards' central arguments are, first, that the missing mechanism that produces the emotional collective effervescence is a musical one. Secondly, he argues that increasingly polyphonic ritual practices are required to constrain the tendency toward homophony in rituals of positive feedback, if the peculiar collective effervescence of enclaving is to be contained effectively. Richards concludes that conflict management must also necessarily be built around polyphonic ritual processes if it is to have any hope of success in emotional containment and entrainment.

In Stephan Feuchtwang's rich case study of spirit writing in Taiwan, the emotional management of collective memory through ritual forms is seen, again from a Durkheimian perspective, to be at once necessary to keep alive all the solidarities within a conflict, but also to negotiate that conflict through the production of an ethic. In Taiwan, the spirit writing performance of history was able, Feuchtwang argues, to generate authority for its local version of collective memory and for its performer. It did so because it was able to articulate some but not all the bitter intensity that could have been at work in sustaining that memory, and that appears even now in larger-scale, political memories and identities. In this performance, historical time was invoked but not flattened. Crucially, the ritual order of performance here channelled emotional memory and collectivity into a form of public moral education. Collective categories were generated and conflict channelled in less fiercely destructive ways than occurred, for instance, with the brutal performances of rigid categorisations described by Richards.

The next chapter begins the book's second part, on 'Intrapsychic and "public" emotions', which takes up the unanalysed aspect of unconscious processes in situations like those addressed in Part I, and develops a complex account of how intrapsychic and 'public' emotionalities inter-relate. Hélène Joffe, in her chapter, illustrates how representations of estranged or even demonised others in situations of incipient conflict or distancing can be explained, in a way that combines Moscovici's (2000) social psychological model of representations of selves and others, with a Kleinian psychoanalytic understanding of the social place of anxiety. With this chapter, then, the book begins its address to the structure and effects of intrapsychic emotionality. Joffe focuses particularly on public reactions to health crises, in particular, African responses to the HIV pandemic. In Joffe's account, the psychic patterning of emotionality is split endlessly, from infancy on, between rigid, ahistorical conflict-defined categorisations of the world, and more ambiguous, fluid and historically sensitive categories. These categories are, however, filled up by the specific varieties of social differences and divisions within which we live – for instance, with western concepts of 'good', controlled, rational, and 'bad', uncontrolled, irrational selves. Joffe's use of both the social representational framework, which traces contingencies and change in the patterns of collectivities and conflicts between categories, and the Kleinian notion of psychic ambiguity, allows her to postulate another, microsociological and intrapsychic route towards understanding the negotiation of emotions within the public realm than those explored in the first three chapters.

Stephen Frosh, like Joffe, invokes unconscious mechanisms associated with psychic rigidity, as well as making a precise analysis of social and institutional histories, in order to examine the emergence and entrenchment of deep conflict within the psychoanalytic community itself. This collectivity, often held together by powerful authority structures, seems in their absence to cohere by strong adherence to common principles, and it is therefore peculiarly vulnerable to schism when rival interpretations of those principles emerge. Frosh shows that the mobilisation of collective memory may not only sustain sectarianism, of the kind described by Freud himself (1963 [1930]) as the narcissism of small differences, but can also support an institutionalisation of conflict that is highly resistant to change, through the construction of identity and other categories in which powerful emotions of pride, fury, bitterness, shame and guilt are invested. Frosh provides another perspective on the entrenchment of rigid, conflicted, atemporal categories that again brings the microsocial and the intrapsychic into convergence.

In Andrew Cooper's chapter, categories drawn from psychoanalysis are deployed more generally to understand the emotional drivers of categorisation processes in the public realm. From a clinical rather than an academic psychoanalytic perspective, Cooper's chapter argues that the processes by which categorisation occurs in fields that are the focus of novel collective concern cannot be understood entirely by reference to the social substitution by power of one categoric scheme for another, or the gradual development of one such scheme out of another. Rather, Cooper suggests, drawing on the ambiguous psychic states described by Joffe, that liminality, inarticulacy, ambivalence and anxiety surrounds processes of public categorisation, especially in matters that touch upon selfhood – states that can only be explained by reference to post-Freudian dynamics of repression, sublimation and the mentalisation of emotions that have infantile roots. As in Joffe's paper, therefore, the emotional dynamics of depressive functioning and its tolerance of social and temporal ambivalence and mobility, provide the emotional ground from which novel categorisations can best be addressed and understood.

Such studies of the emotional processes of categorisation, when the categories are well developed and integrated theories, are perhaps best regarded as part of a psycho-sociology of knowledge. It is in this genre that Michael Rustin's examination of the phases of psychoanalysis, like Cooper's account of the emergence of particular knowledge categories into public life, is situated, and Rustin's chapter too draws on post-Freudian concepts of universal human emotionality, but also, again, pays attention to the social coloration of that emotionality. Rustin argues that the forms of distress that drove people to seek the assistance of clinical psychoanalysis over the course of the twentieth century may well, as orthodox psychoanalysis insists, have infantile roots that are enduring features of human nature, but the relative importance and mix of these disorders seem to have shifted over time in ways that can be explained by the changing emotional pressures flowing from the wider public realm of political and social change. The phases through which the intellectual tradition has developed in Britain since Freud, through Klein, Winnicott, Bowlby, Bion and Britton reflect, Rustin argues, a series of clinical recognitions, albeit sometimes overlaid with the changing ideological biases of the day, of shifting patterns of individual emotional disorder produced by the forces at work in public life. Whereas Frosh emphasises the fissiparous nature of the tradition, Rustin chooses to stress its institutional continuity tempered by flexibility and its remarkable capacity for conflict containment and constrained pluralism over its *longue durée*. This, he implies, may reflect the partially successful achievement of a professional mentalisation of potential conflict that has sustained the British profession in ways that the German profession, on Frosh's account, could not achieve.

The book then moves into its final part, 'Cultural, historical and political formations of emotion,' where previous interests in the social shaping of emotionalities assume the central place in discussions of cultural, historical and political formations of emotion. In the following chapter, the mobility and ambivalence of emotionalised categories in the public realm are addressed from another, more critical perspective, and varieties of psychoanalysis are supplemented with Foucaultian and poststructuralist accounts for the first time in the book. The category of 'trauma', Susannah Radstone argues, has been transformed over the past two decades, loosed from its medical moorings to stand for a variety of emotional responses to individual and collective suffering, acquiring a powerful explanatory force in direct relation to its imprecision and emotionality. Radstone suggests that a combination of Foucaultian and poststructuralist with psychoanalytic perspectives is both possible and desirable. Foucaultian analysis can offer an account of the character of the social construct of 'trauma' at this historical moment within popular and professional representations. A poststructuralist perspective can help explain the social process of diffusion of the collective representation of the so-called traumatic. Psychoanalysis can help explain the appeal of 'trauma' through its abilities to compensate, domesticate and displace emotion, fantasy and action.

Squire's study, drawing on Foucaultian models of analysing discourses and also on psychoanalytically-inflected criticisms of the lacunae in such models, returns to the issue of rigid rather than ambiguous categorisations in the public realm, examining how unwelcome and stigmatised social categories such as HIV positivity are received, or even welcomed; rejected or denied; made the focus of fantasies of absolute power or powerlessness, or used to negotiate a variety of citizenly collective identities with more limited authority and effectiveness. Where Joffe examines HIV 'othering' from the point of view of those demonising, Squire examines those demonised, in order to show how locally relevant concepts such as 'entitlement' become integrated with a variety of emotions that enable people to redefine 'selfhood'. Indeed, following Karstedt's (2002) exploration of emotions as moral claims, Squire speaks of HIV entitlement as itself an emotion that accrues a degree of authority and power. For Squire, there are possibilities of conflict negotiation, and the generation of more inclusive categories, that can be discerned when we analyse the emotional

freight of apparently 'exclusive' and rigid categories, such as HIV positive and HIV negative status, as they are performed in specific social
and historical contexts.

Whereas Radstone and Frosh show the construction of authority
through the investment of emotion in the power of categories, Squire
examines the incipient authority that can build even within unre-
garded social categories through their emotionalisation, and Richards
examines the demolition of authority through the ritual production of
emotions within a positive feedback system, Treacher's study of Egypt
since the revolution of 1952 concerns the failure to establish a coherent emotional basis for authority in the political realm, except by way
of an authoritarianism that neither communicates, negotiates nor
absorbs emotions. Treacher shows that the illegibility of illegitimate
authority (Sennett, 1980) requires the displacement of emotions away
from critical aspects of collective memory. This displacement sustains
emotions of pride and dignity defensively, covering shame at failures
that are too costly to acknowledge publicly. In turn, this begins a collective process which is the close analogue of the individual process of
repression in the psychoanalytic account. Outright conflict is contained and any risks of the kinds of positive feedback that Richards
observed in Sierra Leone, under an order of even more rigid, religiously
emotionalised categories, are avoided. But this public management of
emotion is undertaken at the price of an inability to process frustrated
emotions, which must be locked out of the public and into a private
ahistorical sphere, the boundaries of which become all the more
heavily marked in the process of repression. Once again in this
chapter, psychoanalytic concepts come into use within a frame of historical analysis, a concatenation which leads Treacher to move continually between the different but linked registers of personal and
national emotional trajectories.

Conclusion

The book's chapters provide yardsticks by which particular traditions'
potential contributions to understanding public emotions can be measured. The chapters are also testing grounds on which possible useful
syntheses between traditions have been explored. The sociological, cul-
tural-studies, psychological and psychodynamic accounts of emotions
that appear here remain almost entirely distinct from popular contemporary 'evolutionary' accounts, which have little to say in the specific
field of social and public consequences of emotions. However, it seems

easy to develop combinations of post-Freudian psychoanalysis with poststructuralist or social psychological approaches (Joffe, Frosh, Cooper, Radstone, Squire, Treacher), and of Durkheimian and cybernetic models of dynamics (6, Richards) – but less easy to bring about the kind of rapprochement between Durkheim and postructuralism that is implicitly attempted in Feuchtwang's chapter or to enter into a conversation between Freud and Durkheim (Rustin). Perhaps one of the broader implications is the possibility of an emerging research agenda, focused on the driving force of emotionality in public structures, which will bring together these latter two lineages.

When compared with biological, rational-choice, cognitive-psychological and Weberian approaches, the common recognition of the centrality of emotion in shaping the character of public life, in the Freudian, Durkheimian and poststructuralist traditions represented here, ought to make commerce between them much easier than with many other leading traditions of social thought. We hope this group of chapters will open a space for that conversation to continue.

The five dimensions used here to explore key emotional dynamics of public life – conflict, collectivity, categorisation, memory and futurity, and power and authority – are not found in all these chapters, nor do they constitute a theory. Other dimensions could have been chosen. We are not suggesting, either, that the chapters in this volume themselves represent the final word on questions of how emotions shape public life. Taken together, however, the chapters, read along the lines of these dimensions, cast new light on the emotional processes and structures involved with public life in a wide variety of societies and situations, and on the consequences this emotionality has for public and private lives.

Notes

1   This project developed from a three year national seminar series initiated in 1998, organised by a group of academics then all at the University of East London. The initial series, entitled 'Affect, Ethics and Citizenship' (AEC), aimed to bring together a group of academics and clinical psychotherapists to look at the place of the emotions in public life. Like the subsequent series of seminars, 'Matters of Feeling', supported by the journal *Economy and Society*, that led to this book, that first series was marked by its inter-disciplinary nature. In addition, the AEC series aimed to forge links between academics whose primary interest was in culture and public life and clinicians whose primary focus was the individual and their feelings. Its origins were in the prior annual 'Psychoanalysis and the Public Sphere' conference, which was organised by the Psychosocial

Studies programme at UEL and the journal *Free Associations*. The series of 12 annual conferences offered a unique space in which a group of politically committed clinicians and academics could think across disciplinary and institutional boundaries about the emotional aspects of a variety of political and social issues. In none of these debates was dialogue straightforward. Academics were divided between Foucaultian, neo-Durkhemian and Kleinian psychoanalytic perspectives, while clinicians found all the academic approaches, including the psychoanalytic ones, difficult to relate to their own approach.

2   Similar work has been done, starting from a sociological understanding of evolved human functioning (see Turner, 2000).

References

6 P, 2003. 'What is there to feel? a neo-Durkheimian theory of the emotions'. *European Journal of Psychotherapy, Counselling and Health*, 5, 3, 263–90

Adorno TW and Horkheimer M, 1997 [1955]. *Dialectic of Enlightenment*. London: Verso

Adorno TW, Frenkel-Brunswik E, Levinson DJ and Nevitt-Sandford R, 1950. *The Authoritarian Personality*. New York: WW Norton & Co.

Ahmed S, 2004. *The Cultural Politics of Emotions*. Edinburgh: Edinburgh University Press

Alexander JC, ed., 1988. *Durkheimian Sociology: Cultural Studies*. Cambridge: Cambridge University Press

Althusser L, 1971. *Lenin and Philosophy*. London: New Left Books

Anderson E, 2003 [1978]. *A Place on the Corner: Fieldwork Encounters and Discoveries*. Chicago: University of Chicago Press

Arendt H, 1963. *On Revolution*. Harmondsworth: Penguin

Arendt H, 1969. *On Violence*. San Diego, California: Harcourt Brace

Arendt H, 1992. *Lectures on Kant's Political Philosophy*. Chicago: University of Chicago Press

Barbalet JM, 1998. *Emotion, Social Structure and Social Theory: A Macrosociological Approach*. Cambridge: Cambridge University Press

Barbalet JM, 2004. William James: pragmatism, social psychology and the emotions. *European Journal of Social Theory*, 7, 3, 337–53

Bendelow G and Williams SJ, eds, 1998. *Emotions and Social Life: Critical Themes and Contemporary Issues*. London: Routledge

Ben-Ze'ev A, 2000. *The Subtlety of Emotions*. Cambridge, Massachusetts: Massachusetts Institute of Technology Press

Berezin M, 2002. Secure states: towards a political sociology of emotion, in JM Barbalet, ed., *Emotions and Sociology*. Oxford: Blackwell, 33–52

Bergson H, 1988. *Matter and Memory*. New York: Zone Books

Bion WR, 1967. Notes on memory and desire. *Psycho-analytic Forum*, 2, 3, 271–80

Britton R, 1998. *Belief and Imagination*. London: Routledge

Brown J and Richards B, 2000. An introduction to the psychoanalytic sociology of emotion. *Psychoanalytic Studies*, 2, 1, 31–3

Brown W, 1995. *States of Injury*. Princeton: Princeton University Press

Burkitt I, 2005. Powerful emotions: Power, government and opposition in the 'war on terror'. *Sociology* 39, 4, 679–96

Butler J, 1997. *Psychic Life of Power*. Stanford: Stanford University Press
Butler J, 2004. *Precarious Life: The Powers of Mourning and Violence*. London: Verso
Burgin V, Donald J and Kaplan C, eds, 1986. *Formations of Fantasy*. London: Methuen and Company
Carbanac M, 2002. What is emotion? *Behavioural Processes*, 60, 69–83
Chodorow N, 1999. *The Power of Feelings*. New Haven, Connecticut: Yale University Press
Cohen S, 2002 [1972]. *Folk Devils and Moral Panics: The Creation of the Mods and Rockers*. London: Routledge
Coleman JS, 1990. *Foundations of Social Theory*. Cambridge, Massachusetts: Belknap Press of the Harvard University Press
Collins R, 1986. *Weberian Sociological Theory*. Cambridge: Cambridge University Press
Collins R, 2004. *Interaction Ritual Chains*. Princeton, New Jersey: Princeton University Press
Connors C, 1997. Field and forum: culture and agriculture in Roman rhetoric. In WJ Dominick, ed., *Roman Eloquence: Rhetoric in Society and Literature*. London: Routledge, 71–89
Cosmides, L and Tooby J, 2000. Evolutionary psychology and the emotions. In M Lewis and JM Haviland-Jones, eds, *Handbook of Emotions*. New York: Guildford Press
Damasio A, 2003. *Looking for Spinoza: Joy, Sorrow and the Feeling Brain*. London: Random House
Darwin C, 1890. *The Expression of the Emotions in Man and Animals*. London: John Murray
Deleuze G and Guttari F, 1987. *A Thousand Plateaus: Capitalism and Schizophrenia*. Minneapolis, Minnesota: University of Minnesota Press
Deleuze G, 1990. *Expressionism in Philosophy: Spinoza*. New York: Zone Books
de Sousa R, 1994. Emotion. In S Guttenplan, ed., *A companion to the Philosophy of Mind*. Oxford: Blackwell, 270–6
Dixon T, 2003. *From Passions to Emotions: The Creation of a Secular Psychological Category*. Cambridge: Cambridge University Press
Dolan RJ, 2002. Emotion, cognition, and behaviour. *Science*, 298, 5596, 1191–4
Durkheim É, 1951 [1897]. *Suicide: A Study in Sociology*. London: Routledge
Durkheim É, 1957 [1950]. *Professional Ethics and Civic Morals*. London: Routledge
Durkheim, É, 1995 [1912]. *Elementary Forms of the Religious Life*. New York: Free Press
Dyer R, 1985. Entertainment and Utopia. In B Nicholl, ed., *Movies and Methods, Volume 2*. Berkeley, California: University of California Press
Edelman M, 1985 [1967]. *The Symbolic Uses of Politics*. Urbana, Illinois: University of Illinois Press
Edelman M, 1988. *Constructing the Political Spectacle*. Chicago: University of Chicago Press
Ekman P, 1980. *The Face of Man: Expressions of Universal Emotions in a New Guinea Village*. New York: Garland STPM Press
Elias N, 1994. *The Civilising Process, Volumes I and II*. Oxford: Blackwell
Elster J, 1999. *Alchemies of the Mind: Rationality and the Emotions*. Cambridge: Cambridge University Press

Erskine A, 1990. *The Hellenistic Stoa: Political Thought and Action.* Ithaca, New York: Cornell University Press

Evans D, 2001. *Emotion: the Science of Sentiment.* Oxford: Oxford University Press

Evans D, 2002. The search hypothesis of emotion. *British Journal of the Philosophy of Science,* 53, 497–509

Evans D and Cruse P, 2004. *Emotion, Evolution and Rationality.* Oxford: Oxford University Press

Fineman S, ed., 2000 [1993]. *Emotion in Organisations.* London: Sage

Foucault M, 1978. *The History of Sexuality: An Introduction.* Harmondsworth: Penguin

Foucault M, 1980, *Power/Knowledge: Selected Interviews and Writings, 1972–1977.* Hemel Hempstead: Harvester Wheatsheaf

Foucault M, 1986. *The History of Sexuality, Volume 3: The Care of the Self.* Harmondsworth: Penguin

Freud S, 1963 [1930]. Civilisation and its Discontents, *Standard Edition of the Complete Psychological Works of Sigmund Freud,* Volume 22, London: Institute of Psychoanalysis and Hogarth Press

Friedman E and Squire C, 1998. *Morality USA.* Minneapolis, Minnesota: University of Minnesota Press

Frosh S, 2002. *After Words.* London: Palgrave

Furedi F, 2004. *Therapeutic Culture.* London: Routledge

Gault BA and Sabini J, 2000. The roles of empathy, anger and gender in predicting attitudes toward punitive, reparative and preventative public policies. *Cognition and Emotion,* 14, 4, 495–520

Giddens A, 1992. *The Transformation of Intimacy.* Cambridge: Polity

Goffman E, 1967. *Interaction Ritual: Essays on Face-to-Face Behaviour.* Garden City, New York: Doubleday, Anchor Books

Goleman D, 1996. *Emotional Intelligence: Why it can matter more than IQ.* London: Bloomsbury

Goodwin J, Jaspar J and Polletta F, eds, 2001. *Passionate Politics.* Chicago: University of Chicago Press

Green A, 1986. *On Private Madness.* London: The Hogarth Press and the Institute of Psychoanalysis

Green A, 1999. *The Fabric of Affect in the Psychoanalytic Discourse.* London: Routledge

Greenspan P, 1988. *Emotion and Reason.* London: Routledge

Grossberg L, 1984. 'I'd rather feel bad than not feel anything at all': rock and roll, pleasure and power. *Enclitic,* 8, 1/2, 94–111

Habermas J, 1984. *The Theory of Communicative Action, Volume 1: Reason and the Rationalisation of Society.* London: Heinemann

Habermas J, 1989. *The Structural Transformation of the Public Sphere: An Inquiry into a Category of Bourgeois Society.* Cambridge: Polity

Hall C, 2002. 'Passions and constraint': the marginalisation of passion in liberal political theory. *Philosophy and Social Criticism,* 28, 6, 727–48

Hall C, 2005. *The Trouble with Passion: Political Theory Beyond the Reign of Reason.* London: Routledge

Hall S and Jefferson T, eds, 1976. *Resistance Through Rituals: Youth Subcultures in Post-war Britain.* London: Harper Collins

Hampshire S, 1999. *Justice is Conflict.* London: Duckworth

Harding J and Pribram ED, 2002. The power of feeling: locating emotions in culture. *Cultural Studies*, 5, 4, 407–26
Harré R, 1986. *The Social Construction of Emotions*. Oxford: Blackwell
Heath S, 1981. *Questions of Cinema*. London: Macmillan
Hochschild AR, 1983. *The Managed Heart: The Commercialisation of Human Feeling*. Berkeley, California: University of California Press
Hoggett P, 2000. *Emotional Life and the Politics of Welfare*. Basingstoke: Palgrave Macmillan
Hoggett P, 2001. Agency, rationality and social policy. *Journal of Social Policy*, 30, 1, 37–56
Hoggett P and Thompson S, 2002. Towards a democracy of the emotions. *Constellations*, 9, 1, 106–26
Honneth A, 1996. *The Struggle for Recognition*. Cambridge, Massachusetts: Massachusetts Institute of Technology Press
Hume D, 1969 [1739]. *A Treatise of Human Nature*. Harmondsworth: Pelican
Jagger A, 1989. Love and knowledge: emotion in feminist epistemology. In AM Jagger and SR Bordo, eds, *Gender/Body/Knowledge: Feminist Reconstructions of Being and Knowing*. New Brunswick, New Jersey: Rutgers University Press, 145–71
James W, 1955 [1890]. *Principles of Psychology*. New York: Dover Publications
Jameson F, Eagleton T, Kaplan C and Mulvey L, 1983. *Formations of Pleasure*. London: Routledge, Kegan and Paul
Kalimtzis K, 2000. *Aristotle on Political Enmity and Disease: An Inquiry into Stasis*. Albany, New York: State University of New York Press
Karstedt S, 2002. Emotions and criminal justice. *Theoretical Criminology*, 6, 3, 299–317
Kateb G, 1984. *Hannah Arendt: Politics, Conscience, Evil*. Totowa, New Jersey: Rowman and Allanhead
Kennedy B, 2000. *Deleuze and the Cinema: The Aesthetics of Sensation*. Edinburgh: Edinburgh University Press
Klein M, 1975. *Envy and Gratitude and Other Works 1946–1963*. London: Hogarth Press
Klein M, 1988. *Love, Guilt and Reparation and Other Works 1921–1945*. London: Virago
Kristeva J, 1982. *Powers of Horror*. New York: Columbia University Press
Lacan J, 1977. *The Four Fundamental Concepts of Psychoanalysis*. London: Hogarth Press
Lazarus R, 1999. *Stress and Emotion*. New York: Free Association Books
LeDoux J, 1996. *The Emotional Brain: The Mysterious Underpinning of Emotional Life*. New York: Simon and Schuster
Lerner JS, Gonzalez RM, Small DA, Fischhoff B, 2003. Effects of fear and anger on perceived risks of terrorism. *Psychological Science*, 14, 2, 144–50
Luhmann N, 1986. *Love as Passion: The Codification of Intimacy*. Oxford: Blackwell
Lupton D, 1998. *The Emotional Self*. London: Sage
Lutz CA and Abu-Lughod L, eds, 1990. *Language and the Politics of Emotion*. Cambridge: Cambridge University Press
Lyman P, 2004. The domestic of anger: the use and abuse of anger in politics. *European Journal of Social Theory*, 7, 2, 133–47

Marcus GE, 2002. *The sentimental citizen: Emotion in Democratic Politics.* Philadelphia, Pennsylvania: Penn State University Press

Marcus GE, Neuman WR and MacKuen M, 2000. *Affective Intelligence and Political Judgment.* Chicago: University of Chicago Press

Marcuse H, 1974. *Eros and Civilisation: A Philosophical Inquiry into Freud.* Boston, Massachusetts: Beacon Press

Matravers D, 1998. *Art and Emotion.* Oxford: Oxford University Press

Meštrović SG, 1996. *The Postemotional Society.* London: Sage

Moscovici S, 2000. *Social Representations: Explorations in Social Psychology.* Cambridge: Polity

Mulvey L, 1975. Visual pleasure and narrative cinema. *Screen,* 16, 3, 6–18

Music G, 2001. *Affect and Emotion.* Ideas In Psychoanalysis. Cambridge: Icon Books

Nozick R, 1974. *Anarchy, State and Utopia.* Oxford: Blackwell

Nussbaum M, 2001. *Upheavals of Thought.* Cambridge: Cambridge University Press

Ogden T, 1992. *The Matrix of the Mind: Object Relations and Psychoanalytic Dialogue.* London: Karnac

Orbach S, 1999. *Towards Emotional Literacy.* London: Virago

Panksepp J, 2003. On the animalian values of the human spirit: the foundational role of affect in psychotherapy and the evolution of consciousness. *European Journal of Psychotherapy, Counselling and Health,* 5, 3, 225–45

Pixley J, 2002a. Emotions and economics. In J Barbalet, ed., *Emotions and Sociology.* Oxford: Blackwell, 69–89

Pixley J, 2002b. Finance organisations, decisions and emotions. *British Journal of Sociology,* 53, 1, 41–65

Pixley J, 2005. *Emotions in Finance: Distrust and Uncertainty in Global Markets.* Cambridge: Cambridge University Press

Porter R, 2000. *Enlightenment: Britain and the Creation of the Modern World.* Harmondsworth: Penguin

Quinn E, 2004. *Nuthin' but a 'G' thang: The Culture and Commerce of Gangsta Rap.* New York: Columbia University Press

Rawls J, 1970. *A Theory of Justice.* Oxford: Oxford University Press

Rawls AW, 1996. Durkheim's epistemology: the neglected argument. *American Journal of Sociology,* 102, 2, 420–82

Redhead S, ed., 1993. *Rave off: Politics and Deviance in Contemporary Youth Culture.* Aldershot: Arena

Rhodes K, Furnham A and Frederickson N, 2004. Emotional intelligence. *Psychologist,* October, 574–7

Richards B, 1999. Therapeutic culture and the democratisation of feeling. Paper given at the University of East London seminar series. *Affect Ethics and Citizenship,* 12.2.99, Birkbeck College, London

Ricoeur P, 1981. *The Rule of Metaphor.* Toronto: University of Toronto Press

Rorty AO, 1980. *Explaining Emotions.* Los Angeles: University of California Press

Rorty AO, 1996. *Essays on Aristotle's 'Rhetoric.'* Berkeley, California: University of California Press

Rose J, 1998. *States of Fantasy.* Oxford: Oxford University Press

Rose N, 1996. *Inventing our Selves.* Cambridge: Cambridge University Press

Rousseau J-J, 1973 [1755]. A discourse on the origin of inequality. In Rousseau J-J, 1973, *The Social Contract and the Discourses.* London: JM Dent & Sons, 27–114

Rustin M, 1991. *The Good Society and the Inner World: Psychoanalysis, Politics and Culture.* London: Verso

Schenk HG, 1966. *The Mind of the European Romantics.* Oxford: Oxford University Press

Scherer KR, 2001. Emotional experience is subject to social and technological change: extrapolating to the future. *Social Science Information,* 40, 1, 125–51

Schmitt C, 1996. *The Concept of the Political.* Chicago: University of Chicago Press

Sennett R, 1974. *The Fall of Public Man.* London: Faber

Sennett R, 1980. *Authority.* London: Faber and Faber

Shaviro S, 1993. *The Cinematic Body.* Minneapolis, Minnesota: Minnesota University Press

Shweder RA and LeVine R, eds, 1984. *Culture Theory: Essays on Mind, Self and Emotion.* Cambridge: Cambridge University Press

Smith C and Ellsworth P, 1985. Patterns of cognitive appraisal in emotion. *Journal of Personality and Social Psychology,* 48, 813–48

Spinoza B, 2000 (1989) [1677]. *Ethics,* tr & ed, Parkinson GHR. Oxford: Oxford University Press

St. John G, 2003. *Rave Culture and Religion.* London: Routledge

Sturdy A, 2003. Knowing the unknowable? A discussion of methodological and theoretical issues in emotion research and organisational studies. *Organisation,* 10, 1, 81–105

Tamborino J, 1999. Locating the body: corporeality and politics in Hannah Arendt, *Journal of Political Philosophy,* 7, 2, 172–90

Terada R, 2001. *Feeling in Theory.* Cambridge, Massachusetts: Harvard University Press

Thompson S and Hoggett P, 2001. The emotional dynamics of deliberative democracy. *Policy and Politics,* 29, 3, 351–64

Turner J, 2000. *On the Origins of Human Emotions.* Stanford, California: Stanford University Press

Walzer M, 2002. Passion and politics. *Philosophy and Social Criticism,* 28, 6, 617–33

Weber M, 1958. Bureaucracy. In HH Gerth and CW Mills, eds, *From Max Weber: Essays in Sociology.* New York: Galaxy, 196–244

Weber M, 1976. *The Protestant Ethic and the Spirit of Capitalism.* London: Allen and Unwin

Whyte WF, 1955. *Street Corner Society: The Social Structure of an Italian Slum.* Chicago: University of Chicago Press

Wide Angle, 1988. *The Fantastic Issue,* 10, 3

Winnicott DW, 1964. *The Child, the Family and the Outside World.* Harmondsworth: Penguin

Part I

Emotions, Conflict and Settlement: a New Durkheimian Approach

1
Rituals Elicit Emotions to Define and Shape Public Life: a Neo-Durkheimian Theory

Perri 6

Public life and emotions: basic theses of the Durkheimian tradition

In the public space of consumption and display in the high street, of the fury of the street demonstration, the streetwise bravado and fear of the mean streets and also in the intense publicity of the meeting held off the streets, public life is an emotional affair in which both requisite and inappropriate feelings are achieved, sustained, modulated and controlled by ritual and bodily performance. Indeed, the differing degrees of publicity of these spaces are only defined ritually. Rituals mark them off from each other by the practices of emotional management ritually prescribed and ritually violated in each case. The conflicts that these rituals enact and amplify can readily erupt and polarise, unless other rituals provide the basis for settlements between their competing imperatives and accountabilities.

Durkheim's account of this proposes that all forms of social organisation, whether on the small scale of the totemic group or the tribe or on the large scale of the revolutionary mob of late eighteenth century France, depend for their cohesion upon their capacity to elicit, institutionalise and communicate those emotions that sustain both the capacity for shared classification, belief and belonging (Durkheim and Mauss, 1963 [1902–3]; Durkheim, 1995 [1912]; Marshall, 2002), and that without the appropriate emotions, neither classification nor belief nor belonging are possible (Rawls, 2001; Shilling, 1997). Less intensely felt and expressed emotions may be required for 'organic solidarity', but even organic solidarity ultimately rests on an emotional order (Fish, 2002). Secondly, he argues, those emotions are elicited, cultivated and sustained through institutionalised collective practices of repeated ceremonial or ritual (James, 2003), both in societies of generally low but occasionally high material and high moral density such as tribal systems (Durkheim, 1995 [1912]) and in the more diffuse societies of higher material but lower moral density in the developed world where the cooler forms of belonging required for contract law and democratic life rest on distinct ritual forms (Durkheim, 1957 [1950]). Although in *Forms*, Durkheim studied rituals in which the same emotion was elicited in all participants, and many subsequent Durkheimian studies have analysed the relationship between ritual and the production of emotion as one in which there is convergence in the emotions felt by all involved. However, this is only true if participants are defined as a particular core group: many ritualised activities, especially in political contexts, involve several such groups. In particular, during many rituals of conflict, different and even contrary emotions are elicited among different groups or individuals present or observing or discovering later about the ritual activity (cf. Collins, 2004).

The present theory rests on a third proposition which can be said to be implicit in Durkheim's writing. By defining boundaries around communities of classification, belief and belonging, rituals also define the boundaries that, for each of the elementary institutional forms of social organisation or 'solidarities', are counted as public. Rituals, Durkheim argues (1995 [1912]) mark off in space and time those phenomena that have the special status that, in the religious context, has the status of the sacred, and for which there are a variety of secular equivalents (cf. Smith, 1999). For example, Goffman (1961, 1971, 1967a, b) transposed Durkheim's theory to show how the 'cult of the individual' is produced by quotidian ritual as opposed to formal grand ceremonial. In his theory of the democratic state as a ritual order Durkheim (1957 [1950]) shows that the boundaries of statehood itself are ritually defined. It is a reasonable extension of this theory, and of Goffman's (1963, 1971) work on civil inattention, to argue that what counts as public is in fact defined ritually, whether publicity is a matter of observable physical public space or public institutional accountability. The emotions appropriate to public space and to public life are not only ritually enforced, as Scheff's (2000) argument about the importance of shame would have it, but the emotions that structure public conflict and provisional settlements of conflicts are actually produced by the ritual practices of publicity and public life. Indeed, public life is only possible to the extent that there is sufficient settlement between conflicting emotions, by ritually allowing sufficient public space for the recognition of others' deeply felt commitments. These feelings in conflict are each produced by ritual practices. Crucial here are the cooler rituals of organic solidarity, which provide vital curbs upon the potential excesses of, for example, collective effervescence or indeed hauteur and deference, in order to make viable the ensemble of institutions that define public life.

The chapter builds upon the neo-Durkheimian theory of the emotions available to be felt in particular institutional settings developed elsewhere (6, 2003a). Although it is not necessary to accept that particular theory in order to accept the argument of the present chapter, it would be necessary to accept some taxonomy of institutional forms of that kind, that would elicit different styles of feeling, analogously with the different 'thought styles' available in different institutional settings (Douglas, 1986; Fleck, 1979 [1935]; Lloyd, 1990; Mannheim, 1936 [1929–1931]).

Ritual

A crucial concept in rebuilding a Durkheimian theory of emotions and institutions must be that of ritual. Durkheim (1995 [1912]) argued that rituals serve to produce social cohesion, that cohesion requires ritual, that they are necessary to fix categories and classifications (Rawls, 1996), and that all ritual achieves these functions in large part through the production of styles of management of emotions such as 'collective effervescence'.

Moreover, his account of ritual is central to his political sociology. A central Durkheimian insight is that *all* politics is ritual in character, although certainly not 'ritualistic'. (Collins, 1975, 1981, 1988, 1994, 2004). In lectures on political sociology (1992, 1957 [1950]), Durkheim set out schematically his claim that the democratic state should be understood as a whole system of ritual practices interdependent with those of civil society, and the democratic state in particular understood as a system of rituals that supported two-way communication between élites and citizens. Ritual gives structure and meaning to confrontational practices of politics such as strikes (Rothenbuhler, 1988) or revolutions (Tiriyakian, 1988). Indeed, Durkheim (1995 [1912]) suggested, the peculiar form of rituals in such settings, with their collective effervescence, strong mechanical solidarity, and clear association with specific revolutionary spaces (Smith, 1999), is the product of the informal institutional situation of strikes and revolutions, in which strongly and weakly regulated social formations are highly polarised (cf. Douglas and Mars, 2003; Rayner, 1988). There are special cases where grand public ceremonial is the stuff of all politics, such as the case of classical Bali as analysed by Geertz (1980), but these do not, as is still commonly thought, exhaust the role of ritual in politics.

What, then, is a ritual, that such a claim could be illuminating and explanatory? It is a misunderstanding to think of 'ritual politics' or 'symbolic politics' as something empty or a sham, a tawdry deception, fundamentally dishonest and by implication less important than the serious business of, say, running programmes – a view of ritual that has long been too common in political science (Brunsson and Olsen, 1993; Edelman, 1985 [1967], 1988; Power, 1997). Political anthropologists have long recognised that anything really important in a society will sooner or later have to be ritualised if its importance is to be institutionalised (for instance Douglas, 1966, 1970a, 1982c, and Apter, 1999; Kertzer, 1988; Meyer and Rowan, 1977; Steinmetz, 1999). Rituals, indeed, sustain the possibility of honest communication: for by ritual we establish the credibility of speakers and test the ritual 'key' in which they are making their utterances against the ritually expected ones (Goffman, 1986 [1974]). For in prescribing the forms of speech in semi-private meetings, public ceremonies, interviews, confrontations between groups and individuals, the ritual order of everyday political and social life is what makes political communication and mutual understanding possible, and therefore honest to the degree that it can be so.

Durkheim (1995 [1912]) characterises a rite as a mode of action (p34), rules of conduct that prescribe how people must relate to the sacred (p38), and as 'myths in action' (p79). Cult, he stresses (pp59–60) recurs periodically, and must enact the relationships between the sacred and the profane (p60); he emphasises too the consequential, efficacious means by which the social organisation is – at the very moment of its apparent collapse into emotional anarchy – actually reformed, reinforced, managed both by catharsis and by its obverse, evident mobilisation. Durkheim (1995 [1912], bk III) distinguished between systems of positive rites, which organise prescriptions, and systems of negative rites, which organise proscriptions or prohibitions, arguing that both are necessary and each requires the other. Goffman (1976b) showed that in technologically complex societies, the same is true specifically to sustain social relations of a hierarchical form (at the micro-level, through deference), and also of a more individualistic kind (at the micro-social level, in self-respecting and other-respecting forms of demeanour). A synthesis of neo-Durkheimian definitions of ritual would be the following. A ritual is any

1. repeated practice (*repetition*) (Durkheim, 1995 [1912], p60), although always with scope for innovation (cf. Richards, this volume, *contra* e.g. Rapaport, 1979)
2. with some degree of prior prescription of the acts to be performed (*prescription of forms*)
3. involving marking out a particular space and time (*sacrality 1*) (Durkheim, 1995 [1912], 1957 [1950] XI–XIV)
4. to give elevation and special status to those symbols (*sacrality 2*) (Collins, 2004, pp79–101; Rothenbuhler, 1998)
5. which functions to sustain and/or also to challenge institutions and social relations (*functional explanation*)
6. by mobilising emotion and attention among participants and observers (*emotion production*),
7. and by communication that takes the form of by putting exemplars or symbols before participants and observers, which fix categories and classifications, define social boundaries (*exemplar-based classification*) (Douglas, 1966, Chapter 4; Douglas, 1992)
8. and by investing authority in those emotions and exemplars that sustain those bonds (*authority production*), and
9. it achieves this effect by means of the enactment of social organisation (*enactment*) –
10. typically, indeed, the *bodily* enactment (Bell, 1992, Chapter 5; Douglas, 1966, 1970a), or near-bodily enactment ('near bodily', because there are also rituals for communication at a distance: Denzin (1998) analyses 'flaming' rituals in internet Usenet groups; Romm (Livermore) 1999 analyses ritual behaviour in organisational politics conduced by e-mail: however, these rituals appear at least at present to be largely parasitic upon rituals for face-to-face communication) –
11. where the enactment is conducted in miniature by way of analogies, metaphors, transpositions of forms of social organisation (Douglas, 1986, Chapter 4), and of narratives of the processes of conflict and settlement (Turner, 1995 [1969] 1974, 1982) between these forms of social organisation (*symbolism*)
12. in forms, the overt content of which may be and typically are quite different from the content of underlying social relations promoted

or sustained (non-congruence between explicit content and real social efficacy) (*non-congruence*),

13. whether or not the explicit intention of the actors is to perform this enactment of social organisation (*structural*) (Douglas, 1986, Chapter 3; Westrup, 1996, p30ff);

14. where the practice is not transparent in its causal character, that is, it has effects that are diffuse, hard to predict or model in advance in terms of the causal pathways by which the ritual practice will succeed or fail in promoting those forms of social relations (*diffuse causal efficacy*)

15. which work together as a system of ritual, where each ritual form interacts with others to describe the repertoire of public life in a society (Gluckman, 1965)

16. where the ritual forms encompass both life in the quotidian public spaces (Douglas and Isherwood, 1979; Goffman 1967a, b, 1986) as well as grand formalised and organisational ceremonial.[1]

The general recognition has been borrowed by political scientists working in public administration from organisational sociology (especially Meyer and Rowan, 1977; Silverman, 1984) that small, everyday ritual is essential both to the peaceful and the conflictual functioning of administrative organisations, but it has yet to be absorbed into the study, for example, of that quintessentially political instrument, the meeting (though there is some recognition of this in Schwartzman, 1989 and Feldman, 1989; from an Eliasian perspective, see also van Vree, 1999; see Peck *et al.*, 2004; Peck and 6, 2006). Yet the public worlds of meetings of governmental committees, the partnership boards, campaign groups and of negotiations between police officers and street demonstration leaders are the places in which the emotional tenor of politics is defined, definitions challenged and settled.

What, then, is *not* a rite? The most important element of the answer to this question must be 'a tool, for example'. For even when people conceive their rituals largely instrumentally, they typically organise them in ways quite differently from those with which they organise the use of tools. While ritual forms are necessary, on the Durkheimian account, to the social organisation necessary to wield tools – including the tools of government – effectively, they are not themselves tools. For example, the tools of government – such as tax incentives, or contracts, or regulations to prohibit or mandate or information campaigns (6 *et al.*, 2002; Bemelmans-Videc *et al.*, 1998; Hood, 1983; Salamon with Lund, 1989) – are congruent and transparent and concentrated in their causality. A focus on the deployment of tools in public policy where the aim is to secure institutionalisation is the hallmark of the utilitarian approach, deriving from Spencer, that Durkheim was so concerned to argue against (for example 1984 [1893], 1957 [1950]).

On the Durkheimian view, then, the viability of a polity depends on the ritual forms that sustain the organisation required for using the tools of governance and for understanding and using the communication involved in their use. For these tools are only effective to the extent that they can engage the motivation of citizens, producers, consumers and interest groups, which in turn requires their emotional commitment, for, Durkheim (1984 [1893]) stresses interest alone is too feeble to suffice.

Ritual, accountability and time: taxonomy

At the empirical level, then, four forms of ritual in politics have already implicitly distinguished, namely,

- the formal and public: these include religious, constitutional, judicial, commemorative, civic, (theatrical) forms of grand ceremonial
- the informal and public: in this category, we might identify the recently emerged practices laying flowers at scenes of deaths or disasters and the sending of e-mail petitions
- the formal and private: these include, in the household, family prayer, birthday celebrations or Christmas meal or Thanksgiving; there are also prescribed forms of political rhetoric used in meetings behind closed doors, which come into this category, such as that used in the making of opening negotiating claims between trades unions and employers in national bargaining committees
- the informal and private: this is the terrain examined by Goffman of the micro-politics of handshake, the greeting, the prescribed small talk at cocktail parties, and the ritual styles of 'backstairs' political conversation and deal-making.

However, this empirical level of taxonomy is not really sufficient to make out the Durkheimian argument that institutional viability is dependent on the organisation of ritual, for it does not bring out the features which, on this account, play the important causal role in explaining and predicting viability.

At the heart of the Durkheimian theory of institutions that exhibit requisite structural variety (6, 2003b; Ashby, 1947; Thompson, 1996) is a claim about the importance of ensuring the social organisation of practices that link accountabilities, hopes and aspirations between past, present and future. In short, the Durkheimian thesis is that *the viability of a polity or any system of social organisation depends on the comprehensive organisation of social time, for (a) by organising time, accountabilities are organised, and (b) an adequate range of accountabilities is what makes possible the level of social organisation and capability required for institutional arrangements to be viable.*

Unfortunately, it is necessary to reconstruct the elements of the theory from several writings in which he analyses the consequences of ritual, and to follow the ways his approach has been used by Durkheimian scholars. In his writings on ritual and institutions, Durkheim gives emphasis to several different kinds of ritual. In *Forms*, he identifies several kinds of rites – initiatory, the mimetic (one type of totemic membership rite), representative or commemorative, and piacular (expiatory, for funerals, imminent death, misfortune or disaster), and also identifies the more general and nonperiodic performance of cult. This is mainly an empirical classification, and Durkheim does not attempt to show whether these are mutually exclusive and jointly exhaustive. His interest there is principally in their consequences for solidarity; what is missing from the analysis, though, is a full theoretical statement of their interrelationships; moreover, he provides only scattered hints on equivalent forms in societies with more a ramified division of labour.

In the account in the *Leçons*, however, important clues are provided. He examines there how the institutions of property and contract, including marriage, have remained viable, he places great importance on *performative* rituals, in which the utterance of prescribed words in a certain context binds the speaker's future actions before others; promising is in that text the exemplar of performative ritual. In *Forms*, however, he also analyses rituals that respond to events, and shows that they are essential to the viability of institutions that hold people to account against commitments from the past. Examples include the piacular or funerary rite, and a variety of rites honouring ancestors. We might call these ratificatory.

Briefly in *Forms* but also in popular language in his Dreyfusard essay, 'Individualism and the intellectuals' (1973 [1898]), he gives due recognition to the role that other kinds of ritual can play in transforming institutions. Here, his examples are taken from the revolutionary rituals of the storming of the Bastille and the cult of reason. Although it was left to other social scientists in the Durkheimian tradition such as van Gennep (1960 [1908]) to develop the issue, in *Forms* he also acknowledges that there are rites that transform situations from one stage to another. These include initiatory rites, which change the status of an individual by bringing them into membership of a group. There are also others that pitch a community into a new period or stage, perhaps into crisis: these last, Lockwood (1992, Chapter 2) calls 'hyper-rituals' because of their socially creative role. At the opposite extreme, are those rituals that seem to serve to fix and define institutions, such as those commemorative rites which play a role in maintaining social and political memory (Connerton, 1989; Gephart, 2001 [1998]; Halbwachs, 1980 [1950], 1992a [1925]). The first step in reconstructing a Durkheimian theory is to recognise that these two dimensions should be cross-tabulated. For then it becomes possible to see that four fundamental, mutually exclusive but not quite jointly exhaustive, relationships between ritual action and social or political time are established thereby. Performative and definitive rituals such as signing marriage contracts or international treaties or swearing oaths to give truthful evidence in courts are future-binding, because they seek to bind the behaviour of individuals and groups over significant periods of time. Performative and transformative rituals such as rites of passage or rituals to enter new collective periods are oriented to the present, because they mark the present as a watershed moment to be built up to in anticipation and later remembered as marking a social boundary or distinction in accountability. Ratificatory and definitive rituals such as honouring the commitments inherited from predecessors perpetuate the past (the rituals so beloved of Burke, 1910 [1790]), while ratificatory and transformative rituals such as revolutionary or protest rituals demand the rectification or correction of the past (those beloved of Paine, 1998 [1791]). In each of these cases, the public ceremonial ritual not only seals the accountabilities by fixing certain key emotions, but also provides formal ritual markers to complete or begin or link together a chain of other informal rituals (Collins, 2004) including those of negotiation and preparation and of group remembering, each of which in turn organises emotions in relation to the focal public formal ritual. Each thereby sustains accountabilities to different kinds of institution – which are exemplified respectively, by promises, memberships, traditions and principled justice (see Durkheim's discussion of the need for justice to correct persisting elements of the forced division of labour: 1984 [1893], bk III, ch 2). The first two, sustained by performative rituals are more concrete, and the later two by ratificatory ones, are more abstract.[2]

Of course, as anthropologists have long emphasised, there is no guarantee that rituals will be efficacious, either in their overt purpose or in their implicit social function; in this vulnerability, rituals are no different from any other social practice. Marriages fail, treaties are violated, comrades forget, witnesses mislead and so on. Yet it is the fact that in so many cases, ritual practices are sufficiently efficacious in mobilising the emotions of appropriate accountability, that makes rituals still worth undertaking. For when one spouse deserts or 'cheats on' the other, when one state 'dishonours' its treaty obligations, when witnesses 'perjure themselves', the heightened emotional tenor of the vocabulary with which describe such failures of accountability to the rituals they have performed demonstrates both the greater severity attached to defection from commitments that have been ritually solemnised and the additional ritual productions to which we respond to defections by others, at least in advance of being offered appropriate and also ritually presented apologies, exculpations, and so on.

Durkheim argues that each type of ritual defined by its peculiar time-orientation will produce a different kind of emotion. Funerary rites, even if they involve frenzied grief, are essentially solemn, and this is typical of commemorative rites. Since the aim is to induce reflection upon the institutions of the past that continue to command adherence, this solemnity is appropriate. Contracts for real estate or marriage too, however happy the occasion, are solemn matters for reflection is induced among the participants about the gravity of what they have entered into. Durkheim (1995 [1912]) identifies 'collective effervescence' or that style of the management of emotions in which there is an overflowing of appropriate passions in several kinds of ritual, including the *corroboree*, totemic rites including various Intichiuma, and also piacular (meaning 'expiatory') or those rites which are conducted on funerary occasions, imminent death or occasions of disaster or collective crisis. However, there are marked differences in the form of effervescence that Durkheim diagnoses between these rites. The lack of control and 'transports of enthusiasm' and the sexual freedom that he discusses in the case of the totemic rites are very different from the much more solemn frenzy of the mourning rites and the meticulous care taken over self-wounding and hair removal. He contrasts the unfocused joy of the former with the highly focused sadness and also reflective anger of the latter. Essentially, the key difference lies in the degree of reflectiveness and solemnity attached to *commitment to action* to continue the obligations passed on in the case of the piacular rites and the much less reflective passion attached to *commitment to member-*

ship in the case of the totemic rites. Reading this analysis together with his analysis of the solemnity of rituals of contract in the *Leçons*, it becomes clear that the important difference is between the solemnity and reflectiveness of those rites that define accountabilities and the passion and even rage (in the case of some revolutionary rites) of those which transform them (cf. Turner's 1995 [1969], 1974, 1982 concept of *'communitas'*).

However, the behavioural form that is appropriate to these emotions differs according to whether the ritual is performative or ratificatory. At ratificatory rituals, expressive weeping or fist-waving or shouting is entirely appropriate. In performative rituals, a more impassive demeanour is appropriate (on the expressive impassive distinction in style of emotion management, see 6, 2003a). Although there are sometimes tears of joy at weddings, for example, in most western countries, they are hardly ever considered appropriate at the moment when the officiant administers the solemn vows. At occasions when communities are pitched into crisis, grim stoicism or furious defiance may be appropriate in political and juridical rituals, and is typically produced by the form of rhetoric used (Aristotle, 1991).

Figure 1.1 sets out the classification, with examples from political as well as from wider social contexts. It also shows the basic solidarities or institutional forms of political and social organisation that typically use each of these forms. In addition, it shows how to integrate into the analysis an enriched Aristotelian (1991) appreciation of the institutional cultivation of styles of rhetoric to elicit particular emotions, where that rhetoric is itself understood as a ritualised activity. In some cases, the ritual form is used in the passing of people from one form of institution to another (especially in rites of passage); in other cases, it is used to reinforce a single solidarity.[3]

As we should expect from ritual forms like these four, that stress accountability to institutions all the solidarities are those in the experience of institutions is such as to elicit some type of emotional commitment.

In each of these types of rituals, then, the basic activity is that of holding others – and oneself as participant – to account. Future binding rituals make future accountability against present commitments possible; past correcting ritual holds people to account for claimed errors or injustices; past perpetuating rituals hold people to account for their conservation of an inheritance; present oriented rituals hold people to account as members or persons carrying certain roles. The different emotions produced in each make these basic forms of accountability possible.

Performative
↓

i.e. performance of extensively prescribed acts produces a change of classified state or accountability for individual participants, and so produces a change in the form solidarity between them
Type of behavioural management of affect produced: *Impassive*

Type A: Legal, juridical, paedagogical
Solidarities: Individualist, hierarchical
Time orientation: Future oriented: binding of future action by present action of commitment
Relationship with other ritual forms: Commits to future Type C rituals
Examples from Durkheim: rites of contract and respect for property (*Professional ethics and civil morals*)
Example of rhetoric and Aristotelian type of rhetoric: Tennis Court Oath, deliberative and/or adversarial followed by epideictic
Example from organisational process: Acceptance of the budget report
Examples form everyday comsumption, socialising, working: handshake on borrowing or lending, farewell with promise of reunion, signing personal development objectives statement after appraisal

Type B: Rite of passage e.g., accession into membership (e.g., life stage), marking change in period
Solidarities: Hierarchical, enclave
Time orientation: Present-oriented: succession of periods or stages, opens up options classified appropriate to new classified conditions
Relationship with other ritual forms: Marks classification as capable of participation in future Type A rituals
Examples from Durkheim: Intichiuma (*Elementary forms*)
Example of rhetoric and Aristotelian type of rhetoric: Churchill's acceptance speech 'Blood, sweat and tears'; epideictic
Example from organisational process: leaving party, launch for change of organisational name or logo
Examples from political process: concluding communiqué press release,
Example from everyday consumption, socialising, working: receiving first car, induction of new staff member

Definitive
←

i.e. Defines accountability by closing down or limiting options for participants
Type of affect produced:
Solemnly or reflectively effervescent

Type C: Commemorative
Solidarities: Hierarchical, enclave
Time orientation: Past oriented: binding by perpetuating accountability to past institutions
Relationship with other ritual forms: Fulfils commitments in past Type A rituals

Type D: Political, mobilisation
Solidarities: Enclave, individualist
Time orientation: Future oriented: calls for correction of past actions or institutions
Relationship with other ritual forms: Calls for future Type C rituals

Transformative
→

i.e. Transforms accountability by opening up or calling for opening up of options
Type of affect produced: *Ragingly or non-reflectively effervescent*

Figure 1.1   The four elementary types of ritual forms

Examples from Durkheim: the piacular rite (Elementary forms)

Example of rhetoric and Aristotelian type of rhetoric: Gettysburg address, Pericles' Funeral oration, epideictic

Example from organisational process: Festschrift, award ceremony, plaque

Example from political process: head of state apology for wrongs of previous régime, acceptance of war reparations

Examples form everyday consumption, socialising, working: souvenir purchase and display, family anniversary

Examples form Durkheim: French revolutionary rites (Elementary forms)

Example of rhetoric and Aristotelian type of rhetoric: Zola's j'accuse, demagogic

Example from organisational process: strike

Example from political process: protest meeting, serving of writ in class action

Examples from everyday consumption, socialising, working: fans at match, frontline staff team meeting in support of colleague

→

Ratificatory

i.e. performance of acts not prescribed quite so extensively marks, ratifies, reflects, expresses a prior change of classified state or accountability for individual participants, and so produces a change in the form of solidarity between them

Type of behavioural management of affect produced: *Expressive*

Figure 1.1 The four elementary types of ritual forms – *continued*

Many empirical rituals of course are hybrids, combining two or more elementary forms. Weddings for example involve future-binding and performative vows, but in many societies also operate as rites of passage. Political rituals that hark back to ancient victories – such as some northern Irish Protestant ceremonies about the Battle of the Boyne – are at once commemorative and mobilisatory. There are also political rituals in which large numbers engage in simultaneous commitment or pledging for political action, which represent hybrids along the negative diagonal. And so on.

However, these four core forms do not quite provide a complete taxonomy of the ritual forms observed or that have real social and political importance. Many political anthropologists have laid great stress on importance of rituals of joking, insult, even obscenity, of satire and mockery, and upon the fact that sometimes even in the most solemn ritual cycles, a space is deliberately reserved for them (Bloch, 1989, Chapter 9; Douglas, 1970b; Handelman, 1982; Turner, 1995 [1969]). Political scientists have stressed the importance of television or radio satire including impersonation or, for many centuries but most obviously in the work of Gillray in the eighteenth century or Bell today, newspaper cartoons in providing either a safety valve or a focus of mobilisation. The joker or the satirist is a figure with a certain institutional immunity in many societies: *Monty Python*, *Spitting Image* and Rory Bremner have been shown on national television without censorship, and theirs is of course a highly ritual form of humour, both in the manner of delivery and in the manner of its experience by an audience. The price of that immunity is a measure of distance, or a ritual place of safety from the most active forms of participation in the institutions they send up: the same is basically true of the role of the laugher in ritual forms found in societies using less complex technologies than those of Europe and north America. The role of the joker or satirist is that of the isolate, even if the organisation of their audience may well be enclaved or individualistic. That is, the ritual form here is appropriate to that of the person who is not committed and to a certain extent not even required to be committed to the institutions to which, in the rest of their lives when they are not in satiric mode, they are actually held to account. They are simply expected to survive, to cope, and endure through time under those institutions. Satire has therefore an orthogonal relationship with political and social time. In any society, this is the experience of most people with respect to at least some institutions for at least some period of their lives. Those who are committed individualists, enclave members or

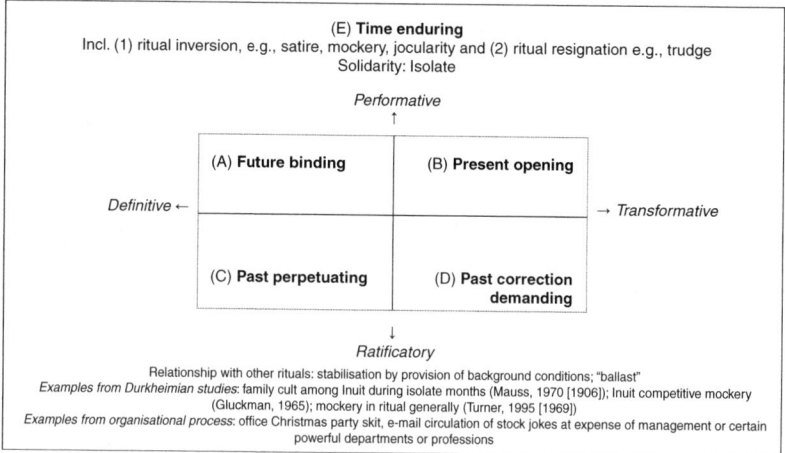

Figure 1.2   Time enduring ritual compared with the four time committed ritual forms

hierarchs with respect to, say, business or governmental or academic or charitable or religious or even familial institutions may find themselves, at least for a time, as isolates with respect to one of the others. Figure 1.2 shows the isolate ritual form surrounding the others as a background, because it does not enter the core set of commitment based ritual forms which are defined by the core of the diagram, and because its pervasiveness makes it inappropriate to show it as appearing on a third dimension or plane.

Ritual forms as an interdependent system

If Durkheim's work offered no more than a taxonomy of important forms of ritual and their relationship with social time and accountability, it would be interesting but not a theory of ritual institutionalisation through the production and mutual containment of different kinds of emotion. The theory offered here is functional, in the narrow sense that it uses functional explanations.[4] However, because it specifically provides for conflict and postulates the high plausibility of dysfunctionality in the absence of special conditions, it is not functionalist.

A central thesis of the theory is that these elementary forms of ritual work as part of whole system, exist only in relation to each other, and that they provide essential political services for each other. The whole set of rituals available to and used in a society can only be understood together, as an interlocking system (Gluckman, 1965; Turner, 1995 [1969]). Figure 1.1 provides a very high level description of the elements of any system of social organisation. For each type organises certain emotions and provides a basis for their communication. Any viable social organisation must contain an adequate level of articulation for each of the five forms of ritual – future-binding, present-opening, past-perpetuating, past-correcting, and time-enduring. To the extent that the polity as a set of institutions maintains itself at all, it must provide a high level ritual order that enables settlement between them.

Durkheim stresses the necessity for future-binding ritual forms if contract, property, the defining of criminal acts and other basic institutions (1957 [1950]) are to be sustained, for by purely utilitarian means they would be unviable. Without past-correcting rituals, it would be impossible to overthrow elements of forced division of labour that still persist (1984 [1893] bk III, ch 2). Without present-opening rituals, social mobility, for example, is very difficult, for it becomes impossible to signify what counts as a change in status: societies without formal *rites de passage* for class mobility must use micro-rituals of the Goffman kind for marking stratification and for achieving change, such as changes in manners, accent, dress, self-presentation. Without past-perpetuating ritual forms, institutions cannot achieve viability because they cannot recognise the fact or absence of continuity with their own past. Organisational memory cannot be sustained, save by ritual forms (Halbwachs, 1992a [1925], 1980 [1950]).

Two kinds of evidence can be adduced in support of this hypothesis. First, one can study cases of collapse, such as failed states or bankrupt organisations or failed policies, to find under-articulated ritual forms and secondly one can study reasonably successful ones to identify the causal contribution that the presence of each form made. Turnbull's (1972) study of the social and political collapse among the Ik was of former kind, and part of his diagnosis was the failure of past-perpetuating and of future-binding ritual forms. Price and Thompson's (1997) study of Alpine villages shows the range of micro-ritual forms and ritual innovation at work in making the villages viable over seven centuries. Past-perpetuating rituals sustain the political organisation of the village and some traditional land-uses; past-correcting rituals enable villagers to engage in collective action against external demands that they felt threatened the viability of their ecological relationship with the forests; future-binding ritual forms have sustained capacity for economic growth in good times and so on; all that is missing from Price and Thompson's study is the role of time-enduring satiric rituals.

For example, the moral and legal capacity to enter into future-binding rituals is marked not simply by chronological age, but by in many countries the ritual forms of the issuance of documents and at least micro-rituals (in the USA, the receipt of the sacred driving licence serves to mark effective entry into citizenship, with all the familial micro-ritual surrounding it). More generally, the classifications of capability for future binding are sustained by such stage-opening ritual forms. Future-binding and past-perpetuating ritual forms are reciprocal: each calls for the other. Past-correcting rituals anticipate and call for future-binding and then, once corrected, past perpetuating forms. Past-perpetuating rituals – both informal ones of access, demeanour and dress and formal ones of commemoration of instaurations and of reconfirmation of laws – confirm the continuing relevance of enduring systems of classification of people by class, by entitlement, by merit, by authorisation to exercise state power, and so on. Figure 1.3 summarises some key bilateral relationships. In addition, there are more diffuse multi-lateral services. The time-enduring rituals of inversion and satire enable the system to avoid hyperactivism and conflict, provide safety valves and also provide essential information that can trigger corrective action before the point that past-correcting rituals become too threatening or even violent.

Moreover, each form of ritual serves to curb the potentially destabilising excesses of the others. Future-binding and past-correcting ritual forms, without the balancing of past-perpetuating and stage-opening, will produce what Durkheim (1951 [1897]) termed *mal de l'infini*, or the inability to limit what is desired to what is feasible produced by insufficient social regulation (see Meštrović, 1993 [1988]) – the hallmark of the millenarian and the bitterly disappointed cynic alike – because they will produce a collective imaginary of wiping clean the social slate, which can never in practice be achieved. Conversely, past-perpetuating and stage opening ritual forms without the rebalancing of the other two, will produce fatalism or the forced division of labour (Durkheim (1984 [1893]), because they will produce only the endless cycling of existing institutions without innovation or change and will, *de facto*, subordinate the regulated to those who can claim to 'own' the legacy of the authoritative past, for example, in age-segmented societies, the young to the old.

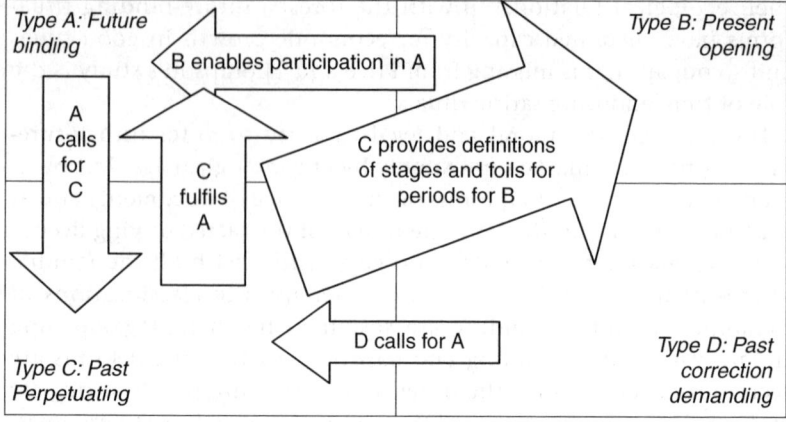

Figure 1.3   Some key specific bilateral relationships between the four core types

In this sense, therefore, the interdependence of the mutually dissimilar ritual forms sustains organic solidarity, the ability of social organisation at any scale to contain the dangerous processes by which people who ritually classify themselves as mutually similar ritually reject others.[5] For each of the basic ritual forms – past correcting, past perpetuating, future binding, present opening and time enduring – when undertaken in isolation from others and repeatedly so as to reinforce its peculiar emotion, can readily produce and sustain mechanical solidarity, or that condition of insistence of the authority of mutual similarity among people that can so quickly become exclusive and intolerant. The risks of such emotions as corrosive pride (C), embittered rage (D), resignation (E), over-commitment etc., are most likely to be contained by a con-strained plurality of all the ritual forms, which is perhaps the best way to think about organic solidarity as a ritual process and not merely as an abstract criterion or as a kind of attenuation of an emotion of group belonging.[6]

Conclusion

The *spaces* of public life at every point on the spectrum from the meeting through the street to the world of the celebrity and the elected politician are marked off by ritually defined affect styles (6, 2003a):

conversely, the forms of civil inattention appropriate in each space define what counts as private in each context. Held together by the overarching system of ritual, public life depends upon adequate variety of rituals to define the forms of publicity which are the basic institutions of a polity. Moreover, the present theory emphasises that the multiple relationships of life in public to *time* and of the emotions which articulate the claims we make of each other in relation to present, past and future are managed by the system of rituals. The feeling orders of the mechanical solidarities risk emotional extremism – the fury of collective effervescence or even *mal de l'infini* in past-correcting ritual, the corrosive cynicism of time enduring ritual, the solemnity of future-binding commitment – in their efforts to enforce institutional definitions of similarity and corresponding pressures for accountability. Organic solidarity, or the institutional condition in which people who classify each other as dissimilar from each other and operating in ritually dissimilar spaces which sustain conflicting emotions, requires a delicate mix of spaces for all of the kinds of rituals – a ritual division of labour in public life – as well as rituals of conciliation, exchange of services between rituals.

A Durkheimian theory of ritual and emotion has real significance for political theory as well as for political science and political sociology. Much twentieth century political theory stemming from the work of Rawls, Nozick, Dworkin, Habermas, Barry and others has been concerned with derivation of more or less ideal arrangements on the basis of principle: it has rightly been criticised as describing a jurisprudence for constitutional courts than defining a genuinely political account of institutions. Real politics is about making settlements, striking compromises and cultivating and containing emotions. Normative political theory really should be conducted in a quite different register, and one that is much more concerned with the institutional capabilities of accommodation, settlement and what Gray (2000a, b) calls *modus vivendi*. The significance of Durkheim's embryonic ritual theory of the democratic state in the *Leçons* is that, read together with the rest of his *oeuvre*, it provides the materials with which we can develop an account of those *modi vivendi* as systems of production and containment of a variety of emotions, as sustained by requisite variety in ritual. These *modi vivendi* constitute practices of organic solidarity, or the capacity of those classified by the prevailing institutions as dissimilar to live together despite. Crucially, the theory argues, sufficient variety in the orientation of ritual and emotion to time is key to the viability of a polity.

Notes

1   This account of ritual is to be contrasted with those, which may as well be called Weberian, following his conception of 'rationalisation', as a historical process of the elimination of non-congruent and non-transparent forms of cognitive practice from social organisation. These views hold that ritual is a separate and rarified category of thought or communication from the everyday, the scientific, the technological or the practical, and generally, following Weber, they regard it as a hangover from 'tradition' and assimilate ritual to magic (for example Beattie, 1970; Bloch, 1989, chapters 2, 3; Horton, 1970) or else root it in 'non-rational biological processes (Bloch, 1998, chapters 1, 4).

2   Durkheim's main discussion of the relationship between ritual and time concerns the extent to which the cycle of rituals defines the structure of time as represented and as experienced in passage (cf. Durkheim 1995 [1912]), 10). In this, he drew on the work of his student Hubert (1999 [1905]). However, the Durkheimian school developed the idea that time orientations of ritual are of fundamental importance in shaping public life. Mauss (1979 [1906]) recognised that the boundary between what was classified as public and private was marked by ritual transitions in the nature and quality of time between the seasons in Inuit society, and went on to explore how in each period, the content of the ritual activity prefigured future and adjusted for past seasons, as well as sustained present commitments. In his work on memory, Halbwachs (1992a [1925], 1992b [1941], 1980 [1950]) examined the importance of ritual processes among religious groups for sustaining either apocalyptic past correcting or past perpetuating styles of memory.

3   Thus, it should *not* be thought that this taxonomy can be reduced to the cross-tabulation of social regulation and social integration that yields the four basic institutional forms used neo-Durkheimians such as Douglas (1982a, b) and Thompson (1996; Thompson *et al.*, 1990): this will become even clearer when an additional element is introduced below. The present taxonomy can work with theirs, but it is not the same. In principle, someone who rejected the Douglas-Thompson taxonomy of institutional forms and preferred some other, could still adopt Figure 1.1.

4   For the argument that, contrary to Elster's (1983) widely cited charge, functional explanations, if properly constructed and adequately evidenced, can be valid, and that they cannot be eliminated from social science, see Douglas, 1986, chapter 3.

5   Of course, Durkheim came to recognise by the time he wrote *Elementary Forms*, as he perhaps has not in *Division*, that similarity of people is not in nature, but is an achievement of social and political institutions that select features that are relevant for their principles of allocation: Douglas and Hull, 1992; Goodman, 1972.

6   Many writers on ritual and emotion treat 'solidarity' as itself an emotion (for instance Collins, 2004). However, Durkheim makes the most sparing use of the term in *Forms*. In *Division*, it is clear that solidarity denotes a form of social organisation defined in respect of the *institutional* types of *structural* bonds and the degree of similarity demanded by such bonds. The

emotional process associated with, for example, the violation of those bonds by different kinds of crime is at most an indicative symptom of the presence of a particular type of institutional organisation. It is this usage that is followed here.

References

6 P, 2003a. What is there to feel? a neo-Durkheimian theory of the emotions. *European Journal of Psychotherapy, Counselling and Health*, 5, 3, 263–90

6 P, 2003b. Institutional viability: a neo-Durkheimian theory. *Innovation: the European Journal of Social Science Research*, 16, 4, 395–415

6 P, Seltzer K, Leat D and Stoker G, 2002. *Towards Holistic Governance: The New Agenda in Government Reform*. Basingstoke: Palgrave

Apter A, 1999. The subvention of tradition: a genealogy of the Nigerian durbar. In G. Steinmetz, ed., *State/Culture: State-Formation after the Cultural Turn*. Ithaca, New York: Cornell University Press, 213–52

Aristotle, 1991. *The Art of Rhetoric*. Harmondsworth: Penguin

Ashby WR, 1947. Principles of the self-organising dynamic system. *Journal of General Psychology*, 37

Beattie JHM, 1970. On understanding ritual. In BR Wilson, ed., *Rationality*. Oxford: Blackwell, 240–68

Bell C, 1992. *Ritual Theory, Ritual Practice*. Oxford: Oxford University Press

Bell C, 1997. *Ritual: Perspectives and Dimensions*. New York: Oxford University Press

Bemelmans-Videc M-L, Rist RC and Vedung E, eds, 1998. *Carrots, Sticks and Sermons: Policy Instruments and their Evaluation*. New Brunswick, New Jersey: Transaction

Bloch M, 1989. *Ritual, History and Power: Selected Papers in Anthropology*. London: Athlone

Bloch M, 1998. *How We Think They Think: Anthropological Approaches to Cognition, Memory and Literacy*. Boulder, Colorado: Westview Press

Brunsson N and Olsen J-P, 1993. *The Reforming Organisation*. London: Routledge

Burke E, 1910 [1790]. *Reflections on the Revolution in France*. London: Dent

Collins R, 1975. *Conflict Sociology*. New York: Academic Press

Collins R, 1981. On the micro-foundations of macro-sociology. *American Journal of Sociology*, 86, 5, 984–1014

Collins R, 1988. The Durkheimian tradition in conflict sociology. In JC Alexander, ed., *Durkheimian Sociology: Conflict Studies*. Cambridge: Cambridge University Press, 108–28

Collins R, 1994. *Four Sociological Traditions*. New York: Oxford University Press

Collins R, 2004. *Interaction Ritual Chains*. Princeton: Princeton University Press

Connerton P, 1989. *How Societies Remember*. Cambridge: Cambridge University Press

Denzin NK, 1998. In search of the inner child: co-dependency and gender in a cyberspace community, in Bendelow G and Williams SJ, eds, 1998, *Emotions in Social Life: Critical Themes and Contemporary Issues*. London: Routledge, 97–119

58   *Public Emotions*

Douglas M, 1966. *Purity and Danger: An Analysis of the Concepts of Pollution and Taboo.* London: Routledge
Douglas M, 1970a. *Natural Symbols: Explorations in Cosmology.* London: Routledge
Douglas M, 1970b. The social control of cognition: some factors in joke perception. *Man*, 5, 2
Douglas M, ed., 1982a. *Essays in the Sociology of Perception.* London: Routledge and Kegan Paul
Douglas M, 1982b [1978]. Cultural bias. In M Douglas, *In the Active Voice.* London: Routledge and Kegan Paul, 183–254
Douglas M, 1982c. The contempt of ritual, in M Douglas, ed., *In the Active Voice,* London: Routledge and Kegan Paul, 34–8
Douglas M, 1986. *How Institutions Think.* London: Routledge and Kegan Paul
Douglas M, 1992. Rightness of categories, in M Douglas and D Hull, eds, *How Classification Works: Nelson Goodman among the Social Sciences.* Edinburgh: Edinburgh University Press, 239–71
Douglas M and Hull D, eds, 1992. *How Classification Works: Nelson Goodman among the Social Sciences.* Edinburgh: Edinburgh University Press, 239–71
Douglas M and Isherwood B, 1979. *The World of Goods: Towards an Anthropology of Consumption.* London: Routledge
Douglas M and Mars G, 2003. Terrorism: a positive feedback game. *Human Relations*, 56, 7, 763–86
Durkheim É, 1951 [1897]. *Suicide: A Study in Sociology.* London: Routledge
Durkheim É, 1957 [2nd edn, 1992; 1950; lectures: 1890–1900]. *Professional Ethics and Civic Morals.* London: Routledge
Durkheim É, 1973 [1898]. Individualism and the intellectuals, in RN Bellah, ed., *Émile Durkheim on Morality and Society.* Chicago: University of Chicago Press, 43–57
Durkheim É, 1984 [1893]. *The Division of Labour in Society.* Basingstoke: Basingstoke
Durkheim É, 1995 [1912]. *Elementary Forms of the Religious Life.* New York: Free Press
Durkheim É and Mauss M, 1963 [1903]. *Primitive Classification.* Chicago: University of Chicago Press
Edelman M, 1985 [1967]. *The Symbolic Uses of Politics.* Urbana, Illinois: University of Illinois Press
Edelman M, 1988. *Constructing the Political Spectacle.* Chicago: University of Chicago Press
Elster J, 1983. *Explaining Technical Change: A Case Study in the Philosophy of Science.* Cambridge: Cambridge University Press
Feldman MS, 1989. *Order Without Design: Information Production and Policy Making.* Stanford, California: Stanford University Press
Fish J, 2002. Religion and the changing intensity of emotional solidarities in Durkheim's *The division of labour in society* (1893). *Journal of Classical Sociology,* 2, 2, 202–23
Fleck L, 1979 [1935]. *The Genesis and Development of a Scientific Fact.* Chicago: University of Chicago Press
Geertz C, 1980. *Negara: The Theatre State in Nineteenth Century Bali.* Princeton, New Jersey: Princeton University Press

van Gennep A, 1960 [1908]. *The Rites of Passage*. London: Routledge and Kegan Paul

Gephart W, 2001 [1998]. Memory and the sacred: the cult of anniversaries and commemorative rituals in the light of *The elementary forms*. In NJ Allen, WSF Pickering and W Watts Miller W, eds, *On Durkheim's Elementary Forms of Religious Life*. London: Routledge, 92–102

Gluckman M, 1965. *Politics, Law and Ritual in Tribal Society*. Oxford: Basil Blackwell

Goffman E, 1961. *Asylums*. Harmondsworth: Penguin

Goffman E, 1963. *Behaviour in Public Places: Notes on the Social Organisation of Gatherings*. New York: Free Press

Goffman E, 1967a. On face-work: an analysis of ritual elements in social interaction. In E Goffman, *Interaction Ritual: Essays on Face-to-Face Behaviour*. New York: Pantheon Books, 5–46

Goffman E, 1967b. The nature of deference and demeanour, in E Goffman, *Interaction Ritual: Essays on Face-to-Face Behaviour*. New York: Pantheon Books, 47–96

Goffman E, 1971. *Relations in Public: Micro-Studies of the Public Order*. New York: Basic Books

Goffman E, 1986 [1974]. *Frame Analysis: An Essay on the Organisation of Experience*. Boston, Massachusetts: Northeastern University Press

Goodman N, 1972. Seven strictures on similarity. In N Goodman, *Problems and Projects*. Chicago: Bobbs-Merrill, 437–47

Gray J, 2000a. *Two Faces of Liberalism*. Cambridge: Polity Press

Gray J, 2000b. Pluralism and toleration in contemporary political philosophy. *Political Studies*, 48, 2, 323–33

Halbwachs M, 1980 [1950]. *The Collective Memory*. New York: Harper and Row

Halbwachs M, 1992a [1925]. The social frameworks of memory. In L Coser, ed., *Maurice Halbwachs on Collective Memory*. Chicago: University of Chicago Press, 37–189

Halbwachs M, 1992b [1941]. Conclusion. In L Coser, ed., *Maurice Halbwachs on Collective Memory*. Chicago: University of Chicago Press, 193–235

Handelman D, 1982. Reflexivity in festival and other cultural events. In M Douglas, ed., *Essays in the Sociology of Perception*. London: Routledge and Kegan Paul, 162–90

Hood CC, 1983. *The Tools of Government*. Basingstoke: Macmillan

Horton R, 1970. African traditional thought and western science. In BR Wilson, ed., *Rationality*. Oxford: Blackwell, 131–71

Hubert H 1999 [1905]. *Essay on Time: A Brief Study of the Representation of Time in Religion and Magic*. Oxford: Durkheim Press

James W, 2003. *The Ceremonial Animal: A New Portrait of Anthropology*. Oxford: Oxford University Press

Kertzer DI, 1988. *Ritual, Politics and Power*. New Haven, Connecticut: Yale University Press

Lloyd GER, 1990. *Demystifying Mentalities*. Cambridge: Cambridge University Press

Lockwood D, 1992. *Solidarity and Schism: 'The Problem of Disorder' in Durkheimian and Marxist Sociology*. Oxford: Oxford University Press

Mannheim K, 1936 [1929–1931]. *Ideology and Utopia: An Introduction to the Sociology of Knowledge*. Orlando, Florida: Harcourt Brace Jovanovich

Marshall DA, 2002. Behaviour, belonging and belief: a theory of ritual practice. *Sociological Theory*, 20, 3, 360–80

Mauss M, 1979, [1906]. *Seasonal Variations of the Eskimo*. London: Routledge and Kegan Paul

Meštrović SG, 1993 [1988]. *Émile Durkheim and the Reformation of Sociology*. Lanham, Maryland: Rowman and Littlefield

Meyer JW and Rowan B, 1977. Institutionalised organisations: formal structure as myth and ceremony. *American Journal of Sociology*, 83, 3, 340–63

Paine T, 1998 [1791]. *The Rights of Man*. Oxford: Oxford University Press

Peck EW and 6 P, 2006. *Beyond 'Delivery': Policy Implementation as Sense-Making and Settlement*. Basingstoke: Palgrave Macmillan

Peck EW, 6 P and Gulliver P and Towell D, 2004. Why do we keep on meeting like this? The board as ritual in health and social care. *Health Services Management Research*, 17, 100–9

Power M, 1997. *The Audit Society: Rituals of Verification*. Oxford: Oxford University Press

Price MF and Thompson M, 1997. The complex life: human land uses in mountain eco-systems. *Global Ecology and Biogeography Letters*, 6, 1, 77–90

Rappaport RA, 1979. The obvious aspects of ritual. In RA Rappaport, *Ecology, Meaning and Religion*. Richmond, California: North Atlantic Books, 173–222

Rawls AW, 1996. Durkheim's epistemology: the neglected argument. *American Journal of Sociology*, 102, 2, September, 430–82

Rawls AW, 2001. Durkheim's treatment of practice: concrete practice vs representations as the foundations of reason. *Journal of Classical Sociology*, 1, 1, 33–68

Rayner S, 1988. The rules that keep us equal: complexity and the costs of egalitarian organisation. In JG Flanagan and S Rayner, eds, *Rules, Decisions and Inequality in Egalitarian Societies*. Aldershot: Ashgate, 20–42

Romm C, 1999. *Virtual Politicking: Playing Politics in Electronically Linked Organizations*. Creskill, New Jersey: Hampton Press

Rothenbuhler EW, 1988. The liminal fight: mass strikes as ritual and interpretation. In JC Alexander, ed., *Durkheimian Sociology: Cultural Studies*. Cambridge: Cambridge University Press, 66–89

Rothenbuhler EW, 1998. *Ritual Communication: From Everyday Conversation to Mediated Ceremony*. Thousand Oaks, California: Sage

Salamon LM with Lund MS, 1989. *Beyond Privatisation: The Tools of Government Action*. Washington, DC: Urban Institute Press

Schwartzman HB, 1989. *The Meeting: Gatherings in Organisations and Communities*. New York: Plenum

Scheff TJ, 2000. Shame and the social bond: a sociological theory. *Sociological Theory*, 18, 1, 84–99

Shilling C, 1997. Emotions, embodiment and the sensation of society. *Sociological Review*, 45, 2, 195–219

Silverman D, 1984. Going private: ceremonial forms in a private oncology clinic. *Sociology*, 18, 2, 191–204

Smith P, 1999. The elementary forms of place and their transformations: a Durkheimian model. *Qualitative Sociology*, 22, 1, 13–36

Steinmetz G, ed., 1999. *State/Culture: State-Formation after the Cultural Turn*. Ithaca, New York: Cornell University Press

Thompson M, 1996. *Inherent Relationality: An Anti-dualist Approach to Institutions.* Bergen: LOS Senteret

Thompson M, Ellis RJ and Wildavsky A, 1990. *Cultural Theory.* Boulder, Colorado: Westview Press

Tiriyakian EA, 1988. From Durkheim to Managua: revolutions as religious revivals. In JC Alexander, ed., *Durkheimian Sociology: Cultural Studies.* Cambridge: Cambridge University Press, 44–65

Turnbull C, 1972. *The Mountain People.* New York: Simon and Schuster

Turner VW, 1995 [1969]. *The Ritual Process: Structure and Anti-structure.* New York: Aldine de Gruyter

Turner VW, 1974. *Dramas, Fields and Metaphors: Symbolic Action in Human Society.* Ithaca, New York: Cornell University Press

Turner VW, 1982. *From Ritual to Theatre: The Human Seriousness of Play.* New York: PAJ Publications

van Vree W, 1999. *Meetings, Manners and Civilisation: The Development of Modern Meeting Behaviour.* London: Leicester University Press

Westrup C, 1996. The play of information systems development: drama and ritual in the development of a nursing information system. *Information Technology and People,* 9, 2, 24–42

2
The Emotions at War: A Musicological Approach to Understanding Atrocity in Sierra Leone[1]

Paul Richards

Introduction

War has such momentous consequences that it is hard to escape the idea it must be driven by carefully calculated strategic objectives. Armed conflict seemingly must have a goal. Special pleading soon takes over the explanation of the phenomena of war. To the religious, war is competition between creeds. To economists, war is 'greed, not grievance'. Durkheim initiated a different line of argument. Group violence (self harm or harm against others – sacrificial mutilations or vendettas, under the category the piacular rite) entrains emotional energies in defence of collectivity. By extension, certain acts of war (and perhaps entire conflicts) may be classed as group reinforcement. Stone (2004) applies the Durkheimian approach to the explanation of the massacres in Rwanda in 1994. In this chapter I will attempt something similar, in regard to atrocities associated with the war in Sierra Leone (1991–2002). But it is necessary to address an evident weakness in the Durkheimian approach. The mechanism underlying Durkheim's doctrine of 'effervescence' is obscure. Recent work on the evolution of musicality as a domain of unassigned intentionality may bring us closer to the identification of candidate mechanisms. Musicality, it has been argued, is an evolved capacity for the production and appreciation of organised sounds (and movements) in which participants dwell upon the very idea of interactive intentionality (that is, it is a means to explore sociality). It seems possible to adapt the argument about musicality to war. War begins as masquerade. It is a performance space in which conflicting social alternatives are 'danced out'. It has long been understood that war is as much posturing as all-out attack. But this posturing requires performance cues. It needs to unfold according to a recognisable pulse. Where the beat is lost there is risk of extraversion. Noise replaces music. Anger boils over and extreme damage results. My argument, in regard to Sierra Leone, will be that war was a carefully orchestrated family feud until intervention by external forces (South African mercenaries) 'scrambled' the music (that is, social signals regarding the nature of the dispute). Rite became bloody riot, with horrific consequences.

A sketch of the war in Sierra Leone[2]

The principal parties to the civil war in Sierra Leone (1991–2002) were, initially, a very small and poorly equipped insurgent entity – the Revolutionary United Front of Sierra Leone (RUF), led by a collective of radical students, and later by a cashiered army corporal, Alfred Foday Sankoh – and the government army. Fighting spread from Liberia, where RUF cadres had earlier assisted the insurgency of the National Patriotic Front of Liberia (NPFL), led by Charles Taylor. RUF units of about 50 fighters each entered Sierra Leone from Liberia at Bomaru and Bo Waterside, points north and south of the Gola Forest, a boundary wilderness separating western Liberia and eastern Sierra Leone. The national army, assisted by Guinean troops under a mutual defence pact, closed roads from the eastern border at Daru on the Moa River and Joru on the road to the eastern provincial capital Kenema, in the south.

Some RUF units in the far south were able to cross the Moa and head towards the southern provincial capital, Bo. The government army had no capacity for jungle warfare, and these southern units threatened for a time, but were later in 1991 pushed back towards the Liberian border by battle-hardened former Liberian soldiers re-armed by the Sierra Leone government from among refugees fleeing the NPFL. Stalemate ensued, during which period the tiny RUF concentrated on recruiting and training impoverished young people it had recruited from rural communities in and around the Gola Forest. Post war studies among ex-combatants suggest the great majority of these recruits were in fact inducted against their will (Humphreys and Weinstein, 2004).

Both the government and outsiders assumed that the loyalty of these conscripted youths (female as well as males) would be suspect.

However, abductees saw their own induction into the RUF as a kind of initiation, in a part of Africa where young teenagers are almost universally 'seized' by two sodalities (so-called 'secret' societies) – Poro (for males) and Sande (for females) – with considerable show of ritual violence. Initiation hardships are conceived to be part of the necessary process of removing children from the emotional bonds of the family and re-attaching them, with revised emotional entrainment, to a wider inter-familial social unit – the sodality – ruled by elders. Initiation involves physical trauma but also a large amount of music and dance. The learning of society songs and cries, through which appropriate emotional states are rekindled in subsequent life crises, forms much of the curriculum of the period spent in seclusion in the bush school (a sacred clearing in the forest). The spirit forces upon which the sodalities depend are manifested as dancing masquerades. RUF trainers relied upon equivalent musical tools of emotional management to forge loyalty to the movement (Richards, 1996, 2005a).

Although constrained within the Liberian border region the infant RUF was able for a time to acquire supplies through its Liberian ally the NPFL. But the Taylor faction was driven out of the western forest of Liberia from 1992 by the Sierra Leone government supported militia ULIMO (United Liberian Movement for Justice and Democracy), and the RUF became increasingly enclaved. During 1991–92 the RUF leadership controlled small border towns (Pujehun in the south and Pendembu in the east) from where it attempted to run civil administration. It appointed its own chiefs, and set up people's courts, well regarded by some villagers who hated the arbitrariness of 'customary' courts presided over by members of major land-owning families. But bombing raids by the Nigerian airforce, informally involved in the Sierra Leone war as an extension of the activities of the West African peace-enforcement mission in Liberia (ECOMOG), forced the abandonment of towns, and later even the remote border village of Sandeyalu in northern Kailahun District where the leadership took refuge early in 2003.

Forced to shelter in a 'bunker' which was no more than a pit alongside a half-built house on a slight hill in Sandeyalu, the leadership decided to abandon its few vehicles and heavy weapons and take to the forests in November 2003. Sankoh went south to Faama, an isolated small chiefdom headquarters in a finger of land connecting to the Moro River, which divides the Sierra Leonean and Liberian Gola Forests, and thereafter to a forest site at the southern end of the Kambui Hills, where a well-protected camp – the Zogoda – became the movement's secret HQ (Peters, 2006). Other military commanders were instructed to make similar camps in the network of hilly forest reserves reaching into the heart of the country. Communication was by radio (Sankoh was trained as an army signals technician) or written instructions and reports ferried along farm paths criss-crossing the country by trusted cadres (Peters and Richards, 1998; RUF/SL, 1995). The camps were established during the first half of 1994, and thereafter daily life for young inmates seized in raids on unprotected rural schools increasingly resembled life in the Poro bush.

Resentful at being forced to confront the RUF in vulnerable forward positions without adequate arms and ammunition young army officers revolted against the government of President Joseph Saidu Momoh in April 1992, and formed a military junta, the National Provisional Ruling Council (NPRC). A number of officers under the protection of the deposed president had managed to avoid service at the war front. In an act of wanton strategic foolishness the new regime posted these officers to the war front to experience the fighting at first hand. Here they soon abandoned positions and connived with the enemy to sell supplies. Some hoped this way to cause the collapse of the NPRC.

The NPRC made a second fatal mistake by reneging on earlier agreements at the war front to include their enemy in a peace process (RUF/SL, 1995). The regime calculated it would consolidate its own position as an unelected junta by quickly ridding the country of the remnants of the RUF. New recruits were found from among the urban unemployed and supplies were poured into the war front. The new recruits were barely capable of fighting, and certainly had no intention of following the RUF into the bush on foot. Of the weapons that were not sold by corrupt officers to the enemy most of the rest disappeared in ambushes and raids. The RUF, to its surprise, found itself re-supplied (RUF/SL, 1995).

Loans and grants extracted from the international community were milked to fight the war and enrich the junta. To keep the pipe of assistance open the NPRC claimed it had beaten the RUF but needed money to demobilise troops and rebuild war-affected communities. Any evidence of actual fighting was put down to disloyal troops. Junta forces maintained road blocks around towns – harrassing civilians – but effectively abandoned the bush and its remote pathways to the increasingly ingenious cadres of the RUF (Richards, 1996; RUF/SL, 1995). The RUF remained quiet during much of 1994, re-grouping in the camps and training for a new phase of its struggle. The Phase II campaign began in November 1994, with a raid on Kabala, in which prisoners were released from the jail, and two international volunteers seized as hostages. Army command degenerated into factional bickering among cliques. Thereafter, small war bands of young RUF recruits roamed the country at will, mounting pin prick raids far and wide. The attacks and ambushes approached Freetown in the early part of 1995, prompting hasty evacuations among nervous international agencies.

All manner of means were used to frighten the populace and convey a much greater sense of power and reach than the movement truly possessed. Villages might be attacked and then burnt, but clear attempts were made to limit loss of life. The movement was often more interested in preaching to villagers than killing them. In some cases populations were ushered in the direction of towns, with instructions to seek the care of humanitarian agencies while the revolution was under way, before a settlement was torched. Cadres scattered letters to explain their struggle, which they conceived to be a popular uprising of disenfranchised rural youth against the abuses of landlords and chiefs (Peters and Richards, 1998). They wrote slogans on walls, often invoking symbols of popular resistance by citing reggae and hip-hop icons. Actions were also designed to sow seeds of dissension. Fighters dressed in stolen army fatigues to convey a sense that the government's own troops had turned against the civilian populace. Houses belonging to only one faction in a land or chieftaincy dispute might be burnt to convey the idea that the rival faction had colluded with the raiders.[3]

Far from the battle zone, capital city elites interpreted these signs differently, developing a shape shifting discourse of 'sobels' (soldiers by day and rebels by night) whereby it was supposed the country was no longer in the grip of a rebellion but menaced only by disloyal junta troops. Attempts to resolve the hostage crisis led to the first clear evidence that the RUF had survived the border bombings of 1992–3 and was sequestered with an increasingly large number of suprisingly loyal young abductees in inaccessible bush camps. A Ghanaian associate of Charles Taylor was recruited by an international conflict resolution agency, International Alert. Through his contacts with RUF civilians in Ghana and Cote d'Ivoire the Ghanaian interlocutor was able to set up a trip from across the Moa in Guinea through forest bush tracks to reach the Zogoda, where he was able to interview Sankoh (later shown on British TV news), film young cadres displaying their 'moves' as forest fighters, and record a performance of camp inmates singing the movement's anthem (see below). The trip led to the release of hostages (some of whom later spoke with some degree of admiration concerning the movement) and the beginning of a peace process leading to the Abidjan agreement of November 1996. The Abidjan process might have led to an ending of the war and a successful peace. It was clear from the RUF's behaviour that it was interested at this stage primarily in projecting its message about political corruption and the social exclusion of rural impoverished youth. The war had been dislocative but primarily dramaturgical. Deaths among civilians and in combat were surprisingly low (agency figures – possibly inflated – put the death toll after nearly six years of conflict at about 15,000 persons). Many of these casualties will have been among the RUF itself, sometimes the result of army massacres or lynchings by civilians. The free-lance actions by local civil defence also became a factor. Junior initiates in Poro have the duty to defend their communities, and a number of war-front commanders, doubting the loyalty of regular troops, began to train Poro auxiliaries. Local hunters also began to initiate apprentices into their guild to expand civil defence. With advice from South African private security experts this later developed into a government-sponsored national civil defence movement (in effect a rival to the national army).

The paradoxical loyalty of abductees to the RUF was no surprise to villagers brought up with the experience of initiation. Children abducted by the movement were seen to have been emotionally reconstructed by their experiences. With feelings of loyalty to the rebel collective forged by the rigours of abduction the children were lost to wider society; some villagers concluded the 'rebel mind' would endure. Amnesty International (1992) documented extra-judicial killing of young people suspected of rebel sympathies. My own fieldwork took me to sites of mass graves where it was said the army had killed abducted children who had succeeded in fleeing the RUF. In Pujehun District in September 1992 I encountered a chief who protected about ten children in his house, fearing they would be lynched by families or neighbours for having fallen into rebel hands. Other accounts spoke of army torture of suspected rebel sympathisers, including amputation of fingers and limbs. After the war, one woman leader in the RUF explained her loyalty to the movement as the result of her husband being mutilated and killed by the army in 1991.

Evidence of the dangers of community re-entry fed back into the movement and future run-aways were deterred. There was now no option but to be loyal. Any faint chances of flight were snuffed out by the movement's practice of marking recruits – especially attempted run-aways – with tattoos or scarification. The hazards of running away and seeking readmission to mainstream rural society are graphically portrayed in the account of a carpenter seized in January 1995 in a raid on the town of Kambia in North-western Sierra Leone (Peters and Richards, 1998). After days on the run from his bush camp he had the appearance of a 'bush creature' – only luck and acts of casual kindness helped him to escape, where a majority met an untimely end, summarily shot by the army or battered to death by the clubs of lynch mobs.

In its bush phase the RUF succeeded not only in 'converting' its mass of teenage rural cadres to its cause but also in winning the circumstantial (and perhaps more durable) loyalty of a number of educated captives. The circumstances of their capture is not always clear, and in some cases it appears they were persons known for their radical or socially progressive views. Not all were grudging in their support for the movement's aims. As delegates from the RUF War Council some became prominent in the Abidjan peace negotiations.

But the Abidjan negotiation was in difficulty even as it took shape. This was due to a new dynamic in the capital. The NPRC – unable to trust its own army – had turned to international private security companies for help. Several were already involved in the Sierra Leone diamond mining sector. One complex of companies – their precise inter-relations remain unclear – became a dominant element in the war. British based Branch Energy (today Koidu Holdings), a subsidiary of Diamondworks of Toronto, acquired a major kimberlite diamond mining concession under the NPRC, and used the services of a South African group specialising in private security, Executive Outcomes. The South Africans responded to the NPRC's request for military help against the RUF, in part to locate and rescue the hostages. Payment may have involved diamond concessions of interest to its mining partners. Executive Outcomes began to stem the advance of the RUF, concentrating in particular on mining areas.

By the end of 1995, however, capital city and international pressure had built on the NPRC to such a point that it conceded elections, and lost power to the formerly banned Sierra Leone Peoples Party (SLPP). The SLPP presidential candidate, Ahmad Tejan-Kabbah, and the electoral commissioner, James Jonah, who later became the Sierra Leone minister of finance, in the regime he helped elect, were seen by some as having being parachuted in by the United Nations, to prepare the way for a UN peace keeping 'success' in the war against the RUF (Kabbah had worked for many years for the UN Development Programme and Jonah had been in charge of the failed UN peacekeeping operation in Somalia).

President Kabbah vowed to keep the Abidjan peace process on track, but increasingly became the victim of competing forces among the various international interests seeking to control the crisis in the country. The British were interested in a democratic transition, considering the factionalised NPRC army the main obstacle and the RUF an irrelevant side-show. The UN was interested in a peace-keeping success as evidence of 'African solutions to African problems' (a mantra of the Clinton presidency in the US). The RUF's main interlocutor in Abidjan – the conflict resolution agency International Alert – was considered problematic by many. It was deemed to be dressing the RUF in borrowed robes, making it appear more significant than it merited from a Freetown perspective.[4] Its executive director was rumoured in some quarters to be a rival for the UN secretary-generalship. The mining companies and their allies in private security were anxious to open mines; Abidjan seemed to imply protracted discussions with the RUF about corruption and transparency over minerals.

Sankoh and the War Council of the RUF signed cease-fire agreements with Kabbah in April and June 1996. But reaching a final agreement in Abidjan proved difficult. This was due to the activities of the South African mercenaries commanding Executive Outcomes.[5] It was at the suggestion of Pine Pienaar, a former South African defence Force colonel, that the president launched a Friday afternoon War Council in State House. Hooper (2003) reports that Executive Outcomes, backed by the Nigerian ECOMOG commander in Sierra Leone, used these meetings to browbeat the president to abandon his cease-fire agreements and authorise all-out bombardments of key RUF bush camps. This proved to be strategically unwise. It scattered the RUF cadres while the leadership was away in Abidjan negotiating peace (the main raid on the Zogoda appears to have taken place in late September or early October 1996). Sankoh lost control of his traumatised ground forces. Under great pressure from the international community to sign an agreement Sankoh made perfunctory helicopter visits arranged by International Alert to three of his surviving camps, fearing for his own life (International Alert, 1997). A stillborn deal was signed (30th November 1996). Sankoh never rejoined his movement in the bush, which became increasingly unstable and atrocity-prone.

It is not clear what strategic vision motivated the South Africans. Clearly, they despised the RUF (see Hooper, 2003), and seem to have assumed that heavy bombardment and air raids would cause panic and surrender. They gambled that the dramaturgy of their firepower would be enough (Richards, 2005a). The British in Malaya discovered that ten times as many regular troops were needed against dedicated insurgents in tropical forest conditions. An apologist for Executive Outcomes claims that there were about 500 RUF cadres at the time (Hooper, 2003). I led a team planning the demobilisation of the RUF in preparation for signing Abidjan, and interviewed a range of RUF fighters, concluding that the movement had between three and five thousand fighters (Richards *et al.*, 1997). To have securely overcome the RUF by military means would have required (if my figure was correct, and the Malayan multiplier applied) about 30,000 regular peace keeping troops. The eventual number supplied by the UN was in total just under 20,000, the largest peace keeping mission on the planet at the time. About 24,000 RUF fighters handed in a weapon to qualify for demobilisation (Humphreys and Weinstein, 2004). Executive Outcomes had a small group of less than ten white officers and about 50 Namibian and South African black rank-and-file, mostly veterans of covert operations in Angola and Namibia during the apartheid period (Hooper, 2003).

Having scattered the RUF, and revealed the cease-fire to be a pretence Executive Outcomes had no chance to restore control. The company was dismissed after the Abidjan accord was signed, and then disbanded. A British replacement, Sandline International, with apparent links to the same nexus of companies holding the kimberlite concession, and mired in controversy in the UK over the Arms to Africa scandal, was never more than marginally effective, operationally. Kabbah, meanwhile, had been deposed by army mutineers, who went into a short-lived alliance with the scattered and traumatised splinters of the RUF. These mutineers were rooted out (in February 1998) by ECOMOG and Kabbah restored.

After Abidjan, Sankoh was arrested in Nigeria, returned to Sierra Leone subsequent to the restoration of Kabbah, and condemned to death. Leaders of the army mutiny were shot by firing squad in October 1998, despite international protest. One of those executed was a woman, Major Kula Samba. Junta loyalists in the bush vowed revenge and planned an attack (January 6th 1999) on Freetown with support from rival international diamond mining interests. They were joined by RUF elements intent on rescuing Sankoh. Atrocities multiplied, including the amputation of hands, feet and limbs of several thousand civilians.[6]

Nigerian contingents in ECOMOG – having failed to prevent the Freetown attack – announced they would withdraw from Sierra Leone, leaving the newly restored Kabbah regime defenceless (the mutinous army had been disbanded in 1998). Sankoh was pardoned, and a new power-sharing peace agreement signed in Lome in 1999. The UN and other international agencies queried pardons offered to those perpetrating atrocities, and a Special Court for Sierra Leonean war crimes was proposed.[7]

A UN peace keeping force, UNAMSIL, was formed and deployed in April 2000 to replace the departing Nigerians. The Lome agreement broke down when the RUF – resisting enforced disarmament – took large numbers of newly-deployed UN troops hostage. The UN reported (wrongly) that the RUF was once again marching on Freetown, causing mass panic. Temporary order was restored by the intervention of British troops, new agreements were reached with the RUF in Abuja in November 2000, and UN forces then spread across the country. Final demobilisation of the warring parties was completed by the end of 2001, amid an atmosphere of general war weariness.

Understanding atrocity as performance

Although all parties in the war in Sierra Leone carried out atrocities and committed grievous abuses it is clear that there was some ebb and flow in occurrence. A minor surge of abuses was particularly associated with the elections of early 1996, from which the RUF was excluded. A major surge followed the South African mercenary interventions that scattered the RUF. A third spate seems to be especially associated with the beating back of the junta/RUF forces in January 1999. There was a definite ebb in abuses in the period 1994–5 during which time the RUF was gathering strength and spreading surreptitiously throughout the country. This was a period during which some informants fleeing the movement reported 'the RUF no longer kills'.

My argument below will concern how we might explain these ebbs and surges. In all cases the destructiveness of war – I submit – derives from a dynamic of performance. There is something urgent and important at stake beyond the scope of language to convey. When the performance is engaged – when the parties begin (as it were) to dance to a single tune – progress towards peace seems possible. Progress towards Abidjan, which would have released the RUF from the bush and rescue the hostages, was accompanied by a scaling down of the movement's destructiveness. Burning of huts replaced killing of civilians. The movement even encouraged the 'flow' of civilians towards temporary safety in camps. But the involvement of first the international community in the election process (based on a capital city concept) and then of

Executive Outcomes in 'enforcing' a peace, seems to have disrupted the 'beat'. The sense that (despite spoilers, free-riders and opportunists) some progress was being made in 'acting out' (or better, 'dancing out') a solution to a deep national crisis was lost. Outsiders pursuing their own interests 'scrambled' a process in which possible new social scenarios were being rehearsed. Excesses of violence began to assume epidemic form, as cadres sought vainly to re-establish an underlying pulse.

I shall argue that the mechanisms controlling this pulse-seeking behaviour (and the behavioural excesses triggered when pulse was lost) are probably better explained in ways that evolutionists have approached the origins of musical capacity as emotional entrainment than through any attempt to provide a symbolic interpretation or rationalisation of acts of extreme violence. There is a clear compatibility between Durkheimian ideas about emotional effervescence and the arguments of evolutionary musicologists regarding the origins of musicality as a sphere of unassigned intentionality within which humans regularly rehearse social scenarios, thus creating the possibility of social solidarity (Cross, 2006). But (in Durkheimian perspective) war is not something alien to society. Combat is inseparable from struggles to attain social solidarity and justice (cf. Rawls, 2003; Lockwood, 1992). Peace and war – I shall suggest – are products of the same musical mechanism.

First I wish to present two brief ethnographic vignettes. The first suggests that atrocity (even at its most horrible) has performative aspects comparable with the self harm and harm to others that Durkheim attributes to the piacular rite, and thus, in some aspects at least, can be understood as an attempt to 'act out' rage at loss of social coherence. The second point concerns evidence that performance is in some respects separable from speech and rational calculation. The apparent independence of music (i.e. the performative aspect of a rite) from linguistic (and thus discursive) capacities is important to the analysis of atrocity. The frequency with which victims in Sierra Leone were required by their abusers to dance or sing is sometimes interpreted as an attempted disordering of rational expectations – the normal turned upside down. But equally, I will contend, it might offer clues as to the importance abusers attach to generating new kinds of social order through certain kinds of performative actions. In seeking to penetrate the mind of abusers, to guard against recurrence, it seems important to ask why it seems so important to make victims 'dance to a new tune'.

Massacre as rite

When interviewed in November 2003 R. was living in domestic obscurity in Kenema, supported by a midwife who had befriended her during a pregnancy. She had a background in the RUF about which she was willing to talk.[8] She entered the movement when 'adopted' in Buedu (in Kailahun District). At first, her work was to carry loads on endless bush marches. She had tried to escape, but was caught. The men helping her were shot. Girls considered 'fine' (as she was) were spared. Leading fighters headed large domestic groups, and girls were potential partners for fighters, or wives of allies. She came under the protection of the head wife of a prominent commander. This meant she was free from sexual molestation. In time she entered into an authorised relationship with a young fighter, and as her man advanced in the movement; she also acquired status. 'Other ranks' were punished unless they addressed her as 'madam', or by her name. Where before she had head-loaded ammunition all day, she now travelled in a hammock, and had the pick of the fine things the RUF redistributed 'to the women they liked'.

The account corrects some popular misconceptions about the RUF. R. talks about the importance of religion in the movement. She describes it as a preoccupation. 'They worshipped a lot...during fast month the rebels kept fast, or...went to church to pray if they were Christians'. She then contrasts a 'moral order' in camp with conditions in the battle zone, where fighters – so sexually constrained in camp that only a 'big man' was allowed to initiate a virgin – carried out rape. Had she, herself, trained for combat, we asked. She remains silent, but her friends in the compound suspect she was also a fighter. The unanswered question switches her thoughts to scenes associated with battle. She talks about the role of *moreh man dem* (Krio, pl., from Arabic *murid*, pupil of the Koran, that is Muslim diviners) from Guinea who prepared RUF fighters by making offerings, *pul saraa* (Krio: to give charity, from Arabic *sadaga*, alms).

Without preamble, speaking quietly and without animation she tells the story of a massacre perpetrated by XX (a colonel and commander of the group in which she lived). She describes the man, fresh from fighting, as disturbed by 'heat' (that is, anger). XX asks the advice of his *moreh man*. He is told to make a sacrifice. He takes some civilian captives. A pit is dug. XX guns his victims into the pit. Under the instruction of the *moreh man*, XX climbs among the dead and dying, collecting five gallons of blood in a container – his 'sacrifice'.

Claims of human sacrifice belong to a long-standing political discourse in the region. The factual basis for such stories can often be doubted. But it seems noteworthy that R. describes the massacre in terms of a rite. Nor is it doubted that atrocity was at times framed as performances. It was noted above how often victim were ordered to sing or dance. Victims of amputation – including young children – have described how they were invited to 'gamble' on their choice of 'punishment', or how victims were chosen by lottery. The lottery has a long history in the region. Poison ordeals undertaken to refute witchcraft accusations – in effect – operated as lotteries (active ingredients in the Sasswood ordeal induced either vomiting or heart attack). The lottery is a performative technique favoured by egalitarian groups to ensure random allocation of benefits or hardships (Douglas, 1993), and it stands in opposition to the personalised favour (or displeasure) of the patron. The RUF leadership often complained about its exclusion from a system of patrimonial rule, and described the randomised levelling associated with its 'operation no living thing' and 'operation revenge yourself' (both 1998) as a vendetta against civilian supporters of the CDF in the wake of the failed Abidjan peace process. Durkheim includes vendetta under his category of the piacular rite since it is violence undertaken not to settle individual grievances but in response to a threat to the group.[9] This offers a line of explanation. Post-Abidjan, and threatened with annihilation, RUF commanders responded to their movement's incipient social collapse by sacrificing the rural civilians they had once intended to save.

The RUF anthem

'Rose', a middle-aged woman, who worked as a secretary in Monrovia before the war, was living in her village on the Liberia-Sierra Leone border when abducted by the RUF during 1994. She escaped around 1996,[10] and was working for a child soldier rehabilitation programme in Freetown when interviewed by BBC radio journalist Tom Porteous late in 1998. The present section is a modified excerpt from Richards (2005b), where a full transcript of the interview can be found.

Rose is asked what the RUF were fighting for: [they told us]...*to move out the rotten system of the APC government...that we have so many minerals in our country, like diamonds, gold, bauxite, rutile, and even so many fishes in the sea, but they said we are suffering in this country...the government is taking care of the money...we don't have free education, even in the hospital people die because they don't have money to buy needle and tablets, pay hospital bills, or consultation fee to the doctor...so they want...need...free education, and want everything to be good in the country.'* Was this sincere? *'Rose'* answers: *'they told us this....but according to their actions...they were killing and threatening people...so we...it was bad for them...[laughs]...you will tell someone to stop doing something, then you are seeing him doing another one which is worst [sic.]...eh?, then how can you believe that person?'* The interviewer persists: *'So what do you think [the RUF was] fighting for?'* Rose sums up the movement: *'To me, maybe they were fighting for what they told us, but they never succeed[ed]... because of their bad acts'.*

However the RUF was more organised than some commentators assert. Literacy was prized, and after her capture Rose was put to work as a secretary-typist in the RUF War Office (adults without such useful skills became slave labourers: Peters and Richards, 1998). The movement, she explained, made considerable use of record keeping. She typed monthly reports from various 'targets' and from all camps belonging to the RUF (detailing *'how many people have been captured in that month, how many women or children, how many died, what kind of sickness have break outs in that month, how many...combatants that have died at the front line...so they send in all the monthly reports in the office and hand it over to Foday Sankoh'*). She also prepared passes to be signed by commanders controlling movements outside camps of both fighters and civilians. The punishment for being caught without a pass was death. When there was no typewriter or ribbon 'Rose' prepared reports and passes by hand.

The movement had its own courts (*'they nearly formed their own government, because when you do any wrong they have their own supreme courts...you have to face in that court if you have done any wrong...if the court states that you will die, then you will die'*). People were judged before being punished: *'in the jungle they judge you before they kill you'.* The purpose was often to control the behaviour of combatants: *'for the boys that can go at the front line, if they kill innocent people, when the commander come in [sic.] he has to bring in his report, so if you are caught, and you killed a civilian, or burned them up in a house, you will be killed.'* But tight discipline also undermined the RUF. *'Some of those boys, when they have done these acts, they will not go back in the combat camp...they will prefer to stay at the front line just fighting...of course, they know that when they will be judged, and be killed...so they will never turn back to the rear, they are always at the front fighting.'* This helps explain strongly divergent views of the RUF, as disciplined movement and murderous rabble: *'Yes, they were disciplined...but some of them can't obey...'*

Every day camp life began at 6 am with compulsory prayers. Those who did not go were *'in jail for three days...[in the]...guard room'*. The prayers were both Muslim and Christian. *'They will appoint one person to pray. After you have prayed then you will say the Lord's Prayer, and then you will say the Alfatiyah'*. The interviewer asks *'how did you...*[long pause]*...reconcile the fact that these people were forcing you...were making you pray everyday, and at the same time were carrying out such terrible things, both to the people within the RUF, and to their enemy?'* Rose is at a loss for an answer. *'Yes, when they...when they will...after the prayers, they have to pick...these boys from the strike force...to go at the front there, after the prayer...but when they go, really they are out of control, now, you see...because when they go they see these wines, this marijuana...so they got out of control, and even at times they won't obey their commanders.'*

After prayers camp inmates were also required to sing the RUF anthem. Rose gives a perfect rendering. The interviewer praises her for singing so well. She explains her mastery in terms of the harsh beatings administered to those who stumbled. She had been beaten four times to acquire the song. Baffled, the interviewer wonders *'How can you sing that song so beautifully, with that memory? You sing it very well, but with the memory that, that this was beaten into you...how can you sing it with such...?* [both laugh]'. Rose replies that *'they taught us that song because we have teachers among us...so during...after prayers...for this anthem song, you are just forced to sing, whether you are hungry, or you feel discouraged, or someone died from you that day, they don't want to know. All they know that you sing the song on the right time...'*. This, then, is a rather dramatic instance of the basic difference Cross (2003) draws between musicality and linguistic capacity (see below). Musical performance is *unassigned* intentionality. It rehearses the possibility of new social orders even when the singer has no commitment. Having been initiated (against her will) into the RUF world, Rose could still respond to its pulse, even though her mind was now miles away.

Peters (2006), who interviewed RUF ex-combatants (male and female and of varying ranks) about life in the bush camps, sometimes in the sites where they had formerly been based, reports that fighters engaged in lengthy sessions of singing and dancing in preparation for attacks. Explicitly, music was used to ensure social bonding, on a pattern associated with the sessions of the sodalities.[11] There seems little doubt that the fighters, in fact, came to view their movement as a sodality. From reluctant abductees many became ardent movement loyalists (Peters and Richards, 1998). In the event, they were stood down only by demobilisation and reintegration paying careful attention to phase and pulse (Peters, 2006).

Explaining the destructive passions: musicality gone wrong?

In this preliminary offering enough has been said, I hope, to indicate that the business of war – even its excesses – is far from being a set of uncontrolled, incoherent events. Yet it seems equally misleading to try and account for atrocity in terms of rational choice. Destructive passions have evidently become engaged, and it would be good to know more about how they can be cooled. The brief account of the war in Sierra Leone and the two ethnographic vignettes were intended to establish the likelihood that atrocity is performed, that performance capacity involves something apart from the 'rational actor', and that clumsy external interruptions of performance, and the injustices such interventions compound, might cause performances to go wrong with disastrous effect. As part of the task of trying to understand atrocity and its triggers we need theories of performance that go beyond agency as often conceived in the social sciences, but without lurching into the terrain of evolved instincts demarcated by some less subtle socio-biologists. This is where it seems to me some recent theorising concerning the origins of musicality may be helpful.

Cross (2006) seeks an explanation of musicality as 'a fundamental part of the human communicative tool kit' that, in parallel with language, can be considered as both a natural and symbolic domain of human thought and behaviour. His approach allows for cultural specificity of musical activity grounded in an evolved human faculty for musicality. His argument parallels the case of language, though he claims that musicality and language represent somewhat different cognitive processing capacities, and have come to serve different social and cultural functions.

In particular, music (in which Cross includes what would normally be considered dance) offers scope to explore what he terms unassigned intentionality – response to music involves pulse-following behaviour, invokes memory and creates a sense of anticipation (see Davies, 1978), but is not specifically 'about' anything. In this it differs from language and the more obviously representative or symbolic art forms. Disagreeing with those (for instance, Pinker, 1997) who treat music as a 'spandrel' (or 'sport') in evolutionary terms, Cross argues that musicality is a key to understanding the emergence of sociality. Social interaction involves coordination of activities in groups. We need complex skills of

"ANTHEM" OF RUF/SL

Verse 1 (of 3)

RuF is fighting to save Sierra Leone

RuF is fighting to save her people

RuF is fighting to save her country

RuF is fighting to save Sierra Leone

Refrain

Go and tell the president that Sierra Leone is my home

Go and tell my parents they'll see me no more

We're fighting in the battlefield and fighting forever

Ev'ry Sierra Leonean is fighting for his land

transcr. PR

turn-taking and the counter-pointing of simultaneous activities. Music offers a 'rehearsal' space in which strategies and moves of potential social significance can be tested. Mothers who send their daughters to dancing or piano lessons – or indeed parents who initiate their children through Poro and Sande – are not misled. The intention is not virtuosity but refined social intelligence – an ability to move through the pitfalls of social life with grace and agility. The scope of Cross's argument needs to be appreciated. He is not explaining why some of us 'like music', but is offering a explanation of the emergence of sociality. He proposes (no less) that 'musicality underpins the intellectual and social flexibility displayed by modern humans'. This includes 'many of the most important abstract concepts that frame and give meaning to interaction'. Specifically (in relation to the topic of the present chapter) he considers that 'social justice, that aspect of morality...concerned with the achievement of equity in human relations' has its roots in human musicality. This is not to suggest that the unmusical are unjust. The significance of the argument is evolutionary. It relates to the origins of the capacity for social justice. Without musicality (he suggests) 'the flexibility in managing social relations that characterises modern humans and that constitutes the matrix within which abstract conceptions such as social justice can take form is less likely to have arisen' (all quotations from p. 1).[12]

I am greatly impressed by the implications this argument holds for the possibility of a 'polyphonic' justice, bridging between differently organised social solidarities. 'Polyphony' (an ability to listen and respond to several distinct strands of argument about justice at once) seems to me a desideratum for a truly global doctrine of human rights. Polyphonic justice would be able to distinguish, and hold within one frame, arguments about the 'rights to combat' (Rawls, 2003) in the face of a persistent unequal division of labour (the legacy of slavery), and address the human rights abuses of those who have had their rights abused (in fact, the kind of situation addressed by the Special Court for War Crimes in Sierra Leone in regard to a number of the accused).

Ian Cross's theory of musicality and its evolutionary origins seems also to offer a way of filling one of the obvious gaps in Durkheimian theory – the lack of any plausible cognitive mechanism to account for the phenomenon of 'effervescence' – the intensification and co-ordination of group emotional excitement leading to the the 'fixing' of collective representations (laws, morality, symbols of identity and such like). Randall Collins has recently revisited the problem, but in labelling the gap in Durkheimian theory 'sub-cognitive ritualism' (Collins, 2004) seems to have proposed not much of a mechanism while losing focus on the excitement and energy that makes social things happen. In proposing we treat musicality as a cognitive processing capacity perhaps similar to language in its evolutionary background but different from language in its (generalised rather than targeted, meaning-rich) domains of application, Cross provides a way of escaping a problem that continues to limit the Durkheimian inheritance in anthropology – inability to move beyond a notion of culture as phenomenal (Douglas, 1996; Kuper, 1999), and a fixation upon ritual (in particular) as a device for communicating culture (Rappaport, 1999).[13] What Durkheim in fact argued is that ritual (worship) energises the group (Durkheim, 1995 [1912]). Belief arises from social energy, not the other way round (Boyer, 2000). Cross has it right – musicality is way of practising moves before we need them. But because 'decoding' ritual has become a cottage industry in anthropology it is perhaps best to abandon the term to these (non-Durkheimian) decoders, and adopt 'musicality' to cover the circumstances Durkheim envisages.

This said we still need to address the dark side of musicality. Cross provides us with a non-dichotomised explanation of music (it is both bio-logically-based and culturally constructed). In this he aligns with recent accounts of emotional capacities by psychologists. Biological explana-tions deal well with emotional reflexes such as fear, and social explana-tions with 'higher' emotions such as love, hope or anger (Averill, 1982). According to Griffiths (1997, p132) the possibility of an integrated approach to the emotions rests on recognition of a psychological pheno-type comprising both 'traditional biological factors such as genes and traditional cultural elements such as stories and norms of behaviour'.

The higher emotions may be enacted. Fear is instinctive, and recog-nised by its symptoms, but a parent disciplining a naughty child may, initially, only pretend anger – performance makes the feelings real. More abstractly, some 'emotions [are] constructions, built up from more elementary units that are not themselves emotional', involving organisation 'on biological, psychological and social levels' (Averill, 1992, p20). Acting out the emotions involves what Griffiths terms 'covert' social construction. By this he means referring certain emo-tional states to entities – such as a god or the nation – maintained in the imagination of a group, and in the name of which behaviour dis-ruptive of norms is licensed as 'spontaneous'. Griffiths (1997) terms the fruits of such covert construction *disclaimed action*. In such cases, a person is commonly described as 'possessed', for instance. by a fervour which switches off normal reflexive monitoring of behaviour, as in spirit possession, or moments of heedless valour in battle. In such cases, the 'emotions fulfil their social functions precisely because they are interpreted as passions rather than actions' (Griffiths, 1997, p149).

This is where we encounter a difficulty. Music allows us to rehearse our sociality in such a way that 'polyphonic' justice becomes possible. But if

Griffiths is right it can also in certain circumstances lead to the switching off of the very social codes through which peace and inter-group equity are maintained – emotional energies are coupled to covert constructions licensed in the name of the group. Reckless behaviours – whether self-harm or atrocity – seemingly result. Durkheim still offers one of the best organised accounts of what may be afoot. Book III ('The principal modes of ritual conduct') of the *Elementary Forms of Religious Life* considers asceticism and sacrifice (the negative and positive cults). Some positive rites produce a sense of joyful anticipation. Others involve great sadness, anger, and harm. Mourning the death of a community member can occasion extreme violence, including cutting the body to the point where the mourner dies. Angry rites also address other kinds of disaster – drought, or the loss of cult objects. The connecting element is threat to community life requiring ceremonies of expiation. Durkheim terms these *piacular rites*, defined (by Karen Fields) as 'rites conducted on the occasion of death, misfortune or collective crisis that are not expressions of individual feeling (Durkheim 1995 [1912], p392 fn).

Mourners explain funerary rituals as necessary to ward off the vengeance of the souls of the dead. But why, Durkheim asks, would a person committed to the community become vengeful after death? Beliefs concerning the pacification of souls are secondary accretions. The rite – as performance – comes before the belief it sustains. The priority of practice over belief is clearly seen in ceremonies to stop famine or sickness. These operate without anthropomorphic entanglements (not even the spirit of the departed, as in a funeral rite). Durkheim concludes that for native Australians 'abstinences and blood-letting stop famines and cure sicknesses, *acting on their own*' (p410, my emphasis).

The observation that anger at burials is focused not on the deceased but on the restoration of community is not confined to the Australian ethnography. In rural Sierra Leone, in-laws in a Mende village attack each other at a funeral, often roughly, seeking assurance the inter-family cooperation facilitated by marriage will not wither. They rehearse their worst fears in a rite that seems, at times, akin to a riot. What seems most original in Durkheim's argument is the notion that the threat to the group, at the death of a member, is loss of social dynamism. In bereavement the true enemy is despair. The fact that piacular rites sometimes involve horrendous acts of self-harm, or harm to others (Durkheim cites the vendetta) shows that the collectivity can be re-energised through fury as well as joy. A group faced with extinction may perform acts of lacerating violence to fan the dying embers of social cohesion.

Conclusion

We are thus left with something of a challenge. The very mechanism proposed to explain how humans have evolved to live in harmony, interacting with grace and justice, is also capable of violent extraversion. Where a way of life is threatened – or perceived to be threatened – with extinction, these same evolved capacities can become a juggernaut of performative violence, consuming both those who dance, and those who stand in their way. Dealing with this challenge requires another occasion, except to say – here – that commonsense suggests peace-makers, looking for early-warning signs, should be sensitive to the sounds of performance rhythms becoming disrupted. Shooting up the safe refuges of the RUF in the middle of a peace process was not tactically sensible. It was also arguably a crime against humanity. And it triggered consequent crimes pursued in the spirit of the vendetta. The polyphonic justice of the Special Court for War Crimes in Sierra Leone should extend to the scrutiny of those who barracked and disrupted the Abidjan peace process.

Notes

1 I wish to thank members of the seminar on 'The emotions and public life' at Birkbeck College, and Filip de Boeck's post-graduate anthropology seminar at Leuven for discussions leading to the binning of several early versions of this paper. Perri 6 and Derek Bolton have been generous in advising on revisions. I also wish to thank Ian Cross for helpful correspondence and an important paper 'in press'.

2 For detailed material on the war and its context see, for example, Abdullah (2004), Keen (2005), Peters (2006), and Richards (1996).

3 The army added to the confusion by driving civilians out of recently attacked areas – claiming a free-fire zone to hunt rebels long gone, but in reality organising extensive looting sprees. One loyalist officer, shooting at looting troops, is supposed to have remarked that 'soldiers do not leave the battle zone carrying TV sets'.

4 Ironically, this was literally true – one of the RUF's first requests in agreeing to open peace negotiations was to ask International Alert to find it decent clothes to take part in negotiations, after years in the bush.

5 An opposite view is that of Shearer (1997) who argues that 'stick' was essential to compel Sankoh to sign the peace deal.

6 The instigators were both regular soldiers associated with the former army and RUF cadres. Similar atrocities were also carried out by irregular civil defence forces.

7 The court appointed an American special prosecutor and a panel of three Sierra Leonean and four international judges, and will conclude its activities in 2007. Those indicted included Sankoh (deceased 2003), several RUF military commanders, and senior civil defence and army figures. No individuals associated with private security companies or ECOMOG have been indicted.

8 The interview was undertaken jointly with a Sierra Leonean colleague James Vincent, who had earlier established rapport with the interviewee. For a discussion of some factors to be considered in interviewing former members of the RUF see Peters and Richards (1998) and Peters (2006).
9 In general, Durkheim thought homicide more likely in groups bound by 'mechanical' solidarity (i.e. in the absence of levels of institutional variety associated with a complex division of labour). His thoughts on homicide are both scattered and subtle (e.g. anomie – sudden loss of social bearings – is a confounding variable). DiCristina (2004) very usefully brings them together, showing them to be consistent.
10 Rose states she was with the RUF for 27 months and escaped in an ambush laid by *kamajoi* [hunter] fighters – the *kamajoi* militia was not a major factor in the war until mid-late 1996.
11 More data on the role of music and musicality in the Sierra Leone war are forthcoming. The anthropologist Marc Sommers is currently investigating the special significance of rapper Tupac Shakur among some groups of ex-combatants.
12 A somewhat related (and explicitly Durkheimian) performative argument (with important implications, requiring separate treatment) is developed by Woodiwiss (2005) who traces a thread linking the emergence of notions of 'human rights' to ancient arguments over 'human sacrifice' (cf. Girard, 1979).
13 A position well captured in Rappaport's claim that 'At the heart of ritual...is the relationship of performers to performances of invariant sequences of acts and utterances which they did not encode' (Rappaport 1999: 405). This seems explicitly to exclude improvisation (and thus the rehearsal and experimentation at the heart of Cross' argument about musicality).

References

Abdullah I, ed., 2004. *Between Democracy and Terror: The Sierra Leone Civil War.* Dakar: Council for the Development of Social Science Research in Africa
Amnesty International, 1992. *The Extrajudicial Execution of Suspected Rebels and Collaborators.* London: International Secretariat of Amnesty International, Index AFR 51/02/92
Averill JR, 1982. *Anger and Aggression: An Essay on Emotion.* New York: Springer-Verlag
Averill JR, 1992. The structural bases of emotional behavior: a meta-theoretical analysis. In MS Clark, ed., *Emotion: Review of Personality and Social Psychology* 13. London: Sage
Boyer P, 2000. Functional origins of religious concepts: ontological and strategic selection in evolved minds. *Journal of the Royal Anthropological Institute*, New Series, 6, 2, 195–214
Collins R, 2004. *Interaction Ritual Chains.* Princeton and Oxford: Princeton University Press
Cross I, 2003. Music and biocultural evolution. In M Clayton, T Herbert and R Middleton, eds, *The Cultural Study of Music: A Critical Introduction.* London: Routledge
Cross I, 2006. Music and social being. *Musicology Australia* (forthcoming)
Davies JB, 1978. *The Psychology of Music.* London: Hutchinson

DiCristina B, 2004. Durkheim's theory of homicide and the confusion of the empirical literature. *Theoretical Criminology* 8, 1, 57–91

Douglas M, 1993. *In the Wilderness: The Doctrine of Defilement in the Book of Numbers.* Sheffield: Sheffield Academic Press

Douglas M, 1996. *Thought and Style: Critical Essays on Good Taste.* London: Sage Publications

Durkheim E, 1964 [1893]. *The Division of Labor in Society.* New York: Free Press

Durkheim E, 1995 [1912]. *The Elementary Forms of Religious Life.* New York: Free Press

Girard R, 1979. *Violence and the Sacred.* Baltimore: Johns Hopkins University Press

Griffiths P, 1997. *What Emotions Really Are: The Problem of Psychological Categories.* Chicago: University of Chicago Press

Hooper J, 2003. Appendix: Sierra Leone. *Bloodsong! An Account of Executive Outcomes in Angola.* London: HarperCollins

Humphreys M and Weinstein J, 2004. *What the Fighters Say: A survey of Ex-Combatants in Sierra Leone, June–August 2003.* CGSD Working Paper No. 20. New York: Columbia University

International Alert, 1997. *A Time of Hope and Transformation: Sierra Leone Peace Process and Reflections.* London: International Alert

Lockwood D, 1992. *Solidarity and Schism: 'The Problem of Disorder' in Durkheimian and Marxist sociology.* Oxford: Clarendon Press

Keen D, 2005. *Conflict and Collusion in Sierra Leone.* Oxford: James Currey

Kuper A, 1999. *Culture: The Anthropologists' Account.* Cambridge, Massachusetts: Harvard University Press

Peters K, 2006. *Footpaths to Reintegration: War, Youth and Rural Crisis in Sierra Leone.* PhD Thesis, Technology & Agrarian Development Group, Wageningen University

Peters K and Richards P, 1998. Why we fight: voices of youth ex-combatants in Sierra Leone. *Africa,* 68, 1, 183–210

Pinker S, 1997. *How the Mind Works.* London: Allen Lane

Rawls A, 2003. Conflict as a foundation for consensus: contradictions of industrial capitalism in Book III of Durkheim's *Division of Labor. Critical Sociology* 29, 3, 295–335

Rappaport RA, 1999. *Ritual and Religion in the Making of Humanity.* Cambridge: Cambridge University Press

Richards P, 1996. *Fighting for the Rain Forest: War, Youth and Resources in Sierra Leone.* Oxford: Currey (additional material 1998)

Richards P, 2005a. War as smoke and mirrors: Sierra Leone 1991–2, 1994–5, 1995–6. *Anthropological Quarterly* 28, 377–402

Richards P, 2005b. Green Book millenarians? The Sierra Leone war from the perspective of an anthropology of religion. In N Kastfelt, ed., *Religion and Civil War in Africa.* London: C. Hurst

Richards P, Abdullah I, Amara J, Muana P, Stanley E and Vincent J, 1997. *Reintegration of War-Affected Youth and Ex-Combatants: A Study of the Social and Economic Opportunity Structure in Sierra Leone.* Unpublished report, Ministry of Relief, Rehabilitation & Reintegration, Freetown

RUF/SL, 1995. *Footpaths to Democracy: Toward a New Sierra Leone.* No stated place of publication: The Revolutionary United Front of Sierra Leone

Shearer D, 1997. Exploring the limits of consent: conflict resolution in Sierra Leone. *Millennium: Journal of International Studies,* 26, 3, 845–60

Stone D, 2004. Genocide as transgression. *European Journal of Social Theory* 7, 1, 45–65

Woodiwiss A, 2005. *Human Rights.* London: Routledge

3
Public Emotion in a Colonial Context: a Case Of Spirit-Writing in Taiwan under Japanese Occupation

Stephan Feuchtwang

Introduction

Lü Lin Wumu was born in a shack by a stream in the mountains of northern Taiwan, near the very small mining town of Shiding. He was adopted into the family of a small shopkeeper in the town as a young married-in son-in-law to a girl who had also been adopted into the family. At the age of 12, in the year 1886, his adopting father died leaving him, as the oldest male in the family, responsible for the public face of the family, including its shop, though his adopting mother remained in the role of the responsible adult.

When Wumu was in his early twenties, he opened a pharmacy in Chinese medicines. These were the years immediately after the annexation and military occupation of Taiwan by Japan (1895). The last imperial Chinese governor organised resistance to the occupation and in rebellion against his own dynastic state by declaring Taiwan a republic. The declaration was also an appeal to Western powers, but it failed. He fled and the island was declared to have been 'pacified' (Lamley, 1999, pp206–7).

To open a shop of Chinese herbal medicines went against the Japanese policy of replacing traditional with Western bio-medicine. Despite this, Wumu was energetic and resourceful enough to make a success of the new business. But he had also become addicted to opium and to visiting prostitutes. In 1995 Wumu's adopted daughter told me that his drug habit was 'stubborn'. Like his traditional pharmacy, he persisted in it, in the face of Japanese authority that had instructed all young people with an opium habit to attend a clinic (Davidson, 1903, p614).[1]

Lü Lin Wumu was also weak in another sense. To be married into a wife's family as an adult was well understood to be a source of shame and an admission of hardship. But to be married in as a child to an already-adopted girl was doubly feminising. Against this patriarchal and patrilineal shame, Wumu kept Lin, his natal family name alongside that of his adopted family. He also maintained contact with his Lin father's family. Indeed, his adopting mother was worried by his too-frequent visits to them. Concerned also about how weakened he had become by illness and his bad habits, she found a way of reminding him of his filial duty to her dead husband. In this way, as we shall see, she linked three quite distinct weaknesses with the colonial regime. Wumu's drug addiction and lack of filial duty were her main concern and they were a characteristic weakness of Chinese existence. But they had already been linked to the Japanese colonial regime by Wumu's persistence. Wumu's masculinity was threatened because of the poverty of his birth. It too had nothing intrinsically to do with the colonial regime. But the eventual self-strengthening solution that his adoptive mother sought turned out to be intimately associated with a defiance of the regime.

She called him to her room together with her remaining birth son, his younger brother, Xinjin. She told them she had been unable to sleep the past few nights, unable to grasp something that was disturbing her. Could it have been her husband, their father, himself unsettled and so giving her no peace? They themselves suggested going to a spirit-writing centre called the Southpointing Palace to find out.[2]

In following this suggestion they joined the three themes of this chapter. The first is a recovery of masculinity, which entailed finding a way to strengthen family obligation and leadership in a situation of divided family loyalties. The second is defiance of colonial occupation by resort to a local spiritual tradition. The third is entailed in the fact that the spiritual tradition is a performance of emotions in a public setting and at the same time a writing of a distinctive kind of history both for a family and for a more general public.

Spirit-writing as a defiance of colonial authority

When Wumu and his brother came to the Southpointing Palace they made a formal request to communicate with their father and were told to wait for his spirit to ascend the mountain and enter a medium. After several hours they were told he had not come, probably because the deity in charge was angry. To secure a response they would need to cleanse themselves morally and medically. On their return, their mother told them to visit the Southpointing Palace regularly. On one visit Wumu vowed to the Three Benefactors, who are the main deities welcomed to the Southpointing Palace, that if they restored his good health and helped rid him of his bad habits he would build a shrine for them in Shiding and publish a compilation of their communications. The first spirit-writing sessions in Shiding took place in a small hall that Wumu established near his shop. Wumu modelled the hall on the Southpointing Palace. He also had a set of 68 wooden blocks made for printing poetic oracles to be chosen by shaking bamboo stalks until one of the 68 came up. They were interpretable as prescriptions. The prescriptions could of course be made up at his pharmacy next door. In 1906 enough writing had been compiled for publication and edification. The next year Wumu had had them printed and published as the promised compilation in five volumes. These books and the genealogy of the family Lü that his adoptive mother commissioned are the documentary sources for the story I am telling.

In 1915 the Japanese regime forbade spirit-writing because of its subversive potential. The regime had that year discovered and killed the leaders of an uprising organised through spirit-writing and lay Buddhist vegetarian halls in the south of the island. This was among the last incidents of sporadic armed resistance that continued after the island had been 'pacified' (Lamley, 1999, p211; Katz, 2005). The spirit-writing prophets of the Xilai Hermitage incident had rallied celestial generals and their troops to protect them and their followers from bullets in preparation for an attack on the colonial occupation (Jones, 2003, pp21–2). The colonial government learned about it before any attack was mounted, crushed it and implemented strict island-wide controls and a census of religious activities. A register of all temples, with the names of their responsible managers, was compiled and kept. But the spirit-writing hall in Shiding continued with its activities. Indeed, Wumu organised its rebuilding at the back of the local temple. The new venue merited a new name and a higher status than a Hall (Tang): it was renamed Palace of Luminous Virtue (Mingde Gong). Wumu and its other managers inaugurated new public ceremonies honouring the main god of the Three Benefactors. The ceremonies were held openly. But, judging from the dates on some of the sessions printed in the genealogy, spirit writing continued to be held in secret. None of the leaders of the spirit-writing group were named as the temple's managers. Instead the three officially registered managers held local posts in the colonial government. The most prominent of the three was head of the School Committee and was an older friend of Wumu.[3] Wumu was the moving force, but he was hidden behind this official façade.

Wumu was not a revolutionary leader. He compromised with the Japanese regime. He promoted schooling, even though it was in Japanese, as a way of advancement not only for his own son but also for other people's children. He raised funds for them to be able to afford it. But in promoting the spirit-writing of The Three Benefactors and their pantheon he also sustained a patriotic mission to help spread a Chinese synthesis of the three teachings, Buddhism, Confucianism and Daoism, which eventually became the mode of worship in the most popular temples in Taipei city, linked to the Southpointing Palace (Feuchtwang, 1974, pp296–7). For Lü Lin Wumu it was a religious teaching to restore himself and his other literate compatriots. In this they defied condemnation by Japanese literate authority.

The Japanese headmaster of the school made a hand-written report on Shiding's temple in 1915. Some of the tension between school and temple can be gathered from the second to last paragraph. He notes there that in 1912 the temple had been used as classrooms by the school. Then, two years later 'the building was entirely refurbished and the managers of the temple proposed that the school should be moved to another place'. The school was moved, but only a year later 'borrowed part of the temple to use as classrooms' again. The headmaster comments that in this 'we see the influence of education and cultivation' one of whose tasks is to 'pay attention to superstitious misinterpretation'.

Condemnation of religious beliefs and the rituals practised by common people as 'errant' (*mi*) and as 'heterodox' or 'evil' (the translations into English of the Chinese *xie*) has a tradition as old as the Chinese imperial state. But the differences between a Japanese colonial regime's condemnation, as written by the headmaster, and condemnation by those educated into the literate orthodoxy of the Chinese imperial state is the difference between the assertion of a central Chinese civilisation and the projection of a modernising (Japanese) mission. The Japanese colonial mission in Taiwan was unlike most European colonial missions in being part of a self-modernising mission. And it was not a civilising mission of the kind that the Chinese imperial state itself conceived in relation to its tributary borderlands, which had included Japan. Japanese modernising reforms, referred to as the Meiji reforms, had begun just six years before occupation of Taiwan.

The Meiji reforms did not become a republican movement of modernisation as did those that eventually took place in mainland China. Instead they successfully reinforced imperial, as distinct from noble, rule. They included the building of a modern standing army, state-led armaments and other industries, liberal educational and legal reforms, including primary schools modelled on those of the USA, a German-modelled constitution, and limited powers of an elected legislature. Taiwan became part of the territory of the Meiji reforms. How to govern the island was an issue for the reforming currents in Japan, whether to assimilate it into metropolitan Japan giving Taiwanese equal status as citizens of Japan, whether to reserve the privileges of Japanese hierarchy only for a few Taiwanese, whether to tolerate a movement for Taiwanese home rule. Each governor after 1915 had a different tendency, but they all pursued the policy begun by the first governors after military occupation was established of making Taiwan a part of the Japanese modernising economy. One sign of its success is the writing of a Taiwanese who visited the mainland in the 1940s in which the reassurance of finding a thriving Chinese life is disturbed by finding it to be so selfish and degenerate (Lin Peiyin, 2000, referring to Zhong Lihe).

Wumu's ambivalent defiance could be interpreted as an earlier example of the same absorption of the modernising mission of the colonial regime alongside pride and longing for a resurgence of his own Chinese, as distinct from Japanese, reference to a centre of civilisation.

Public emotion in China

A key concept of Chinese civilisation is *li*. *Li* is usually translated as 'rites'. But it has a much broader reference. One way of interpreting it is 'conduct', so long as conduct is also understood as an organisation of appropriate emotions (*qing*). Good conduct is the habitual knowledge, learned through experience, of when and to whom to show feelings of closeness, when and to whom to show respectful distance, or when to remonstrate vociferously (Kipnis, 1997, chapter 6). This is not judged according to an ideal of authenticity, in which a show of sincere feeling must always be accompanied by appeals to believe that it accords with a spontaneous and subjective source. It is instead judged as responsiveness to others and to situations, both well observed or well created and maintained. The cult of sincerity and originality that comes with the Romantic tradition in Europe contrasts with the

Chinese ideal of responsiveness to finely discerned categories of person as well as to objects.[4] The Chinese ideal is no less centred in the self than Romantic authenticity, but the self is always conceived to be at the centre of a set of relationships and in a setting of response and of respect (or face). Chinese concerns with responsiveness and face may well have an equivalent in the public life of Europe lamented by Richard Sennett (1977), replaced by the cult of private sincerity. Romantically authentic feelings (in Europe) are expressed as a self responding to and about others according to nature, not as a self already bound in a relationship of responsiveness that is adjusted, renewed and re-created by its actions. But do not conclude that Chinese responsiveness is bound by great formality and rhetorical rigidity. It is felt, flexible and creative (Chang, 2004).

Charles Stafford (2000, chapters 7 and 8) has written well about Chinese conduct of greeting and parting. At its core is the manifestation of transient joy and then of sorrow at meeting and separation. Longing for the joy of reunion is the appropriate sentiment of parting and separation, celebrated both in everyday behaviour and in classical poetry, some of which is learned early and remains in the repertoire of people with only elementary education for recital at appropriate times. The ultimate separation of death is similarly accompanied by an evocation of appropriate feelings, but its conduct in rituals requires different media to seek and perform separation and reunion. Chief among them are the burning of incense and the writing of petitions or the offering of other paper tokens whose burning is an act of transmission. Beside such rituals there are a number of techniques of transmission and the divination of response. Spirit-writing is one of them.

The tradition of spirit-writing shares with the tradition of history and other kinds of writing in Chinese a pointed reference to inner feeling combined with a didactic purpose. In her study of the prefaces to the collections of stories of strange and ghostly occurrences, Frances Weightman (2004) has reviewed the genre of prefaces to Chinese compilations of writings by one or more authors. The prefaces justify publication by the didactic needs of the reader and the emotional needs of the author. The needs of the reader are for education and enlightenment or awakening. The obligation or unavoidable, sometimes explosive, need of the author is to vent indignation about injustice, to convey insights into the nature of things, or just to pass on something strange that came to attention.

The first preface to the five volumes, written by one of the Shiding spirit-writing Hall's chief collators, follows this genre of didactic feelings. It describes the achievement for which Wumu was recognised.

It praises the collective effort of the members in setting up the branch, then places the shrine in its sacred landscape. It describes the hall's situation, spectacularly placed on the confluence of streams in Shiding, and at the foot of a slope of the same range as the peak of Houshan where the Southpointing Palace is situated. Next, it turns to the volumes themselves:

> Through the phoenix pen hearts find expression, by the rising medium mouths find words. Poems and songs tell cases (*an*) which weave brocades to mend the body and reflect the person (*xiu shen jinghui zi*).

Note the partial differentiation in the pairing of body and person, physical health and moral well being. Note also the reference to cases. It is a reference to the courts of purgatory before which cases of the recently dead, such as Wumu's father, are tried. The same word (*an*) also stands for altars to the deities in the celestial pantheon. Such cases are not simply about personal reform. As the preface demonstrates, they contain general lessons of the need for what it calls moral revolution (*ge*).

> These days [the preface continues] luminous virtue is ignored, virtuous merit has no place, lechery blazes, the sun of correct principle is smudged, disasters erupt everywhere, plagues break out incessantly. When will we rise together to the shore of enlightenment from the paths of confusion? Luckily the Shiding members [of the Hall] do not shirk hardship, the gentry and masses of Wenshan [the district including both Shiding and the Southpointing Palace's mountain] dare to face difficulties. ...By their will (*yuanjiang*), they gallop with immortals and steep themselves in the world so that people can get rid of old ways and powerfully grasp the new.

Among the spirits addressed were those who could bestow just and benevolent recognition of the worth of the recently dead. They were placed in a hierarchy of judicial authority and command over demons, and in these rituals of writing they heard petitions and raised selected people from the living and the recently dead into their own ranks.

Canonisation

The Lü genealogy (a book containing the family tree, description of origins, graveyards and ancestral homes of a lineage as well as eulogistic biographies of some of its members) contains the spirit-writings that concern the raising of Lü Lin Wumu, his adoptive younger brother Xinjin, and his adopting father Lü Sanen into the lowest ranks of the celestial hierarchy. After the name 'Sanen' comes the information that, on a date given both in Japanese (Meiji) and Chinese (Guangxu) reign periods:

> in our Middle Street of Shiding, Xinjin and his adopted elder brother Wumu established the three sage emperors Guan, Lü and Zhang [the Three Benefactors] in the Hall of Luminous Good and issued the five volumes of Enlivening the World for Renewal.

It moves on to the significant occasion of their recognition and canonisation some years later:

> 'By the merciful order of the three sage and benevolent lords, they [Xinjin and Wumu] were appointed seal holders for the celestial officials in the Hall of Luminous Good. So on the 15th of the Second [lunar] month the three sage and benevolent lords instructed Xinjin and Wumu to go the Southpointing Palace to inquire about a case. On the same night of the 15th, ancestor Yuhu rose to the Southpointing Palace and descended into a medium to make his presence known. At the first hour of the 16th day of the second month of the *jisi* year (1929), he appeared as the Blue-clad Boy to say:

> 'On this golden night I am commanded to guide Lü Sanen, deceased father of chief wielder Lü Xinjin, up to the Southpointing pen. Lü Sanen now arrives from the Building of Joyful Good and Lofty Azure Happiness.'

Lü Sanen's words then appear in eight poem-songs from which I shall select the two that are most emotional:

Poem 4
From beginning to end, my sons' childish cries weigh with me.
That your good deeds (have been) like sand by the water cannot be denied.
It is fortunate that the dissolute son returned to the head of the family
And from then established virtue and the praise of ten thousand people.

Poem 5
Bringing up the feelings of mourning, my tears are bitter pearls,
The span of a human life is like a mayfly's.
From beginning to end, the great weight [of my fate] is still at its
root,
The Lü household relied solely on my worthy wife.[5]

The Lü genealogy then informs us that after some weeks Sanen returned, this time in the Shiding branch hall. His approach was announced at two removes. First the god Su, in charge of rites, announced the Xiahai City God, a celestial official. The temple to this particular City God still presides over the district of Dadaocheng, which was the centre of trade for Shiding's products and source of its retailers' stocks, down river in what is now Taipei City. The City God pronounced:

Instructed to mount the stylus of this Hall
As a minister of a celestial court
[I proclaim] This one-in-a-thousand rare occasion.
The seal of approval has been given by the celestial court to
Lü Sanen

Lü Sanen then appeared through the stylus, which wrote that he had been released from the purgatory of Gloomy Dreams (*Sen Meng*) and given a seal-holding office in the Southern Ministry. Again he expresses his overwhelming feelings of gratitude.

Performance of written emotion

The mediums were hands and voices physically apart from Wumu, in séances whose personnel were at least three in number – wielder, communicator and scribe – beside Wumu and Xinjin as direct addressees. In all likelihood there was an outer audience of the members of the Hall. They heard the communicator slowly convey celestial messages to Wumu and Xinjin as part of a performance framed by rituals of invitation, sacrifice, record and seeing off. Within this formal frame[6] the 'voice' of their father was called out in the florid language of responsive feeling (*qing*) and tears. Lü Sanen spoke-wrote with sorrow of the brevity of his lifespan, but by speaking he transcended it. Wumu, 'the dissolute son returned to head the family', heard-read the voice of his father thank and praise him.

The inward emotional reality brought to poetic light in the collection of spirit-writings significantly entitled *Renewal* is the personal reality of what was by now a past, Yin life, that of the dead father. But it extended to the renewed, praised and thanked son who was alive. Beyond him it was evidently extended to something more general, the principles of human feeling as a moral reality. By these dramatisations of emotion, a scene of identification was performed, whose principal live authors (or roles) were Xinjin, Wumu, and their mother, even though she was not present. A performance of powerful emotions is most powerful for the most directly addressed; they are interpellated by name or by description and themselves must visualise the figures addressing them. But through these principal addressees, the others present, and eventually the readership of the printed cases must also have been affected. The ritual is a manifestation to prompt visualisations in them all of a son recognising his father and being recognised in turn, with gratitude.

The trance is a transition from Yin to Yang, past to present, and is the key rite in a chain of inscription that commands moral authority over its readers. Its authority, both juridical and other-worldly, crosses into a judgement of this world. It consists in this factive, historical but also eternal truth. Plainly the authority of spirit-writing is in dialogue with co-existing forms of political authority, such as the colonial government of Taiwan under whose regime Lü Lin Wumu became ill and at the same time defiant. Through spirit-writing Wumu became a leader. Having done his filial duty by the family into which he had been adopted, Wumu in fact returned to his natal name and was inscribed in its genealogy as well. Thus he redeemed himself and his two family names. But renewal went beyond his achieving patrilineal masculinity. Tensions between collaboration with and opposition to the colonial regime and a ritual remedy for social malaise were bound up with each other.

History, memory and personae

This is not just a personal story. It is also a spiritual history published as a case for the edification of Taiwanese readers. It is a link between past and present, a relation between memory and history. This relation is taken up by Michael Lambek (2002 and 2003) to mount a critique of the unique authority of individualised memory and evidential historiography. In the course of his critique he raises the issue of how feelings, ethics and the recalling of the past into the present are linked. He bases his critique on the spirit mediumship he observed among Sakalava in northern Madagascar. I want to take up this issue on the basis of this case of Chinese spirit-writing and suggest an expansion and a criticism of Lambek's critique.

Lambek's starting position for a comparison of the making and maintenance of history is to bring into question distinctions that are axiomatic in the Graeco-Roman philosophical tradition that has spread with the West. One distinction is between *poeisis* (expressive creativity) and a rational, dispassionate representation of the past. Another is between *praxis* (action out of practical reason) and *theoria* (reflective or pure thought). Many further distinctions are inferred from these two. The extent and manner in which such distinctions are upheld – between expressive creativity and reason based on evidence, between practical performance and reflective speech and writing, between a burden of moral obligation and the task of pure factual description and analysis – should therefore become a comparative project rather than simply isolated for criticism. But a critical part of that project is certainly to question the distinction between history, an account of the past, and memory, a clinging to what has happened and bringing it into a living moment with its attendant emotions. Lambek suggests that the distinction between history and memory is a product of the sharpness of the distinctions made for modern historiography and psychology. It does not exist for Sakalava spirit mediums.

They are not just possessed to speak. In possession they dress and act the part and even when not possessed they conform to the likes and dislikes, demeanours and emotions of the beings that appear through their bodies. The past is brought into the present vividly. Often several pasts are simultaneously present because beings from different times are made present by their mediums and they interact. Every possession is also an adaptation to and comment on current circumstances. It is the telling of history by the performance of characters, which then make history by their new encounters, in which they nevertheless observe genealogical prerogatives, the service and deference that juniors owe seniors.[7]

By contrast, Lambek points out well, the written narrative of the past and its documentation by modern European and now world-wide professional historians is far more concerned with events and deeds than with characters. He could have added that entry into character is left to biography and historical fiction. Dress and relics are left to heritage museums, re-enactions of battles, displays of events, waxworks of people, archaeological remains, old tin mines, reconstructed shopping streets, and so on. Another point he makes holds even when we have widened the range this far. Audiences are left to find their own understandings of the emotions in play. But in yet other genres of historical representation, such as music theatre, spoken theatre, and song, emotion is performed. By opening the comparison made by Lambek to a range of representations of the past that can be found in contemporary UK, it may be that equivalents to the various things that are unified in the Sakalava spirit possession that he observed do in fact exist in the UK but are distributed and differentiated instead of being unified.

I will not take this range comparison further. It has already made the point that we are engaged in a comparative anthropology of the organisation and distribution of public emotion. I want to conclude by addressing an important argument, which Lambek thinks his observations support. He thinks that performance of public emotion dissolves the distinction between memory – bringing the past into the present – and history, placing the past in the past. The spirit-medium brings to public occasions, the presence of the past characters that they celebrate, and to individual clients the same spirit-characters hear the client's personal stories and suffering. The spirit-writing equivalent is the more public ritual of annual celebrations of a deity, and the more enclosed and invited audience of the same deity or deities presiding over a 'case'.

We should not write of emotion as such. Each genre is a selection of emotions. In the example of spirit-writing I have described there is a notable contrast between the sobriety of the ritual, the solemnity in which the higher deities introduce the much more recent dead and their feelings, and the drama of their emotions. Full-body spirit possession also occurs in Taiwan and it is a much more violent performance of the character of a deity. But ancestors cannot be raised into the present by full-body spirit possession. Spirit-writing is at once grand and directed to personal 'cases'. It aspires as a genre of writing to the status of the great issuing of dynastic histories, as a reminder and a return to the rule of sage gods while recounting 'cases' of the recent dead and responding to cases of the living. All three – full body possession, spirit-writing, and the issuing of official histories – are variant genres of *li*, acts of revelation, making visible the principles of universal order and the part humans play in harmonising and recreating it in new circumstances. But each genre screens and selects emotions and the kind of evidence relevant to it, just as courts of law and courts of etiquette do.

The crucial point to note is that the feelings and personal memories of the living about those from whom they are separated are filtered or omitted. They may of course be evoked within both those addressed and the audience who can associate their own memories with the address. But the public emotion performed in spirit-writing is restricted to a demonstration of righteous power, indignation about injustice and misdemeanour, and the sorrow of separation.

These performances of public emotion resulted in two kinds of writing, a genealogy and a published compilation that was distributed as a book of moral renewal. The spirit-writing activities also formed an institution, the local cult of the central Benefactor, which now has its own history performed in festivals. Through spirit-writing, Wumu became for a time a figure in the local history centred on the temple in Shiding where these festivals took place and helped define it as a place. In fact he became a recognised person by creating a role in which he helped to form four solidarities, the two patrilines of his family names, the Taiwanese Chinese solidarity to which his case was an exemplary spiritual renewal, and the locality of the Shiding temple. The performance of public emotions in this instance conveyed the authority to make the history of these different solidarities. In sum, the spirit writing inaugurated a local history and displayed selected public emotions to that end.

Having made all these necessary qualifications, I turn at last to the main argument that the performance of emotion dissolves the distinction between history and memory. It seems to me that spirit-writing is *public* memory and emotion and that it did not dissolve the distinction between *personal* emotions (memory) and the formation of a past. On the contrary the performance of emotions authorised a past and its records in which personal memories and their interpersonal transmission could find recognition. To do this, a distinction between personal memory and public, emotional, memory had to be made in the first place for that recognition to occur.

A national coda

The Japanese defeat in the Pacific war brought a Chinese republican and modernising government to Taiwan. It gave some authority to the Southpointing Palace and the syncretic temples to which it was linked (Feuchtwang, 1974, pp294–300). But it fiercely repressed the more political movements of the islanders. Now, the most intense public emotions in Taiwan are displayed in the assertions of a Taiwanese collective identity in the rewriting of histories and the reorganisation of museums on the island against the former military Chinese rule, emotions similar to those of national movements. Opposing them are the strong emotions of unification of the sacred territory of China, coming not just from political and military leaders but also from ordinary people living on the mainland, including students abroad when they meet Taiwanese students.

Charles Stafford cites a Taiwanese news commentator advising the leaders of his government to resist the sentimental appeals of Communist mainland leaders using the classical poetry of separation and longing for reunion (2000, pp171–2). The article commends practical sobriety in the pursuit of the interests of Taiwanese people. But the emotional complement to these interests is the thrill and passion of a unifying common identity of Taiwan that is being forged, and anxiety over its recognition internationally.

In relation to such political emotions, the emotions of spiritual reunion and renewal evident in Lü Lin Wumu's spirit-written volumes are redundant and forgotten. But the sense of history and memory conveyed in them nevertheless continues in *local* commemorations of persons, ancestors, and gods, incorporated into the celebration of local cultures whether or not they are subsumed into Taiwanese people and its heritage.

I have been arguing that at any one time there is a gamut of institutions that channel and form the display and recognition of emotions. The gamut can itself be transformed by slow and revolutionary structural changes of institutions of public life and of the distinctions between domestic and larger scales of social life, such as those that have occurred in post-colonial Taiwan. I have also tried to suggest that at any one time the gamut is divided according to status and aspirations to status. Wumu's spirit-writing was a lowly aspiration to the *Li* of high literacy. But they shared the combination of a measured display of great emotion with a didactic, moral elevation.

A history of such transformations could also be written of fourteenth to twentieth century China. It would parallel the conventions of Christian asceticism and of other (chivalric, court, charivari) late medieval Europe and its transformations into conventions of the public and the private from the fifteenth century onwards. But I do not think there is a European equivalent of the continuity through transformation of *Li*.

Notes

1 At the same time his adopted daughter remembered two military leaders from the Shiding of the early and middle Japanese period. They were bandits who resisted the Japanese. But one of them, Chen Jiesheng, gave up his arms for a lot of gold, a large house and the headship of the newly created (*zhuang*) government of Shiding. In that position he was reputed even in the late 1960s when I was first in Shiding to have protected local farmland by persuading the Japanese authorities not to build a road through the Shiding mountains. It may have been economically short sighted, but he thus earned the gratitude not only of his own but also of subsequent generations. He is remembered as a flawed local hero. Lü Lin Wumu's adopted daughter said that Jiesheng remained a man of conscience who used his office to protect local interests. Lü Lin Wumu was an associate of Chen Jiesheng. Just as Jiesheng was strong but greedy, good and bad, so was Wumu a mixture of weakness and strength. The other bandit, Chen Qiuju had no such lapse.

2 In the spirit-writing tradition, transcription of revelation is by a forked stick with a stylus at the other end resting on a tray of chaff (*kangpan*). The forked stick is called a phoenix medium (*luanji*) and it is held by two people, one or both of whom are in trance. They hold the office of Phoenix Wielder (Luansheng), and one of them is the principal. Each graph they trace is called out by a Communicator (Quanluansheng) and written down by a Recorder (Luluansheng) as the possessed holders move the stick to the next graph. Collators (Jiaosheng) collect the results for subsequent reading by Cantors (Songjingsheng) and exposition by Expositors (Luanxuansheng). They are further prepared for printed publication.

3 This information comes from someone who knew them both when he was a young man, interviewed by me much later, in his ninetieth year.

4 For responsiveness in the high arts of calligraphy, painting and poetry, see for instance Clunas 1996. There, he writes of the increasing commercialisation and commodification of the economy in sixteenth century China, which allowed increasing social mobility into an elite that consequently took to distinguishing itself by the cultivation of taste, separating what had formerly been unified: use and the senses, agronomy and the landscape. Taste was a refinement of self-cultivation as a recluse, moved by strong emotions in response to rocks, trees, bamboos and water. At the same time it was always an appreciative response that gathered together a social network of friends and family (pp80, 98 and 111). For the less elite the two, use and responsiveness, were not as distinct. But for all statuses property was associated with a capacity to create and maintain a social network of relations. Elite cultivation in seclusion could turn into heroic withdrawal from and censure of a politically unjust and corrupt world. Commoners were more likely to form bands of brothers, whose romances are acted and told and collected into a vernacular novel of the fourteenth century the Shui Hu Juan (The Water Margin or Outlaws of the Marsh).

5 The style of these verses is not refined. By comparison with the felicity of élite verse and its allusions, they are made of clichés which do not build well on each other. They are more like what in English genre terms would be called melodrama. In fact with their stage directions and hyperbolic flourishes they are more like plays than poems. The flowery genre of inner

feelings was widespread. It can for instance be found in the records of Singapore spirit mediums in 1950 where Elliott (1955: 121) described the process of recording and publishing the verses of a spirit-medium in trance. The medium used a brush on paper or on rice, which is scattered on the lid of a basket. A recorder stood by to write down the characters he thought he could see. An appendix contains Elliot's translations of four of the resulting poems. They all start with the lament 'Life is short, life is short. When I think again on the shortness of life I cannot help but weep.' They then go on to general admonitions not to be ensnared by the love of life and its material rewards but to concentrate on the fate of the soul and prevent its ending in torment and causing trouble, by concentrating instead on meritorious deeds, cultivating a spiritual life. They are not personal 'cases' as in Shiding, but the expression of inner feeling is similarly written as a personal witness of suffering in floods, rivers, and seas of tears.

6   The frame would have to include the formal properties of the verse, couplets, in which the first line would expect a completion of the next, which must have influenced the caller's recognition of characters in the marks made by the stylus on the chaff.

7   Spirits are also seen and heard, embodied and as their former selves, in the UK. But here, interestingly the medium is still and the action is seen and heard by her audience. A séance was rebroadcast on Christmas Eve on BBC Radio 4, 2003, 50 years after its first, experimental broadcast from a home in Derbyshire. A woman medium behind a curtain made spirit children appear to her family and guests, ringing the bells on the Christmas tree, and then the spirits of recently dead relatives appeared and greeted those present. The language used for their presentation was not historical but scientific. The world of the dead is present but can materialise only through acquiring powers to do so in a non-material material that the husband of the medium in the scientistic language of mediumship called 'ectoplasm'.

References

Chang Xiangqun, 2004. *Lishangwanglai* – Social support networks, reciprocity and creativity in a Chinese village. City University, London: dissertation submitted for a PhD

Clunas C, 1996. *Fruitful Sites: Garden culture in Ming dynasty China*. London: Reaktion Books

Davidson, JW, 1903. *The Island of Formosa 1430–1900*. Taipei: Wenhsing Shutien

Elliott A, 1955. Chinese Spirit-Medium Cults in Singapore. Monographs on Social Anthropology No. 14. Department of Anthropology, London School of Economics and Political Science

Feuchtwang S, 1974. City temples in Taipei under three regimes.' In GW Skinner and M Elvin, eds, *The Chinese City Between Two Worlds*. Stanford, California: Stanford University Press

Jones CB, 2003. Religion in Taiwan at the end of the Japanese colonial period. In P Clart and CB Jones, eds, *Religion in Modern Taiwan; Tradition and Innovation in a Changing Society*. Honolulu: University of Hawai'i Press, 10–35

Katz P, 2005. *When Valleys Turned Blood Red: The Ta-Pa-Ni Incident in Colonial Taiwan.* Honolulu: University of Hawai'i Press

Kipnis AB, 1997. *Producing Guanxi: Sentiment, Self, and Subculture in a North China Village.* Durham NC and London: Duke University Press

Lambek M, 2002. *The Weight of the Past: Living with History in Mahajanga, Madagascar.* New York and London: Palgrave Macmillan

Lambek M, 2003. Memory in a Maussian universe. In S Radstone and K Hodgkin, eds, *Regimes of Memory.* London and New York: Routledge, 202–16

Lamley HJ, 1999. Taiwan under Japanese Rule, 1895–1945: The vicissitudes of colonialism. In MA Rubinstein, ed., *Taiwan; A New History.* Armonk and London: ME Sharpe

Lin Peiyin, 2000. Dream, pursuit and loss: the Chinese experience in the work of Zhong Lihe (1915–1960), paper presented to the annual conference of the British Association for Chinese Studies

Sennett R, 1977. *The Fall of Public Man.* London: Faber

Stafford MC, 2000. *Separation and Reunion in Modern China.* Cambridge: Cambridge University Press

Weightman F, 2004. Pretext of authority: self-justification in the Chinese authorial preface, paper presented to *Goutong*: Communicating, conference of the British Association for Chinese Studies, University of Durham

Part II

Intrapsychic and 'Public' Emotions

4
Anxiety, Mass Crisis and 'the Other'

Hélène Joffe

Introduction

This chapter sets out a way in which an emotion – namely, anxiety – shapes the response to mass crises, such as potential epidemics, threats of terrorism, and influxes of refugees. The sense in which the term 'anxiety' is used in this chapter can be defined in relation to fear: fear is said to have a specific object to which it is a reaction, whereas anxiety is defined by the absence of a specific object.[1] It often relates to a *potential* danger. This chapter argues that the anxiety evoked by the threat of mass crisis elicits 'othering' or the location of negative aspersions, and often blame, with 'the other'. The chapter synthesises a number of theories to foster understanding of the exacerbation of 'othering' at times of crisis.

Since the concept of 'the other' is central to the chapter's thesis, its connotations must be made explicit. Broadly speaking, the chapter adopts the notion of 'the other' widely used in cultural theory and, in particular, in the theories of Said (1978), Gilman (1985) and Crawford (1994). Here 'the other' generally applies to those outside of, and implicitly subordinate to, the dominant group. 'Others' may be less powerful groups within a particular society (such as women) or identified out-groups (such as, in many societies, gay people) and 'foreigners'. A now classical example of 'the other' is described in Said's (1978) writing concerning 'the Orient' – an entity constructed by European culture. Said proposed that members of 'the Orient' did not represent their own emotions, presence or history. Rather, 'the Orient' was filtered through the lens of European culture. The superiority of European identity was constructed and affirmed by way of this process. The Oriental 'Other' came to be associated with derogated practices

and values. This 'Other' provided the dominant culture with a repository into which it could project the values and practices from which it
sought to distance itself.

While the debasement of a range of 'Others' and ascription of
debased qualities to them forms a constant dynamic in many societies,
in periods of potential mass threat and crisis the focus on the negative
and threatening qualities of 'Others' intensifies. One only has to think
of the amplification of anti-Semitism in the German economic crisis of
the 1920s and 1930s to be reminded of this. The escalation of western
anti-gay sentiment from the time when AIDS and its potential to
become a pandemic were identified in the 1980s provides an example
with less severe consequences. More recently, the ongoing workings of
this process have been highlighted by suspicion of and violent attacks
on 'Orientals' in the West when threats of a global spread of the SARS
virus emerged.

It will be argued that anxiety is the driving force behind such
intense responses and that during times of mass crisis[2] it assumes a
more paranoid quality. In such periods those associated with undesirable qualities move from being represented as mildly threatening,
a challenge to the core values of the society, to being seen as the
purveyors of chaos. Thus while the 'Other' is defined in terms of difference and inferiority in relation to normative values in an ongoing
sense, the social representations that arise at times of crisis intensify
this distinction. They reflect a powerful division between a decorous,
righteous 'us' and a disruptive, transgressive 'them' (Douglas, 1966).
Vivid representations that declare which groups and practices
'pollute' the order and decorum of the 'us', of the community,
proliferate (Douglas, 1992) such as the equating of Jews to vermin,
bacteria and maggots in the key Nazi text *Mein Kampf* (see Bar-Tal,
1990).

Such representations can lead to the desire for the removal of the
so-construed 'polluting' presence. The prototypical act that symbolically rids a community of impure elements, those represented as the
source of chaos, thereby restoring order and a positive sense of identity, utilises scapegoats for the ritual transfer of evil from inside to
outside the community (Douglas, 1995). Scapegoating has its coun-
terpart within the individual psyche in the defence termed projection (Joffe, 2004). The chapter moves on to explore this response
to anxiety, first in the context of the individual psyche – drawing
primarily on ideas put forward by Melanie Klein – and then, at a
societal level.

The roots of othering in individuals: a micro-social focus

Klein (1946, 1952) developed her psychodynamic theory of the affective roots of human subjectivity from Freud's writing, particularly his formulation of the duality between the life and death instincts, set out in *Beyond the Pleasure Principle* (Freud, 1974 [1920]). Her developmental theory can be drawn on to provide insight into the link between emotion and public life, specifically anxiety and the treatment of 'the other' at times of mass crisis.

Klein was one of the early pioneers of the notion of object-relations within the psychoanalytic literature. She emphasised the salience of the interaction between the primary caregiver – usually the mother – and the infant, particularly in the first year of life, as the basis for development, including the development of thinking. In the early months, the infant's experience is characterised by feelings of satisfaction or frustration. These feelings are related in large measure to the mother's capacity to anticipate and respond to the infant's gamut of needs, both physical and emotional. At those times when its needs are fulfilled, the infant experiences the caregiver as loving. However, when its needs are unfulfilled, such as when hungry or upset, the infant experiences frustration. This introduces a more persecutory experience into the infant's mind in which it feels a mortal threat to its survival. Of course such feelings occur in a context in which the infant is thoroughly dependent on the caregiver. At times, when needs go unfulfilled, the caregiver is experienced as a hated, threatening object.

During this phase, termed the 'paranoid-schizoid' position by Klein, the infant is unaware that the loving mother is the same figure as the hated one. This enables the infant to keep the experience of the good mother separate from that of the bad mother.[3] In the vein of Freud, Klein believes that infants are orientated towards maintaining more positive feelings. Therefore, the infant not only splits the good from the bad in an effort to protect itself from bad feelings, it also projects the bad outward, away from the self, and into the caregiver. In ordinary mothering the caregiver is able to contain these feelings – usually anxiety, frustration or anger – by way of words of consolation and physical containment, thereby enabling the infant to introject (or take back into its mind) a positive experience and good feelings.

At a slightly later stage of development, around six months of age, the infant is able to perceive that the loving maternal object (the object of satisfaction) is also the hated object (object of frustration), and that the recipient of its loving feelings has also been the recipient of its hateful feelings. This Klein termed the 'depressive position'. Here the infant is faced with anxiety of a more depressive nature, linked to an emerging concern about the state of the object, with a growing drive to repair any perceived damage. This 'position' is based on a greater capacity for integration within the infant's mind of different feelings (good/bad, love/hate) and of different perceptions of the maternal figure.[4]

Thus the structuring of the adult's representational world stems from the affects present in the earliest moments of infancy. Anxiety, in particular, forms an organising concept in the Kleinian psychodynamic understanding of humans. It is experienced from birth onwards. The maturing process revolves around strengthening and organising the self against anxiety. From the earliest stages of infancy splitting, introjection and projection are brought into play unconsciously, to reduce anxiety, thereby ensuring a sense of safety and security for the maturing being.

Most salient for a theory of how affects shape public life is that the earliest representational activity sustains a lack of integration of different feelings, within the developing being: one side of its experience is all good, and the other all bad, with the two kept separate in the infant's mind and available only as alternatives. In addition, the infant endeavours to keep the bad outside of itself, while clinging to the good. This early representational system establishes a way of viewing the world in simplistic terms: either all good or all bad. When one splits a middle ground or 'grey area' with which to think about self, others or experiences is missing. Residues of the split early picture of the world remain in the individual's pattern of representation even once subsequent psychic development (i.e. the 'depressive position') allows for apprehension of complexity, of the 'grey areas'.

A key emphasis of the Kleinian outlook is that the individual experiences similar anxieties and employs similar mechanisms for managing them throughout life. Rather than passing through phases and leaving them behind, each phase of development leaves its mark on the developing individual and each individual oscillates between these two 'positions' during their lifespan. Therefore, these early developments make up a template underpinning adult emotional and cognitive life. Importantly, when changes in the social environment make for insecurity, thereby raising levels of anxiety, forms of this early representational activity – in which 'the other' functions as the repository for the individual's own unwanted thoughts – re-emerge.

The pattern of representation that allows infants to handle anxiety is then reproduced in adult life.

Particularly relevant for theories concerned with the location of threat within 'the other' is a further concept developed by Klein (1946) and her followers, the notion of 'projective identification'. This concept describes a more complex dynamic that develops to deal with anxiety. Projective identification determines that parts of the self which one does not want to own are not only projected into external objects, but that these external objects are then seen to be possessed and controlled by, as well as identified with, the projected parts. Thus, for example, the objects or humans onto which people project their aggression become feared as a source of belligerence (Frosh, 1989; Moses, 1989). In this way, a cycle of persecutory anxiety is maintained, with the consequent need to defend against it.

Projective identification can be more fully demonstrated with reference to a study of Zambian adolescents' shared representations of AIDS (see Joffe and Bettega, 2003). In line with the inferior status of females in the society, and a consequent history of linking a range of illnesses to them, women form the representational repository in which this unwanted disease is lodged. Teenage girls are viewed as the propagators of HIV via their liaisons with 'sugar daddies' – older men who have sex with the girls in return for gifts or money – and with teenage boys. Men of varying ages who are involved in unsafe sexual liaisons are not held culpable for their consequences by Zambian adolescents: all responsibility lies with the girls. Within the representations that dominate, men – adolescent and sugar daddy alike – are threatened by HIV but do not transmit it; they are not actors in the spread of the epidemic. The adolescents – male and female alike – view girls as the dangerous vectors of AIDS and boys and men as helpless in the face of these diseased, contaminating females.

Male identity, as well as the male superiority that characterises the social system, is largely protected by way of such widely shared representations. Conversely, the young women onto whom the bad event is projected, are rendered dangerous. This speaks to the projective identification process and the role played by 'othering', to how a group can buttress a positive sense of identity and power via projection/othering. However, the projected material can return to haunt the group. That which is placed outside the space of the self comes back to torment it. One comes to fear that which one gets rid of in the project of representation construction. Therefore, rather than gaining a firm sense of safety and comfort from the projection of undesirable qualities onto others, as is its unconscious aim, 'self' comes to experience 'other' as a threat by way of 'other's' association with polluting, contaminating qualities. The bad qualities that 'the other' is left to carry threaten to 'leak' back into the space of the self.

How else might people respond to crises? The earliest way of responding to anxiety, detailed above, develops the infant's capacity to order chaos by splitting good from bad objects and experiences, at the level of representation. However, in Klein's (1952) second, depressive developmental position, infants move into a space in which the ability to tolerate ambivalence forms. It is here that the capacity to deal with anxiety in a less split way develops. To be emotionally ambivalent is to be able to hold, simultaneously, positively and negatively charged feelings. This ambivalence is particularly difficult for the developing psyche since it must link and reconcile states that have previously been held apart to defend the core of the self. Complex, rather than simplistic and polarised, representations become possible. Radley's (1999) work on representations of ill people can be drawn on to elucidate the second position. Radley shows that theory that focuses on the exclusion of stigmatised groups, overlooks the compassion that is regularly shown towards those who suffer. In particular, a 'care ethos' is germane to the response to the ill, though it may coexist with a more blaming orientation. This shows that there are alternative ways of responding to heightened anxiety, such as might be evoked by the potential mass illnesses AIDS or SARS. However, it must be noted that the 'care ethos' is linked to those seen to have become the 'victims' of misfortune through no fault of their own. When 'choices' such as practising unsafe sex are seen to inform misfortune, the more blaming response may come to dominate.

In sum, early infantile representations, which leave their mark on the adult psyche, are orientated towards protection of the self from anxiety. To accomplish this protection, 'the other' becomes the repository of material that the individual seeks to push out from its own space. As the container of such associations, 'the other' can become an object of fear. These early building blocks of what is to be associated with others, rather than the self, leave their mark on the developing individual. Adults can be plunged back into the most basic of defences, the persecutory response, when mass threats raise levels of anxiety. It is useful to distinguish between persecutory anxiety, which is evoked when the individual's survival is felt to be under threat, and depressive anxiety, which is more likely to be constituted by care and concern. More than one type of anxiety can be evoked by the same crisis; for instance, concern for those living in a region affected by SARS can occur simultaneously with paranoid anxiety about passing through that region. In addition, though beyond the scope of this chapter, following the clinically derived theory, variations will occur in accordance with individuals' defensive structures.

While psychodynamic[5] theorisation is often seen as solely concerned with the intra-subjective sphere, this chapter argues that it also has social relevance. From infancy to later life, the subjective management of anxiety springs from a relational process in which the self has a tendency to strive for protection from the negative feelings by dumping unwanted material onto 'others' at the level of representation. Holding onto these representations in relation to threatening phenomena has a self-protective motivation. However, crucial to a more social reading of psychoanalytic theory is the point that such representations also come to be constituted by the values and ideologies that circulate in the particular communities, cultures and societies in which individuals are embedded. The chapter moves on to elaborate this more social process.

From the psychodynamic to the broader social world

Psychodynamic theory provides a useful account of the source of representations of 'the other', yet it does not explain what the contents of that material might be. It does not offer insight into the specific representations that people hold about 'others', such as those about females or Jews touched upon above. This is social representations theory's domain. The chapter will show how social representations establish what the individual can comfortably associate with self and in-group, and what is unacceptable and must be placed outside, with 'the other', in the service of identity protection. To make this leap, the chapter draws on strands of cultural and social theory compatible with the more clinically derived psychodynamic model set out above, but so far rarely linked to it.[6]

According to psycho-dynamically oriented cultural theorists, factors within individuals' social environments either activate or constrain their use of defence mechanisms such as projection (Sherwood, 1980). Events that get portrayed as particularly threatening trigger representations that contain elements of inter-group projection. However, in addition, the extent to which it is permissible to project onto certain groups is regulated by the social order, which is constituted by a range of phenomena including laws (for instance, anti-racism laws), norms that can have policy implications (for instance, political correctness, sometimes linked to affirmative action policies) and socially circulating representations. This chapter highlights the final of these aspects.

Social representations theory, instigated by social psychologist Serge Moscovici in the 1960s (see Duveen, 2001), sets out to explain how representations that circulate in the social environment come to impact upon individuals. Popular media are seen to hold a key place in the contemporary social environment and to play a central role in the transmission of information and knowledge concerning mass risks. Media portrayals of a risk event can generate blame, for instance.[7] Yet the media do not construct the targets of blame anew. Each individual and each media story is preceded and surrounded by a world of existing representations, a world in which certain groups have already been represented as respectable and others as degenerate. Representations that circulate in a particular social group prior to the individual's entry to it, influence who and what the individual chooses as the repository[8] for their responses to anxieties.

In the ideas they pass down through the generations, groups store not only a sense of which their disfavoured 'other' groups are, but what aspersions are to be linked to such groups. The groups and aspersions chosen are mutually informative of one another and are underpinned by the core values in the society. For example, Westerners mark out what it is to be a 'good' and upright citizen precisely by way of designating as 'other' that which does not represent western values (Crawford, 1994). A core western value is self-control. The body is the symbolic terrain upon which desire for and display of control are enacted (Crawford, 1985). In particular, the health of the body has come to act as a central metaphor for self-control, self-discipline, self-denial and will power (Crawford, 1994). 'Being healthy', and the appearance of being so has thereby become a metaphor for being a responsible, 'good' citizen. Conversely, 'the others' – smokers, obese people, alcoholics, drug users, people with AIDS – are all associated with excess and indulgence, with a loss of the West's most cherished qualities (see Joffe and Staerklé, in press).[9] Their contravention of the values that are held dear sets them up as repositories for projection of society's ills.

Social representations theory proposes certain mechanisms for the assimilation of new events, such as mass risks, into people's thinking. A key process in the formation of social representations is objectification (Moscovici, 2001 [1984]), which permits abstract ideas – such as the potential for a major escalation of syndromes such as SARS and AIDS – to be assimilated into representations. Objectification, which is highly analogous to symbolisation, involves people making something abstract easier to grasp, by transforming it into a more concrete entity. This process can occur in a number of ways (see Moscovici and Hewstone, 1984), including abstract ideas being substituted with people (personification) or groups. The process is instantiated in SARS and AIDS immediately bringing certain groups to mind. Even the Ebola virus, which has affected only a handful of westerners, has been widely symbolised in Britain in terms of African's rampant illnesses and inadequate medical systems (see Joffe and Haarhoff, 2002). Widespread ways of thinking, or social representations, regarding 'the other' are grounded in such common points of reference. They are repeatedly dredged up at times when mass crises threaten in the service of protecting the inner space and, often, the superiority of dominant western groups.

Discussion: a theoretical integration

In certain respects the social representations vision and the Kleinian psychodynamic framework are incompatible. The idea of representations pre-dating the individual, and the individual merely being born into a location within them, is very different from the notion of the infant constructing a representational system that is identity-protective and then slotting material in the environment into its own pre-existing system of thought. However, the two perspectives can sit together more comfortably if one differentiates between the structuring of people's representations, and the socially shaped contents that constitute these representations. I hope to have shown that even if proclivities towards certain patterns of representation are forged in the early years (that is, the structuring of people's representations), these proclivities in no way diminish the role played by the slowly unfolding social world's particular representations (that is, the contents) in constraining or exacerbating defensive responses to mass risks.

The theorisation of response to crises in terms of the two early Kleinian positions – paranoid-schizoid and depressive – is at odds with the contemporary psychology of responses to risk events, with its assumption that the individual is a self-regulating, largely rational thinker who makes certain systematic errors (for instance, see Slovic, 2000). In contrast, this chapter proposes a model of the individual responding to crisis as an essentially emotional and social being whose motivations are not easily fathomable due to their unconscious source (see Joffe, 1999, 2003, for an elaboration of this contrast). Even though there is increasing attention within psychology to non-conscious processes, which harks back to ideas suggested by Zajonc (1980), among others, the links between such processes and responses within public life are under-developed. Furthermore, contemporary social psychology is reticent in relation to psychodynamic thinking for a range of reasons, including its doubt that the patterning of adult representations is largely forged in infancy, before the individual has knowledge of the macro-social world. However, if one is concerned with the interaction of the ideas that circulate in public life, and the emotional systems that originate with individuals, socially oriented psychodynamic theorisation is invaluable. This chapter has argued that patterns of representation are established very early on, and that subsequent social material shapes the manifestation of these patterns in specific groups and individuals.

Theorisation of this process is not only important in itself, but also for understanding and minimising the powerful and damaging effects of 'othering'. Expressions of distaste fulfil unconscious emotional needs for those who express them, and those who are the recipients of these expressions receive 'powerful doses of bad psychic stuff' (Rustin, 1991). These transactions are so potent and damaging precisely because they do not operate merely at a cognitive level, like the statements of opinion that 'othered' groups and individuals also have to deal with. Therefore, informing people of their 'othering' tendencies at times of crisis may have little effect, since the tendency's force derives from the level at which it operates: the unconscious. This level of functioning is difficult to address and resists argument precisely because it does not engage with conscious levels of functioning. This line of thought is very similar to the one that stresses the power of social representations. Social representations are so powerful precisely because they are taken for granted and therefore appear to be logical, necessary and natural (Oyserman and Marcus, 1998).

Summary and concluding remarks

A framework for understanding how people use 'the other' at times of raised anxiety has been forged in this chapter. The positive identity of 'us' is sustained through imbuing others with devalued properties. When faced with anxiety provoking situations there is a rearrangement in people's representations of themselves and of others. People organise their representations in accordance with the struggle for a boundary between an inner space whose purity they hope to maintain, and a polluted, outside world. The foundations of this process lie in unconscious responses. Freud's bodily metaphor for the projection of 'bad' outward – spitting out bad-tasting food – becomes layered with wider social and moral connotations as the human being becomes acculturated, and such connotations are integrated into his/her identity. Identity is forged, at least in part, by a sense of difference from others, and by excluding those whom the individual, and the culture in which the individual is located, associates with undesirable qualities:

> If the aim of a system is to create an outside where you can put the things you don't want, then we have to look at what that system disposes of – its rubbish – to understand it, to get a picture of how it sees itself and wants to be seen (Phillips, 1995, p19).

This statement is highly complementary with the claim, made by cultural theorists such as Said, that the way that a culture defines the 'Other' discloses how it characterises itself. One particular social representation that is linked to an array of 'Others' in western culture is their lack of self-control (Joffe and Staerklé, in press). Since social representations regulate the extent to which it is permissible to project onto certain groups, those pertaining to lacking control single out certain group for scapegoating. The extreme and growing stigmatisation of obese people and smokers is illuminated by this finding. Clearly, western culture seeks to characterise itself as restrained, and in control, regarding the body. Self-control over mind – symbolised by scientists with their mastery in the face of risk – also forms a key part of the western conception of itself.

In conclusion, it must be emphasised that according to psychodynamic theorisation responses to mass crises need not be solely tied in with othering. The chapter has established that ongoing tensions between 'us' and 'them' are intensified at moments of potential danger and crisis. At such times, the early splitting mechanism of defence reappears in adults, and the 'other' becomes the target of a rich array of projections, which contain those aspects of experience from which individuals seek to distance their 'selves'. Othering is a way of protecting self and in-group; it is defence by way of representation. It also serves the function of status quo maintenance, in that each society perpetuates existing values by the ways in which it responds to crises – for instance, by asserting which groups contravene the self-control ethos, in western contexts.

The particular characteristic of the early, split state that is reinvoked at such times is that contradictory feelings cannot sit together. Were they to do so they would facilitate a rather complex orientation towards threats and towards other groups. However, it is important to highlight that in the course of early development people learn to think in this complex way, to reconcile the split parts. This subsequent aspect of development and its consequences for mass responses is often neglected in theories of 'othering'. It lends hope that splitting is neither inevitable nor unchangeable. It has implications not only for those hoping to rectify social exclusion, but also for opposing the notion that currently pervades psychological theory, that negative stereotyping and prejudice are an inevitable and routine part of what it is to be human.

Notes

1 It must be noted that this does not correspond fully with the Freudian distinction (Laplanche and Pontalis, 1973), but is fairly widely used in the psychoanalytic literature.

2 However, caution is called for in relation to framing the litany of 'hate crimes' or acts of genocide as responses to crises. Rather, a sense of threat and imminent crisis can sometimes be engineered in order to justify the harsh treatment of 'Others'. While bearing this in mind, many of the writings in the field subscribe to a notion that the negative representation of the Other intensifies as the response to a material crisis, such as an escalating epidemic.

3 For Klein, the embryonic nature of the infant's cognitive capacities mean that it is unable to relate to the mother as a whole object, incorporating all aspects of her, but relates to her on the basis of part-objects. For Klein, these primarily involve aspects of the mother's body, especially the breast, which is often linked to the first experience of the maternal object via the feeding relationship.

4 Part-object relationships are replaced by whole object relationships.

5 It must be noted that the Lacanian School of psychodynamic theory and psychodynamically rooted cultural theory are not drawn upon in this chapter.

6 A rich tradition of British sociological thought also extends psychodynamic thinking into the broader social world (see for instance Rustin, 1991; Richards, 1989), though this tradition has not engaged with social representations theory.

7 Of course those who construct the event within popular media are also influenced by the defences outlined above. In addition, they construct the event in accordance with their audiences' preferences.

8 Thus each social group has various 'repositories' (Sherwood, 1980), which it maintains as potential targets for its projection: 'Every social group has a set vocabulary of images for this externalised Other. These images are the product of history and of a culture that perpetuates them ... From the wide range of the potential models in any society, we select a model that best reflects the common presuppositions about the other at any given moment in history' (Gilman, 1985, p20).

9 A counter-trend is also in evidence. Crawford proposes that in western culture the self is not just associated with control but with a release from it. Pleasures, desires, gratification and play are intrinsic aspects of consumer culture. However, rather than holding these two antithetical components together, the culture expunges its association with the uncontrolled aspects – such as addictions – linking them with disparaged 'others'. These 'others' are blamed for bringing their ill health upon themselves, and held outside of the culture symbolically, so that the self cannot be morally infected.

References

Bar-Tal D, 1990. *Group Beliefs*. New York: Springer

Crawford R, 1985. A cultural account of health – control, release and the social body'. In JB McKinlay, ed., *Issues in the Political Economy of Health Care*. London: Tavistock, pp60–103

Crawford R, 1994. The boundaries of the self and the unhealthy other: Reflections on health, culture and AIDS. *Social Science and Medicine*, 38, 10, 1347–65

Douglas M, 1966. *Purity and Danger*. London: Routledge and Kegan Paul

Douglas M, 1992. Risk and Blame. Essays in Cultural Theory. London: Routledge

Douglas T, 1995. *Scapegoats: Transferring Blame*. London: Routledge

Duveen G, 2001. Representations, identities, resistance. In K Deaux and G Philogene, eds, *Representations of the Social: Bridging Theoretical Traditions*. Malden, Massachusetts: Blackwell Publishers, 257–70

Freud S, 1974 (1920). *Beyond the Pleasure Principle. Standard Edition of the Complete Psychological Works of Sigmund Freud* Volume 1. London: Institute of Psychoanalysis and Hogarth Press

Frosh S, 1989. Psychoanalysis and racism. In B Richards, ed., *Crises of the Self: Further Essays on Psychoanalysis and Politics*. London: Free Association Books, 229–44

Gilman S, 1985. *Difference and Pathology: Stereotypes of Sexuality, Race and Madness*. Ithaca, New York: Cornell University Press

Joffe H, 1999. *Risk and 'the Other'*. Cambridge: Cambridge University Press

Joffe H, 2003. Risk: From perception to social representation. *British Journal of Social Psychology*, 42, 1, 55–73

Joffe H, 2005. 'The Other' and identity construction. In L Licata and M Sanchez-Mazas, eds, *The Other: Psychosocial Outlooks*. Grenoble: Grenoble University Press pp95–116

Joffe H and Haarhoff G, 2002. Representations of far-flung illnesses: the case of Ebola in Britain. *Social Science & Medicine*, 54, 955–69

Joffe H and Bettega N, 2003. Social representations of AIDS among Zambian adolescents. *Journal of Health Psychology*, 85, 5, 616–31

Joffe H and Staerklé C, in press. The centrality of the Self-Control Ethos in western aspersions regarding outgroups: A social representational approach to stereotype content. *Culture & Psychology*

Klein M, 1946. Notes on some schizoid mechanisms. *International Journal of Psycho-Analysis*, 27, 99–110

Klein M, 1952. Some theoretical conclusions regarding the emotional life of the infant'. In M Klein, P Hemann, S Isaacs and J Riviere, eds, *Developments in Psycho-Analysis*. London: Hogarth Press, 198–236

Laplanche J and Pontalis J-B, 1973. *The Language of Psychoanalysis.* London: Karnac Books

Moscovici S, 2001 [1984]. Why a theory of social representations. In K Deaux and G Philogene, eds, *Representations of the Social.* Oxford: Blackwell Publishers, 8–35

Moscovici S and Hewstone M, 1984. De la science au sens commun. In S Moscovici, ed., *Psychologie Sociale.* Paris: Presses Universitaires de France, 539–66

Moses R, 1989. Projection, identification and projective identification: Their relation to political process. In J Sandler, ed., *Projection, Identification, Projective Identification.* London: Karnac Books, 133–50

Oyserman D and Markus H, 1998. The self as social representation. In U Flick, ed., *The Psychology of the Social.* Cambridge: Cambridge University Press, pp107–25

Phillips A, 1995. *Terror and Experts.* London: Faber and Faber

Radley A, 1999. Blame, abhorrence and the social response to suffering. Health, 3, 167–87

Richards B, ed., 1989. *Crises of the Self: Further Essays on Psychoanalysis and Politics.* London: Free Association Books

Rustin M, 1991. *The Good Society and the Inner World: Psychoanalysis, Politics and Culture.* London: Verso

Said EW, 1978. *Orientalism: Western Conceptions of the Orient.* London: Penguin

Sherwood R, 1980. *The Psychodynamics of Race.* Sussex: The Harvester Press

Slovic P, 2000. The perception of risk. London: Earthscan

Zajonc R, 1980. Feeling and thinking: Preferences need no inferences. *American Psychologist,* 35, 151–75

5
Another Repressed Returns: the Re-Branding of German Psychoanalysis[1]

Stephen Frosh

Introduction

Coming to terms with the past is never a straightforward affair, for individuals, organisations or whole societies, particularly when that past is traumatic or remains subject to contentious dispute. Under these conditions, past events continue to stir up strong emotions that, if unacknowledged, can come to dominate the present and the future, unspoken passions that circulate without end. In the case of organisations, this can mean the construction of institutional defences attempting to 'contain' or manage these emotions, but it can also result in the construction of these organisations along the lines of the hidden past; that is, failures to deal with what is 'repressed' in institutional life can lead to the repressed itself being constitutive of the institution. A bad history tends not to die quietly when denied, but rather to poison the body within which it lies. In relation particularly to institutional pasts felt to be shameful – and there are many of these, often taking the form of collaboration with an oppressive power – denial of what has happened and prolonged refusal to look it squarely in the face can result in the institution distorting its history and its aims, and losing credibility in its own eyes as well as in those of others.

The idea that disturbing emotions connected to the past have in some way to be 'faced' clearly owes a great deal to psychoanalysis. In some respects, it can be argued that psychoanalysis is founded on the question of how this difficult task might be achieved: how might people exorcise the ghosts that inhabit them, how might they deal with repressed impulses or memories, how might they be freed from endlessly repeating their mistakes? The interpretive and therapeutic vocabulary and procedures of psychoanalysis purport to offer some help here, the basic model being one in which the past is invoked, with all its extravagant emotion, and *worked through*; that is, when the past is allowed to 'come alive' in the present, the possibility is created for its sting to be drawn. When applied to organisations, this involves exploring the unconscious motivations of individual members of the organisation; but it also requires attention to be paid to the organisation's own 'unconscious', the ways in which its processes and structures represent unspoken, often defensive, practices aimed at reducing anxiety and preserving the organisation itself from unmanageable conflict, fragmentation or dissolution (Obholzer and Roberts, 1994). Psychoanalytic concepts and interpretive practices offer a way into these organisational processes, in principle making it possible for them to be recognised and revised.

Psychoanalysis, however, like everything else, has its own institutional past, included in which are a fair number of traumatic events and at least partially repressed emotions. One might think that the psychoanalytic movement is well equipped to deal with this situation, given that easing the past is its stock-in-trade; but as will be seen from the 'case study' presented in this chapter, facing one's own trauma in the way one might help others to face theirs is not necessarily an easy thing to do. For this reason, the case study can be seen as exemplary in the sense that it shows what can happen even when one is dealing with an institution founded on notions of emotional honesty and historical awareness. Faced with a deep historical trauma, which brought up strongly ambivalent feelings about its own conditions of emergence (specifically, here, its Jewish roots), psychoanalysis as an organisation and many psychoanalysts as individuals stepped back from acknowledgement and took refuge in denial and repression. As will be seen, this worked for a while in preserving a sense of unity, but at the cost of a disturbing undercurrent of unease that eventually made itself felt. Whether this always happens, in every institution with such a past, is a moot point; but one might think that if it can happen in psychoanalysis, it can happen anywhere.

Psychoanalysis in Nazi times

Amongst the delicate moments in the history of psychoanalysis, its encounter with the Nazis in the 1930s and 1940s is one that continues to provoke discontent. The history of psychoanalysis in Germany during the period of the Third Reich has been relatively well documented in the past 20 years, particularly following the exhibition on the subject put together for the 1985 International Psychoanalytic Association Congress in Hamburg (Brecht *et al.*, 1985; Cocks, 1997 has provided an extensive account of psychotherapy during the Nazi period). This work has shown clearly that the psychoanalysts followed a policy of 'appeasement' towards the Nazis, characterised by an attempt to distance psychoanalysis from its 'Jewish' elements (Frosh, 2003). Under the leadership of Felix Boehm and Carl Müller-Braunschweig, but with the support of Ernest Jones (then President of the International Psychoanalytic Association) and to some extent Sigmund and Anna Freud, the attitude of the Germans was to try to preserve the psychoanalytic movement there even if it meant compromising with the Nazis. This involved the forced resignation of the Jewish analysts from the German Psychoanalytic Society, the Deutsche Psychoanalytische Gesellschaft (DPG) in 1935; it also involved an intellectual effort to distance psychoanalysis from the Freudian focus on sexuality and the opposition between the unconscious and the social order, replacing it with the project of releasing the potential of the German unconscious in the service of the state. In 1936, the psychoanalysts joined with other psychotherapists under the leadership of Matthias Heinrich Göring to form the German Institute for Psychological Research and Psychotherapy – known, colloquially and lastingly, as the Göring Institute. By 1938, the DPG had been dissolved, but its members continued as 'Work Group A' within the Göring Institute, and some of them – including Boehm and Müller-Braunschweig – retained senior positions. Through their involvement with the Göring Institute, which had the privileged status of a 'Reichsinstitute', they occupied an important place in the Nazi state, offering treatment to homosexuals and to war-traumatised members of the Luftwaffe, and participating in the construction of a 'New German Psychotherapy' based, at least in name, on a non-Freudian and anti-Semitic ideology, and certainly dedicated to the construction of model citizens of the Nazi Reich.

The impact of collaboration between psychoanalysts, psychotherapists and the Nazis continued until well after the demise of the Third Reich. For many years, this history was largely hidden, as the psychoanalysts set about rebuilding their organisation and their myths, specifically presenting themselves – like many other Germans – as always having been victims and possibly opponents of Nazism. Karen Brecht, whose role in clarifying history has been very significant, notes about the situation in the 30 years after the war that, 'Most German publications on the history of psychoanalysis during the Third Reich, originating as they did from contemporary witnesses who presented the analysts as victims, were apologetic and not really informative ... The picture of German psychoanalysts presented by oral history was one of secret resistance fighters and inner emigrants' (Brecht, 1995, p291). In fact, the process of uncovering the history of psychoanalysis in Germany in the Third Reich had to wait for a considerable time, and required a rude shock to get it going. This shock was the product of a remarkable piece of political incompetence on the part of the German psychoanalysts. In 1977, at the International Psychoanalytic Congress held in Jerusalem, the Germans proposed that the next Congress should take place in Berlin. One might have thought that they would realise that raising this issue at a Congress held in the Jewish state would not be a wise move, and perhaps it is an indication of just how much the Germans were out of step with general opinion that they did not realise the furore they would unleash – though it has to be said that the Executive Council of the IPA initially supported their request (McLaughlin, 1978). Chasseguet-Smirgel (1987, p434) represents the events as follows:

> Those who took part in the Jerusalem Congress in 1977 will no doubt remember that our German colleagues then invited us to Berlin. This aroused an outcry because the majority of the members of many of the world's psychoanalytical associations are Jewish. One after another, well known and respected analysts took the stage, saying: 'It's too soon for Germany' or 'Never in Germany'.... It must be said that our German colleagues – of course, it is not easy to be German today – facilitated matters by not connecting their invitation with the highly symbolic venue of that particular Congress.

In the event, the German analysts' request was turned down, provoking a period of difficult self-examination culminating in the exhibition held at the first post-war Congress that did actually take place in Germany, the Hamburg Congress of 1985, an exhibition which also built on the pioneering critical work of a young German psychoanalyst, Regine Lockot. The Hamburg Congress, as will be described below, was far from successful in dealing with the relationship between the German psychoanalysts and the Nazis, but it did reveal the degree to which psychoanalysis had been compromised by its involvement with the Nazis and with the Göring Institute. However, before considering the implications of this, it is important to outline another strand of what happened in Germany: the actual emergence of psychoanalysis from the ashes, that is, its non-sanitised and rather sordid path back to international acceptance.

Reinventing psychoanalysis

At the International Psycho-Analytical Congress held in Zurich in August 1949, the first after the war, Ernest Jones initiated a debate at the business meeting on whether the Deutsche Psychoanalytische Gesellschaft should be allowed back into the International Psycho-Analytic Association. His introduction laid bare the issues facing the IPA and the DPG, and made it readily apparent that what was exercising the psychoanalysts was not the question of how to deal with the possible and actual connections between the German psychoanalysts and the Nazis, but rather how to manage a situation in which, because of the enforced amalgamation of psychoanalysis with psychotherapy in the Göring Institute, there were doubts about the purity of German psychoanalysis as a theoretical and practical system. Indeed, in an act of appropriation of history in line with the tendency to make the analysts into resistance heroes, Werner Kemper is quoted in the minutes of the meeting as describing,

> some of the difficulties of practising psycho-analysis in Germany when, for instance, to treat a Jewish patient invited being sent to a concentration camp. Their group was formerly stigmatised as Marxist, and more recently as a Bourgeois deviation. But they had not a single Nazi among them, which could be said of no other German Society (Freud, 1949, p186).

Kemper was arguing for the readmission of the Germans into the International Association; the leaders of the DPG at this point, and those pressing most strongly for entry, were two well-known names from negotiations with the Nazis, Carl Müller-Braunschweig and Felix Boehm. Müller-Braunschweig was the key figure here, having reformed the DPG as early as October 1945, although the candidates of the DPG were actually being trained in Kemper's Institut für Psychotherapie – a matter of great significance as this Institute was state supported and offered trainees regular or freelance employment at a time when most of the medical establishment was hostile to

psychoanalysis (Thomä, 1969). It was important for the psychotherapists that they drew on the name of the DPG as an organisation that
had been disbanded under the Nazis, rather than acknowledge any
continuity with the Göring Institute, but in fact the traditions and
the persons involved in the new DPG were very much the same as
those who had worked and trained together during the war. Even
some of the ideology was not yet completely hidden: for example, at
a Committee meeting of 7th August 1945, Boehm, in response to a
query from Müller-Braunschweig about how the practice in the new
organisation might differ from that of the old Berlin Psychoanalytic
Institute, is recorded as saying 'what was on his mind, that personally
he had always suffered from the preponderance of Jews in the old
Institute' (Brechet *et al.*, 1985, p195). What was particularly problematic, however, was not the perpetuation of anti-Semitic attitudes, but
rather that the outstanding figure in the Institute was Harald Schultz-
Hencke, who in fact took over its directorship when Kemper went to
work in Brazil in the late 1940s. Continuing the 'deviation' from
Freudianism that had begun well before the war, Schultz-Hencke
and the majority group within the 'new' DPG promoted a form of
'neo-analysis' that very happily chimed with the other psychotherapy groups in Germany, including the Jungians. This, for Müller-
Braunschweig and the majority of analysts outside Germany, was
anathema, a more threatening betrayal than anything that was
admitted so far about the links between the pre-war analysts and the
Nazis, and Müller-Braunschweig's efforts were thenceforth steadily
along the lines of trying to (re-) establish a properly Freudian basis
for the DPG. However, within the DPG itself Schultz-Hencke was a
very significant figure, and he had benefited during the Nazi period
from being allowed to continue teaching and recruiting students,
unlike both Boehm and Müller-Braunschweig. In a critical account,
Thomä (1969) describes how this special position, alongside his
central place in the post-war training Institute for Psychotherapy,
meant that 'Psychoanalysis was represented most strongly by Schultz-
Hencke, and naturally in the manner understood by him' and that,
'The students around Schultz-Hencke were linked to him emotionally
as well as intellectually and thus favourable conditions were created
for forming a group' (p685). Boehm was largely supportive of Schultz-
Hencke, perhaps enacting a wish for unity amongst the Germans
arising as a defence against being torn apart by recriminations; this
meant that the putative director of the DPG, Müller-Braunschweig,
was actually in a minority position.

Jones set up the debate at the Congress in his usual direct way, reviewing the history and provocatively giving expression to his doubts. The question was, how pure ('true, real') could the German Society be given its history of involvement with other psychotherapeutic groups? The previous day, Schultz-Hencke had given a powerful defence of his post-ideological approach and Müller-Braunschweig had responded by criticising him for 'dogmatic conceptual narrowness' in a reply tendentiously entitled 'The neoanalysis of Schultz-Hencke seen from the perspective of psychoanalysis' (Eickhoff, 1995, p952) and including as its opening summary statement the claim that 'Neoanalysis has resulted from drastically eliminating from psychoanalysis all those points which in the course of the development of psychoanalysis aroused resistance' – one of the standard ripostes of traditional Freudians to new departures (Brecht *et al.*, 1985, p203). This debate clearly weighed heavily in Jones' scales: in his introduction, he singled out Müller-Braunschweig's contribution for praise and, by implication, damned Schultz-Hencke.

The German Society was dissolved before the war, just as the Vienna Society was. After the war, Dr Müller-Braunschweig in 1946 notified us of its reconstruction and we naturally welcomed this information, which was tantamount to a provisional acceptance. Since then, however, information about the state of the German Society has been very mixed... It would appear that steady pressure in the direction of amalgamating different forms of psychotherapy – Jung, Adler, Freud, Neo-Analyse *(sic)* – under one heading must have some effect in ten to twelve years on the members. It would not be human to expect otherwise. The probability is that some analysts have remained true, real, genuine analysts and are clear about its relation to other work. Dr Müller-Braunschweig gave an excellent example of this yesterday. At the other extreme there would appear to be some who we should not consider to be psycho-analysts. In between there is also an indefinite number (we do not know how many or how confused), and so the total picture is undoubtedly somewhat bewildering. Discussion in the Central Executive was therefore to the effect that this large Society which still works under the Institute of German Psychotherapy, so that the training is therefore mixed, is not altogether what we should call a psychoanalytical Society. The question is what steps our colleagues from Germany think they should take to remedy this complicated state of affairs. (Freud, 1949, p186)

In response, Müller-Braunschweig expressed his disappointment that there was any difficulty concerning readmission, claiming that the psychoanalysts 'preserved their own autonomy and independence' and planned to establish their own Institute, but after some debate about how best to manage the situation with Schultz-Hencke, the decision went against him, with acceptance of Heinz Hartmann's motion 'that the Central Executive pursue its investigation further, that provisional acceptance of the German Society be continued, and that the Central Executive report to the next Congress' (Ibid., p187). This rebuttal seems to have come as a shock to the Germans, who were heavily invested in the idea that they had saved psychoanalysis during the Nazi period and that, as Thomä (1969, p687) puts it, 'They had been unable to prevent anything, and everything that was done on their part as a result of the demands of the regime always had Freud's sanction or the approval of the representatives of the International Psycho-Analytical Association.' The public revelation that the DPG was severely split was a narcissistic injury that was particularly hard to deal with, resulting in feelings of betrayal that became increasingly overt. Müller-Braunschweig, as the representative of orthodoxy and the IPA's preferred model of a psychoanalyst, bore the brunt of these hostile feelings.

Subsequent to this meeting, Müller-Braunschweig renewed his efforts to make the DPG more psychoanalytically orthodox. Schultz-Hencke not only opposed this, but refused to leave the DPG himself in order to restore it to psychoanalytic credibility. The degree of acrimony between the protagonists in this dispute became increasingly marked, with Schultz-Hencke claiming that Müller-Braunschweig had deliberately misrepresented his position in Zurich. After Schultz-Hencke turned down an initial approach by Müller-Braunschweig suggesting a face-to-face private meeting, their correspondence rapidly degenerated into personal abuse. On 10th November 1949, Schultz-Hencke wrote to Müller-Braunschweig that, 'I want to tell you quite frankly that in my opinion you are under a total illusion about the motives for your actions and words, and always have been' and went on to argue that his version of neo-analysis was such that 'I am as completely justified in describing myself as a psychoanalyst as I ever was, at any rate as the Americans in question call themselves Neo-Psychoanalysts' (Brecht *et al.*, 1985, p206) – a legitimate point. Three days later, Müller-Braunschweig responded: 'How could you let yourself go as you did in your last letter? It is bristling with slanders, misrepresentations and insults. I was tempted not to reply at all' (Ibid., p207). The battle lines hardened, with the majority group supporting the idea that psycho-analysis could operate within the broader remit of the DPG and the Institute for Psychotherapy, whilst Müller-Braunschweig's group tried to resituate the centre of gravity in a more purely psychoanalytic direction. By January 1950, Müller-Braunschweig was writing to 'all members of the DPG' the following non-conciliatory tract:

> I should like to draw your attention to a question of organisation which has been worrying our Berlin members in particular for a long time. It concerns the relationship of Schultz-Hencke and his friends with our society. A number of our Berlin members see in Schultz-Hencke's membership of the Psychoanalytical Society a problem urgently demanding a solution. The participation of Schultz-Hencke and his friends in the work of our meetings is seen by a number of our members as scarcely productive and adding nothing to the particular objects and tasks of a psychoanalytical society. The group of members who take this view feel that if the work of the Society is to continue to be undisturbed and fruitful, it is desirable that Herr Schultz-Hencke should give up his member-ship of the Society. (Brecht *et al.*, 1985, p209)

Perhaps not surprisingly, this did not resolve the situation and Schultz-Hencke refused to leave quietly. Eventually, Müller-Braunschweig gave up his attempt to gain control of the DPG and initiated a move that once again provoked the language of betrayal. On 10th June 1950 a new organisation, the Deutsche Psychoanalytische Vereinigung (DPV) was formed by Müller-Braunschweig and a few others; its existence was announced in a circular to the members of the DPG in September. At this time, Müller-Braunschweig was still Chairman of the DPG, and the members of the new organisation did not actually resign from the old one, hoping instead to provoke a split. Matters came to a head at a General Meeting of the DPG of 3rd December 1950 (Brecht *et al.*, 1985, pp 211–13). Müller-Braunschweig reported on the situation, Schultz-Hencke responded, saying that his theory was 'two-thirds Freud' and implying that Müller-Braunschweig had been plotting (which he had). Boehm, in the first of a series of increasingly vitriolic interventions, commented that, 'The outsiders among us must be wondering what sort of a scientific life the DPG has been leading in the last two and a half years. The whole of Müller-Braunschweig's report and the discussion up to now must give the idea that there is no Society, but two men with different viewpoints.' Franz Baumeyer accused Müller-Braunschweig, 'Is it not drastic for a Chairman like you to fail so grossly in his duties? So gross a violation justifies measures of distrust.' Müller-Braunschweig defended his actions, explaining that the DPV group had not resigned from the DPG because they wanted to continue their collaboration and wished to have a 'friendly discussion'; however, 'instead of that I was answered with massive countermeasures which confirmed our fears.' Boehm then gave an extraordinary report on Müller-Braunschweig's five year period as Chairman of the DPG, minuted as a series of 19 points, which included praise for his work in some areas, but also contained the following criticisms.

5) Müller-Braunschweig as a representative in the public eye: Boehm had constant complaints that Müller-Braunschweig always gave the impression that he had not prepared his lectures, lost the thread, often repeated himself, etc.
7) Müller-Braunschweig brought dissension into every kind of collaboration.
11) Müller-Braunschweig had staged a public quarrel that was no longer objective. Müller-Braunschweig's appearance before the international public in Zurich was, he said, a typical humiliation of Germans in front of foreigners. Müller-Braunschweig's behaviour had been justly criticised in the press and in letters from foreigners. The IPA's rejection was Müller-Braunschweig's fault.
15) The alienation exists because Müller-Braunschweig is doing everything to eliminate his mortal enemy, Schultz-Hencke.
19) In 1945 Müller-Braunschweig took over a flourishing Society. As a result of his 5 years of activity he leaves a ruined Society, a mere rump.

Given the actual situation in Germany in 1945, this last accusation was especially egregious. After this assault, the proposal 'not to exonerate' Müller-Braunschweig was carried by ten votes to seven (recorded in the minutes as 'Müller-Braunschweig's friends'), with two abstentions; Müller-Braunschweig and seven others then resigned. Thus a split in German psychoanalysis became institutionalised, with the DPG representing neo-analysis and alliance with other psychotherapies, and the DPV representing psychoanalytic orthodoxy. In the years to come, the former was to be portrayed as continuing the tradition of the Göring Institute whilst the latter was credited with restoring psychoanalysis to health; but in fact both organisations were deeply implicated in the past, and the founders of the DPV had actually themselves been members of the Göring Institute, and had exerted influence within it. At the 1951 International Psycho-Analytic Congress in Amsterdam, the question of the admission of the German psychoanalysts into the IPA came up again for reconsideration. This time, the Congress President was Leo Bartmeier, who summarised the issues as follows (Bibring, 1952, p253):

> You will remember that during the last Congress we gave only provisional recognition to the German Psycho-Analytical Society (Deutsche Psychoanalytische Gesellschaft) because of problems concerning its composition and the scientific trends in the group. The main question under discussion was the role which Dr Schultz-Hencke's neo-psychoanalysis played. The last Congress felt that this should be clarified and that the German Psycho-Analytical Society should first re-establish its psycho-analytic orientation before a final decision could be made. After unsuccessful attempts to carry out these suggestions, Dr Carl Müller-Braunschweig organised a new group, the German Psycho-Analytical Association (Deutsche Psychoanalytische Vereinigung). The membership has now increased to eleven, and Dr Müller-Braunschweig has applied to the International Psychoanalytical Association for recognition of this new organisation. The Executive Council suggests to the Congress acceptance of this application for full recognition.

Müller-Braunschweig then explained the background more fully, stating that he had 'tried to influence analysts of this [DPG] group to leave [the DPG] and form a new group based exclusively on psychoanalytic principles' (Ibid.), but the majority of analysts had refused this suggestion, leading to the decision to break away and form the DPV with 'a small group of colleagues'. The resolution to accept the DPV 'under the direction of Dr Müller-Braunschweig' was unanimously accepted. There then followed a debate on what to do about the DPG, which was now under the chairmanship of Boehm. Bartmeier proposed, on behalf of the IPA Executive, that its provisional recognition should be withdrawn. In reply, Kemper gave a historical review of the development of the German Psychotherapeutic Institute, which was, he claimed, 'at the time when the existence of psycho-analysis was threatened in Germany, the only place where the work could be continued' (Ibid., p254). He proposed continuing with the DPG's provisional recognition, a request Boehm supported, arguing that he had only taken on the chairmanship of the DPG in October 1950 and claiming that it 'would be able to prove its scientific value for psycho-analysis between the present Congress and the next one' (Ibid.). He also protested about the view that there were in fact two groups in the DPG – the psychoanalysts and Schultz-Hencke's group – and 'raised the question of the basic meaning of the contemplated rejection of the old German Psycho-Analytical Society. He felt that this implied a rejection of himself, as if his teaching and writing had shown a deviation from the system of psycho-analysis, and he protested against this implica-tion' (Ibid.). Anna Freud then intervened to say that it had never been a personal issue; rather, 'It would be a unique occurrence if the International Psycho-Analytical Association were to accept an institute that was not working independently' (Ibid.); on this basis, the resolu-tion not to extend the DPG's provisional recognition was passed with only four votes against. The new German psychoanalysis was ready to begin. Later on, faced with the trauma of the 1977 Congress and ques-tioning by young German analysts, controversy over the role of both Müller-Braunschweig and Boehm re-emerged in Germany, and the shame of appointing Gerhardt Scheunert, who had been a Nazi, as the DPV's second President was openly revealed. There was also a process of reconciliation between the DPG and DPV, although it was not until 2001 that the DPG was readmitted to the IPA as a 'provisional society'. For a long period what was dominant was a motivated forgetting of history and a focus on how to purify psychoanalysis, not ethically – not, that is, to make up for its involvement with Nazism – but in terms of its disciplinary and professional autonomy.

Even a cautiously psychoanalytic reading of the events of these con-gresses might suggest the triumph of a defence over something rep-ressed, in line with the argument proposed by some of the younger German analysts: rather than deal with what had happened to psycho-analysis under Nazism, including the possibly collaborationist activ-ities of its leaders, the IPA attended to the preservation of the supposed purity of psychoanalytic theory and practice against the depravities of other psychotherapeutic groups. Schultz-Hencke, who probably did have a certain amount to answer for, was made into the necessary bad object; Boehm, who did not distance himself quickly enough from Schultz-Hencke, became contaminated; and Müller-Braunschweig was cleared. 'After a series of organisational manoeuvres, he succeeded in having himself and a small group of colleagues accepted back into the IPA, leaving Schultz-Hencke out in the cold as not only the neo-Freudian – which he was – but also as the displacement object for their common guilt, the designated sole Nazi collaborator – which he was not.' (Antonovsky, 1988, p227) The psychoanalytic movement could carry on, apparently reconciled, though as usual the repressed always threatened to return, and eventually did. The immediate effect, however, was to aid German psychoanalysis in its continuing silence about history, through offering instead an alternative set of myths relating to various ways in which psychoanalysis was saved and betrayed.

Reckoning with 'Our Hitler'

The meeting of the International Psycho-Analytic Association in Hamburg in 1985 included in it the exhibition on psychoanalysis in Nazi Germany recorded in Brecht *et al.* (1985), and thus was to some extent set up as a reckoning with the past. The Congress was opened by the Mayor of Hamburg, Klaus von Dohnyani, who gave a remarkably well-informed and direct presentation of the issues and feelings that were involved in holding the Congress on German soil, which included a summary of what the situation had been like both for non-Nazi Germans in general and for psychoanalysts in particular.

It therefore is my opinion that your colleagues who have described the weaknesses of psychoanalysts and their associations in the years leading up to and during National Socialism have helped to free us from historical entanglements by showing us how it really was – with respect to psychoanalysts, too, even Sigmund Freud. For fear of losing everything, bit by bit was sacrificed, every step being rational – and yet at the same time always in the wrong direction. Here a compromise concerning persons, there a compromise of principles, but always in the pretended interest of preserving the whole – which in the end was lost. (Von Dohnyani, 1986, p4)

Von Dohnyani then asked whether psychoanalysis could 'help us not only to understand ourselves better, but also to be and act better' (Ibid.); his doubts on this subject were clear for all to see. And finally, looking the issue of owning the past straight in the face:

It seems we Germans remain a nation in danger, always fearful of being left behind, of being unloved, of not being appreciated sufficiently. It is probably not by accident that the three great innovators Marx, Freud and Einstein all spoke German as their mother tongue. But then, it is also no coincidence that they all were driven out of the country and regarded English as a language of liberation. Whoever says: our Bach and our Beethoven, must also say: our Hitler. This, too, will be one of your topics. (Ibid.)

This powerful speech, however, was not matched by anything of equivalent power from the psychoanalysts. It is clear from the accounts of those present that the hoped-for reckoning with the past was not made; instead, in what might perhaps be seen as a conventional defensive move, the past was invoked precisely in order that it should be denied. Rafael Moses and Rena Hrushovski-Moses (1986) spoke on behalf of many Jewish analysts when they expressed their unease and disappointment at the way in which the impact of Nazism had been so contained in a seminar on 'identification and its vicissitudes in relation to the Nazi phenomenon' as almost to disappear: that is, the IPA's reluctance to deal with anything but *clinical* issues surrounding Nazism can be seen as a way in which they could claim to be dealing 'scientifically' with the past without dealing *emotionally* with it at all. Moses and Hrushovski-Moses begin their paper commenting, 'We left Hamburg before the official farewell party. We were feeling vaguely depressed. The general atmosphere was that something had been missed. The central issue of this Congress – that it was the first one to be held in Germany since the Second World War and since the Holocaust – had been very much in the air but had not been adequately dealt with' (p175). They note that a similar 'papering-over' had occurred in the 1969 Congress in Vienna, which had been opened by Anna Freud, whose 'opening speech did not tackle in a very direct or forthright way the problem of her relations with her country of birth and with the city in which she had been born and raised. Wounds that were not yet healed were covered over and hidden rather than given acknowledgement and care. The feeling with which many people – many analysts – were left was then, too, one of something missed, of a courageous stand not taken, of politeness and lip service, of things left unsaid' (Ibid.). The parallel here with what actually happened in Germany – a 'courageous stand not taken' – are striking enough.

Moses and Hrushovski-Moses go on to describe a sequence of events during the Congress in which both German and non-German (including Jewish) analysts stepped back from actually enunciating and confronting the feelings swirling below the surface of the Congress, as if they did not want to risk blowing something fragile apart. The theme on 'identification and its vicissitudes in relation to the Nazi phenomenon', they note, was part of a series on identification and various pathologies, thus diluting its specificity; in any case, 'to call the events of the Nazi era, to name what was done by human beings to human beings, a phenomenon, is to elevate brutal events into the realm of more intellectualised abstractions... It is a watering down of something we are looking in the face' (p176). This watering down process could also be seen in the tendency to equate the Nazi Holocaust with other 'holocausts' in different parts of the world, or even in patients' family histories, referring to the way their parents treated them: in the specific context of the Hamburg Congress, these were ways of avoiding dealing with what everyone could feel. Even where 'reality aspects' of the situation did surface – in the discussion groups, for example, when people did speak about their responses to being on German soil – they were dodged: 'they could be sensed, but they were not talked about' (p177). Moses and Hrushovski-Moses suggest that behind all this there was a complex of dynamic forces, including particularly a fear on the part of German analysts that they were going to be attacked, which meant that they and the organisers of the Congress worked hard to avoid confrontations; and a complementary sense amongst non-German analysts that they wanted to move on, 'that the Germans of today could not and should not be held responsible for what their parent generation had done; that peace must be made and the past put aside' (p179). The concern then became that the Congress should 'go well' rather than deal with the issues, the kind of thing that often happens both in individual psychoanalytic sessions and in organisations and meetings of all kinds. 'The main emotional subject was placed in the middle of the Congress, padded on all sides' (Ibid.); nothing could be grasped hold of, with the consequence that no resolution could be achieved, but the cancerous mistrust and disturbance of unacknowledged yet deeply felt emotions continued to fester. Kijak (1989, p218) adds to this the suggestion that, 'there was another important factor which I believe was not discussed: the obligation of coming face to face, not only within the Congress, with the colleagues who are children of the generation that perpetrated the Holocaust, but also outside the Congress with the very Nazi assassins who actually carried out the genocide and who are now enjoying a happy and prosperous life, many of them remembering proudly how they served their fatherland, with no conflict in a society which, in part unconsciously and sometimes consciously, approves and legitimises their history.' *They should be disturbed*, one might think, in need even of psychoanalysis; but instead they are happy and it is the victims who continue to suffer.

Silence over this issue too, Kijak implies, hung densely over the Congress participants.

It has to be said that there was some recognition of this problem at the Congress itself. For example, Ostow (1986), responding to the papers on 'identification and the Nazi phenomenon', prefaced his remarks with the following justification for the focus on clinical work.

It is no secret that this Congress assembles with a certain degree of tension that reflects the unresolved residue of mutual reserve between those of us who were actual or potential victims, and those of us who failed to distinguish ourselves sufficiently clearly from the persecutors during the Nazi apocalypse. It is also obvious that all of us hope this meeting will go far toward overcoming this reserve, by virtue of collaborative work on professional problems, and open and co-operative discussion of the kinds of issues that have come between us. It would seem to me that our panel this morning is designed as just that kind of reconstructive endeavour. (p277)

Treating the Nazi period as a kind of aberration, Ostow went on immediately to 'infer' that 'those Germans who have associated themselves with the Nazi movement, and who have returned to the historically normal way of thinking since its collapse, face a ... need to account for the discontinuity in their mental life, and to make some sense of the bizarre, unnatural, and in fact delusional views that they espoused and promulgated – or at least tolerated – during this episode' (Ibid.). By the end of his subtle paper on the clinical issues, Ostow was arguing that preventing 'another apocalypse and [defusing] prejudicial tensions' could be psychoanalysis' 'contribution to *tikkun olam*' – that is, the healing or perfection of the world (p284). The clearly deeply felt movement here, from acknowledgement of the tension in the Congress, through clinical work, to the idea that psychoanalysis could through these mechanisms of professional understanding of 'delusion' be a major force for good, is symptomatic of a certain kind of slippage in the thinking of the psychoanalytic movement as a whole. The tension, which was real enough, gives way to the distancing of the phenomenon either through focusing on explanations of Nazism itself or on discussions of how Nazism affected *patients*; the point at issue – the implication of *psychoanalysis* in Nazism – consequently is covered over or lost. Psychoanalysis might indeed be a force for moral good, for *tikkun olam*, in many of its aspects, but it also has a darker side, just like the unconscious itself.

A startling and provocative account of all this is given in a compelling paper by Janine Chasseguet-Smirgel (1987). She comments that even though it was agreed that the Congress would focus on an 'essentially clinical exercise', and that several German analysts had written to the President of the IPA demanding that Germany's past should not be concealed at the Congress, 'Nevertheless, when the day devoted to the Nazi phenomenon was announced, I received a telephone call from Germany accusing me of wanting to put the Germans in a concentration camp' (Chasseguet-Smirgel, 1987, p435). Some Germans told her that they were staying away from the Congress 'because they feared hurtful attacks by colleagues, which they were already experiencing daily' (Ibid.). A storm brewed: it became obvious at the Congress both that psychoanalysis had not been 'liquidated' in the Nazi period, but rather had found ways of participating in the Third Reich, and *also* that the degree of passion and vituperation surrounding this hidden history was not conducive to dealing with it. In fact, as Chasseguet-Smirgel points out in her summary comment (p437), both denial and split-off blame can serve the interests of repression.

We must regretfully conclude that our analytical identity is fragile and that courage and independence of mind are rare. If the German psychoanalysts lost their souls during the twelve years of the Nazi regime, the new generation of analysts will not gain them by failing to show sorrow or pity. On the contrary, the hatred expressed in some documents – for example, the collection of letters on this matter published by the DPV, couched on both sides in outrageously violent terms and exchanged hell-for leather like as many blows – shows that those involved are principally concerned with getting rid of their guilt by projecting rather than confronting it. As it happens, the word 'guilt' hardly ever features in these documents. The word that recurs insistently is 'shame'. This is to say that it is not a matter of assuming responsibility – by identification with the parents, and possibly with the analytical parents – for what happened in Germany. When opening the Congress, Klaus von Dohnanyi exclaimed: 'If we say "our Beethoven, our Bach", we must also say "Our Hitler".' Thomas Mann entitled one of his articles 'Bruder Hitler'. After all, the problem is one of identification .... *What is one to do with a Nazi father?* Apparently, the only solution is to reject him. If you speak of the need to integrate your identification with that father, you are immediately treated as a Nazi yourself ... In order to become a human being in the full sense of the term, we have to be able to discover, confront and own, the *Hitler in uns*, otherwise the repressed will return and the disavowed will come back in various guises.

This complex argument is worth examining closely. The DPV set itself up as some kind of clean break with the past, leaving the old DPG to carry the blame of association with the Göring Institute and through that with the Nazis – despite the fact that those involved with the DPV, including its President, were deeply implicated in the Göring Institute. Discovering this past, and more generally realising that the institutions of psychoanalysis could not be idealised as bastions of resistance to the Third Reich, led to bitter acrimony and the rejection of their predecessors by a new and searching generation of German analysts. Chasseguet-Smirgel's argument is that the terms of this were such as again to replicate the splitting between 'good' and 'bad', rather than to create ownership of what had happened and the possibility of working it through, accepting guilt and promoting reparation. In particular, what is not acknowledged is 'the *Hitler in uns*', both at the ordinary level of the question, 'how would we have behaved?' and at the unconscious level of identifying the temptation towards hatred in everyone. Specifically, for the non-Jewish analysts, this means identifying and owning anti-Semitic hatred. Reflecting on the impact of the Shoah on German psychoanalysis, Kreuzer-Haustein (2002), Vice President of the DPG, argues that deep ambivalence towards the 'Jewishness' of psychoanalysis and towards Jews continues on the German scene, in large part as a consequence of guilt at having betrayed psychoanalysis during the Nazi period. Psychoanalysis might have been a German-language creation and therefore something to take pride in; nevertheless, Kreuzer-Haustein suggests, the post-war psychoanalysts were still affected by their own hostile and guilt-ridden associations with psychoanalysis as a 'Jewish science' that had been developed by Freud, a Jew, and was persecuted under National Socialism. Reviewing a book edited by J-L Evard on 'Psychoanalysis Under the Third Reich', Chasseguet-Smirgel (1988) discusses a comment from the editor that Freud 'never showed a will to face up to events ... Despite the fact that he is endowed with all the necessary moral authority, he lets the institution that he has created become enmeshed in abjection and allows it to endorse the pogrom that was required of "Aryan" analysts by the Hitlerian regime ... "Yes to psychoanalysis with the Nazis" say the psychoanalysts of Germany, faced with the abstentionism (tinged with cynicism) of Freud' (p1063). Chasseguet-Smirgel takes issue with these 'reproaches' on a variety of practical grounds, such as Freud's age and the complexity and intensity of the Nazi phenomenon. But her more spirited critique arises from teasing out the anti-Semitic aspects of the attack on Freud, aspects that have resonance in relation to wider (and wilder) accusations that the Jews were in some way responsible for the Holocaust.

> But most suspicious of all is that Germans (although they are not alone in this) reproach Freud for the fate of Jewish analysts and for Germany's agreement to become *Judenrein*. What a convenient solution to the whole problem! And how reminiscent – after the War, was it not rumoured that Hitler was a Jew? Could there be a better way of washing one's hands of the genocide than to reduce it to a Judeo-Jewish affair? Six or seven million Jews were exterminated by a Jew. This proves that Jews are indeed diabolical ... (p1065)

The point here is a general one: without acknowledging quite how pervasive anti-Semitism might have been in the psychoanalytic movement, and the various forms it might have taken, it is hard to see how the past could ever be securely put to rest. Furthermore, without an open encounter with this past, psychoanalysis remains tainted, and its claim to offer the tools with which troubling emotions can be alleviated is correspondingly called into question. More generally still, this 'case history' reveals how a deeply traumatising institutional history can give rise to emotions all the more powerful for being repressed. These may find themselves re-enacted within the institution itself, and if they remain hidden and unacknowledged may result in the whole organisational edifice becoming riddled with disturbance. In the case of German psychoanalysis, personal recriminations, fragmented and split institutions, organisational rivalries, and anti-Semitic scapegoating were all consequences of the failure to attend to the events of the Nazi period. How often this has occurred in other institutions may be a source of debate, but it seems unlikely that this distressing history is in any sense unique.

Notes

1 This chapter is based closely on Chapter 5 of Stephen Frosh's book, *Hate and the 'Jewish Science': Anti-Semitism, Nazism and Psychoanalysis*, London: Palgrave, 2005.

References

Antonovsky A, 1988. Aryan analysts in Nazi Germany: Questions of adaptation, desymbolization and betrayal. *Psychoanalysis and Contemporary Thought*, 11, 213–31

Bibring G, 1952. Report on the Seventeenth International Psycho-Analytical Congress. *International Journal of Psycho-Analysis*, 33, 249–72

Brecht K, Friedrioch V, Hermanns L, Kaminer I and Juelcih D, eds, 1985. *'Here Life Goes On in a Most Peculiar Way': Psychoanalysis before and after 1933*. Hamburg: Kellner Verlag/London: Goethe Institut

Brecht K, 1995. In the Aftermath of Nazi-Germany: Alexander Mitscherlich and Psychoanalysis – Legend and Legacy. *American Imago*, 52, 291–312

Chasseguet-Smirgel J, 1987. 'Time's White Hair We Ruffle': Reflections on the Hamburg Congress. *International Review of Psycho-Analysis*, 14, 433–44

Chasseguet-Smirgel J, 1988. Review of J-L Evard, ed., Les Années Brunes. 1. Psychoanalysis Under the Third Reich. *Journal of the American Psychoanalytic Association*, 36, 1059–66

Cocks G, 1997. *Psychotherapy in the Third Reich: The Göring Institute (Second Edition)* New Jersey: Transaction Publishers

Eickhoff F, 1995. The Formation of the German Psychoanalytical Association (DPV): Regaining the Psychoanalytical Orientation Lost in the Third Reich. *International Journal of Psycho-Analysis*, 76, 945–56

Freud A, 1949. Report on the Sixteenth International Psycho-Analytical Congress. *Bulletin of the International Psychoanalytic Association*, 30, 178–208

Frosh S, 2003. Psychoanalysis, Nazism and 'Jewish Science'. *International Journal of Psycho-Analysis*, 84, 1315–32

Kijak M, 1989. Further Discussions of Reactions of Psychoanalysts to the Nazi Persecution, and Lessons to be Learnt. *International Review of Psycho-Analysis*, 16, 213–22

Kreuzer-Haustein U, 2002. Psychoanalysis and Psychoanalysts in Germany after the Shoa: Points for Discussion by the Panel. *European Psychoanalytic Federation Bulletin*, 56, 16

McLaughlin F, 1978. Report of the 30th International Psycho-Analytical Congress. *Bull Int Psyan Assn*, 59, 64–130

Moses R and Hrushovski-Moses R, 1986. A Form of Group Denial at the Hamburg Congress. *International Review of Psycho-Analysis*, 13, 175–80

Obholzer A and Roberts V, 1994. *The Unconscious at Work*. London: Routledge

Ostow M, 1986. The Psychodynamics of Apocalyptic: Discussion of Papers on Identification and the Nazi Phenomenon. *International Journal of Psycho-Analysis* 67, 277–85

Thomä H, 1969. Some Remarks on Psychoanalysis in Germany, Past and Present. *International Journal of Psycho-Analysis*, 50, 683–92

Von Dohnyani K, 1986. Opening Ceremony, 34th IPA Congress. *International Journal of Psychoanalysis*, 67, 2–4

6
Surface Tensions: Emotion, Conflict and the Social Containment of Dangerous Knowledge[1]

Andrew Cooper

Introduction

In public life, how do we know that we know what we think we know? Trust, whether personal or social, depends upon a framework of confidence in our epistemological relationship to the world around us, and to ourselves. For the conduct of everyday life we need to believe that we are in possession of reliable ways to distinguish fact from fantasy, truth from lies, fiction from documentary, evidence from interpretation, knowledge from belief, possibility from probability – in fact the daily shopping list of epistemological essentials is rather long when one reflects upon it. Knowing, or at least believing, that we know how to know is a precondition of a trusting rather than a suspicious relationship to reality. But from time to time our received social framework of confidence in these matters is profoundly shaken. Episodes or periods of radical doubt are both necessary for social change as well as reflecting such change, and this chapter attempts to illuminate some features of these processes.

In particular, the chapter explores the role of affective conflict in shaping what is available or not available to be known, and the reciprocal interplay of desire and the conditions for its social representation when conflict about what is or can be known surfaces in the public sphere. Thus the chapter explores the nature of social and psychological processes which occur at the boundary of the private and public domains, at the boundary of different kinds of symbolic systems or sites of symbolic propagation, and therefore at the boundaries of the known or knowable, the thinkable and the unthinkable. The focus is on the emergence into public awareness and discourse of events and phenomena which may transpire to have been 'there' all along but which were previously unknowable, denied, unrepresented or unrepresentable; but also with the process by which such knowledge or awareness may recede and become once again unrepresented or unrepresentable. The concern is with phenomena which become the object of claims to legitimation as 'real'; which may succeed or fail to achieve the recognition they seek; which seek such recognition but the claims remain undecided or undecidable; or over the course of time all of these. The connection between representation and affect in the public sphere concerns social capacity, and willingness, to know about painful and conflictual matters at the level of social discourse – or not.

One could say that the founding insights of psychoanalysis, never yet fully unfolded in their relevance for social life, are about how we deal with unwelcome or seemingly dangerous knowledge. Ideas or representations, it might be said, can never be in themselves a source of trouble. It is the feelings, especially the anxieties, associated with them that give rise to the need to deny, disavow, repress, split or operationalise any of the other mechanisms of defence that psychoanalysis has described. As Laplanche and Pontalis summarise it:

> Psycho-analysis speaks of conflict when contradictory internal requirements are opposed to each other in the subject. The conflict may be manifest – between a wish and a moral imperative, for example or between two contradictory emotions – or it may be latent, in which event it is liable to be expressed in a distorted fashion in the manifest conflict, emerging especially in the formation of symptoms, behavioural troubles, character disturbances etc. (1988, p360)

When in the context of clinical work an individual's defences are relaxing, the emerging capacity for new self-knowledge may relate equally to experiences of historical events and truths, or psychic experiences and truths, or to complex and ambiguous inter-lacings of each. In this chapter I suggest that the same conditions of ambiguity pertain in the social field when hitherto repressed or denied dimensions of psychosocial experience become available for symbolisation. In both cases, the emergent phenomena may be understood as being structured like dreams, and as standing in need of decoding (or 'interpretation') if they are to find a place within ordinary discourse. During those periods of disruption in which new phenomena seek symbolisation and a discursive register via which they can be socially integrated we see evidence indicating that 'historical truths' – everyday social processes –

may always be organised by unconscious desire, phantasy, and the primary process. Indeed, one part of the special interest of such unusual emergent phenomena is that they can reveal the symbolic structure of the everyday, the epistemologically taken for granted. In this sense I propose they function rather like 'natural' experiments in the social or natural sciences, revealing aspects of the quotidian through the provision of special conditions that expose the unstable inner logic of the apparently stable and mundane.

The larger, and more tentative, claim of the chapter is that a social epistemology embracing both a concept of the historically 'real' *and* a simultaneous concept of the inherent ambiguity, representational multiplicity, and undecidability of the 'real', is capable of resolving some of the more obstinate tensions in social theory about the status of 'truth' and truth claims. On this view, it is because social life and history are both real and determinate in certain respects, but also structured by symbolic ambiguity and indeterminacy of meaning, that disputes about the nature of truth and truth claims in this area arise in the first place. Indeed, I propose that only if we accept such a view can we hope to disentangle those phenomena which represent something 'beyond' themselves from those which represent only anxiety or desire itself, or are efforts to 'hallucinate' experience as a cover for there being 'nothing there'. This holds out hope that we can evade familiar polarisations in social theory and practice between empiricist and reductive stances on the one hand, and idealist, radical constructivist or relativist ones on the other.

The key anchor point in this way of seeing matters is emotion, and especially emotional conflict. Where social experiences or processes are imbued with emotional conflict, they require a social 'container' if they are to become available for thought in society, as distinct from enactment, denial, repression and so on. In this sense 'discourse' functions as a form of containment, constituting as it does a set of conditions, a language, for representation. Psychoanalytically, the analogy here is with Wilfred Bion's (1967) concept of 'thoughts in search of a thinker'. Bion held that in human development the 'apparatus' for thinking – the mind – succeeds rather than precedes the availability of thoughts to be thought. Difficulties arise for us as individuals to the extent that we have not developed a capacity to make certain kinds or intensities of thought 'thinkable'. Emotional experiences can be 'there', and 'real' but not knowable or thinkable because of the absence of a mental container robust enough to enable symbolisation. Mostly, he suggests it is frightening, painful or conflictual areas of experience which we may have trouble symbolising; but also the failure to develop an apparatus for such thoughts renders them yet more terrifying.

The chapter is therefore concerned with a view of social theory not as a project of explanation, or even primarily 'interpretation', but of discovery or revelation. Following Bion's 'theory of thinking' again, it suggests a variety of social theory framed by the question, 'Which states of social being can be known, and which not, by virtue of the provision or lack of provision of an apparatus for thinking about them?' In its focus on 'liminal' states of social being, that is states of emergence towards representation or representability there is a further analogy with the process, familiar to all of us, of waking with awareness (but not yet 'knowledge') of a dream that has been dreamt, and of rendering this experience knowable through the act of narrativising to ourselves, or others, its process and contents.

Spaces for the unknown – the clinical and social management of child sexual abuse

The paradigm case which informs the argument of this chapter is child abuse and especially child sexual abuse. Perhaps, as Ian Hacking (2000) has also suggested, it is *the* paradigm case simply because sexual relations between adults and children are organised, or not, by the most fundamental psycho-social barrier – the incest taboo. But even this statement begins to open up the complexity of the wider field. Are sexual relations between parents and children, between siblings, between close cousins, and between adults and children not related through family membership, all prohibited through the agency of the same kind of psychic or psycho-social 'law'? One may suspect not, but what are the differences and distinctions involved? Some psycho-analytic thinking would refer a wide range of superficially distinct prohibitions and transgressions to the operation or failure of a basic taboo or law – the Oedipus complex and the mechanisms of repression associated with it. If we want to investigate the wider field of social repression and de-repression, and the ambiguities of ontology and epistemology in this wider field, we might do better to work with a notion of 'family resemblances' among different but related varieties of knowledge, representation, and defences or prohibitions against representation and representability. The value of investigating this terrain by examining 'boundary cases' is that the specific character of what is at issue may be particularly clearly revealed as a particular phenomenon becomes a site of struggle for legitimation or de-legitimation. Writing in similar vein about the history of the concept of child abuse and the conundrums of construction and realism, Ian Hacking observed:

> It is not so often that we can experience a concept in rapid motion…. We shall see more than evolution in three decades of child abuse; we shall see mutations worth calling revolutions, conceptual displacements worth calling explosions. (2000, p132)

In the following pages I first offer an account of a clinical experience in which aspects of 'knowledge' of child abuse come to the surface for an adult in therapy. Their emergence into fuller awareness is attended by what can be described as epistemological uncertainty about aspects of historical truth. Therapy, it is suggested, provides the conditions under which new or revised representations of historical events are developed. But these representations are not pure constructs. They are alternative accounts of realities that may never be independently checkable, although there is every reason to suppose that one set of representations more accurately captures the historical truth than does the other, partly because both cannot be historically accurate with respect to the same set of events. There is also good reason to suggest that it is the powerfully traumatic, conflicted nature of the emotional experiences in question that generates the epistemological confusions that afflicted the patient. Subsequently, I discuss aspects of the emergence into fuller social awareness of the whole phenomenon of child sexual abuse, and propose that the kind of crisis of knowledge that attended this process can equally be explained by reference to the potency of the emotional conflicts involved, but at a social level.

Who did what to whom? Child abuse and the indeterminacy of memory

A man who had been quite severely and repeatedly physically assaulted by his father up until his early adolescence came to a psychotherapy session one day and recounted a memory in which at the age of about four, during a family visit to some relatives, he had lost control of his bladder and bowels causing his father to beat him. The therapist listened and made some tentative observations about the painfulness of the experience and the recollections. The patient returned next day and said that he had gone away and felt able to think more clearly about the memory, and it now seemed to him that events had been the other way round – that his father had beaten him, perhaps because he had been pestering to go home, and he had lost control of himself as a result of the beating. Soon after, it began to emerge that in the present this man suffered occasional near psychotic lapses, in which he experienced catastrophic anxiety arising from a belief that he had made some kind of a mistake, which he had not in fact made. For example, he turned up on time at a supervisor's room for an appointment, and not finding him in, collapsed into a state of anxiety believing that today was tomorrow and that the appointment had therefore been the previous day, that the supervisor would be furious and his career would be in ruins. He returned to 'reality' only when the supervisor phoned him in his room enquiring if he was coming to the appointment.

However, rather characteristically, and hopefully, the patient was able to regroup himself and bring these states of mind to therapy where he and the therapist could look at them together. As it became possible to work with these states of mind more directly a whole area of very confused psychological functioning opened up for exploration.

Writing in 1925, about trauma and memory Pierre Janet says:

> *Memory*, like belief, like all psychological phenomena, is an action; essentially it *is the action of telling a story*. Almost always we are concerned here with a linguistic operation, quite independent of our attitude towards the happening ... A situation has not been ... fully assimilated, until we have achieved, not merely an outward reaction through our movements, but also an inward reaction through the words we address to ourselves, through the organisation of the recital of the event to others and to ourselves, and through the putting of this recital in its place as one of the chapters in our personal history. (1925, pp662–3)

The patient's recitals in psychotherapy are of a special kind in a special situation. Memory of the events brought by the patient were not exactly 'recovered' in therapy. Rather, in the presence of someone who he presumably experienced as sufficiently able to hold his anxieties in mind, important uncertainties and confusions about the veracity of his beliefs about the *ordering* of events became open to re-examination; he was able to reconstruct and develop a new narrative for this episode, in which he takes up a different position in the constellation of events from the one inscribed in the original; one in which he is in some sense less 'to blame' for his punishment and better able to see the connection between his past experience and his contemporary tendency to believe that he brings catastrophe down on himself.

What is 'recovered' here, is something more like a spontaneous capacity to 'see things differently'. That 'something happened' involving a beating by his father and his own loss of control is not in doubt in the patient's mind, but who exactly did what to whom in what order, is in doubt, and in his contemporary experience frequently remained so. The therapist believed that the patient's new narrative almost certainly accorded better with events 'as they actually happened', although in the absence of corroborating evidence it is right to suspend absolute judgement about this. Via his concept of *Nachtraglichkeit*, rather unsatisfactorily translated for us as 'deferred action' or *après coup*, Freud held that 'the material present in the form of memory-traces (is) subjected from time to time to a *re-arrangement* in accordance with fresh circumstances – to a *re-transcription*' (Freud, 1896). Laplanche and Pontalis suggest in their discussion of this concept that,

> It is not lived experience in general that undergoes a deferred revision but, specifically, whatever it has been impossible in the first instance to incorporate fully into a meaningful context. The traumatic event is the epitome of such unassimilated experience. (Laplanche and Pontalis, 1988, p112)

In the example above, the fresh circumstances to which Freud refers as providing the occasion for re-transcription might be the therapeutic context itself. Inside himself, this patient retained sufficient trust to enable him to make good use of a co-operative therapeutic alliance. His recall of abuse is available to him, and to us, but arguably has only been transformed into true *memory*, by virtue of the presence of another mind able to help process and think about psychic experience in a new way. Yet how tenuous was this possibility became evident much later in the therapy when he told his therapist he had been afraid to let him know of his revised version of events in childhood, in case the therapist was angry because he had lied the previous day. Once again as Janet remarks:

> Strictly speaking, then, one who retains a fixed idea of a happening cannot be said to have a 'memory' of the happening. It is only for convenience that we speak of it as a 'traumatic memory'. The subject is often incapable of making with regard to the event

the recital which we speak of as a memory: and yet he remains confronted by a difficult situation in which he has not been able to play a satisfactory part... (1925, p663)

We arrive then, at an initial formulation which suggests why psychoanalysis is so uneasily and ambiguously positioned with respect to child abuse. True memory, on the view advanced here, is *indeterminate* with respect to the question of the 'real event' or 'what actually happened'; *Nachtraglichkeit* or 'retranscription' is not about recovering a determinate or mimetic relationship between memory and historical events, but a meaningful and essentially creative one. And yet where trauma has occurred by virtue of external impingement, or assault, events clearly are, or were, *determinate*. In some sense it happened this way, or that; it happened, or it didn't. Usually therapists are primarily concerned with meaning, but in cases involving trauma necessarily at times find themselves preoccupied with questions of historical accuracy. In the public domain and especially the courts, where child abuse is concerned the focus or direction of concern may often be the reverse.

Because there is little doubt that some version of the childhood events recounted by the patient involving an assault by his father did 'happen', and even less doubt with respect to the contemporary muddles he reported, we could characterise his state of mind as involving systematically distorted beliefs about causality and sequence held (even if temporarily) with complete conviction. But the more general lesson we may draw from this episode, and from the theorisations of Janet is that there is no form of memory which provides a privileged, certain, or mimetic relation to 'the facts'. The facts are often in principle and forever beyond recovery or even access, mediated or partly constituted as they are by imagination, hallucination, delusion – by the desire which all actors bring, but differentially, to the same 'event'.

In which case, what status can we possible assign to the effort to 'establish the facts', as we frequently must, and for the sake of psychic health, need to be able to? The man described is in possession of a fact which can be represented as something like 'On a particular day, my father beat me and something terrible happened which may have been cause or consequence of his actions' but by itself what meaning does this have? We may notice that both accounts of his childhood events have a common narrative structure or structure of meaning which can be summarised as 'Somebody did something to someone, which occasioned a catastrophic reaction'. In the Kleinian psychoanalytic tradition this relational configuration is seen as the basic, inalienable structure of meaningful experience, the elementary form of all unconscious phantasy. On this view, unconscious phantasy is the earliest form of mentation, and plays across the field of early experience, providing it with what we can later see as meaning. Early experience is frequently, and ordinarily, charged with powerful feelings, mostly of a bodily kind. 'The bodily parts are suffused with active suffering' (Hinshelwood, 1994). But the structure of phantasy is *relational* and attributes both benign and malign intentionality to (some) other person(s) as the sources and objects of feeling states. However, attributions of causality, and perhaps causal sequence, are only gradually and precariously informed by 'reality' and may reverse or fluctuate in the manner illustrated by the experiences of the patient described above (Hinshelwood, 1994; Isaacs, 2003).

This notion of a primitive but continually active process of psychic structuring of reality is captured at a more parochial level by the concept of 'the drama triangle'. Karpman (1968) described the triangle comprising the three positions 'persecutor', 'victim', and 'rescuer', showing how in the structure of myths and fairy-tales but also everyday social realities these positions can be fixed or can be rapidly reassigned. Indeed, we see this process in action in a graphic way in the illustration below at the level of social emergence of knowledge of child abuse during the so-called Cleveland affair.

From a psychological perspective then, we may propose that 'things happen', but that 'things' always happen mediated by phantasy to a greater or lesser degree. Phantasy is structured and gives meaning to experience, but the relationship between meaning and historical truth understood in terms of causes, action sequences determining responsibility, and so on, is frequently inherently ambiguous exactly *because* historical events are always mediated by phantasy. When events or realities are charged with emotional tension or conflict between 'good' and 'bad', then ambiguity and reversal of meaning can become the agent of epistemological uncertainty, crisis, or confusion as the various conflicting (psychic or social) agencies battle it out for supremacy over what version of reality, if any, shall prevail.

As a final illustration of this, it is worth citing the work of WRD Fairburn on 'the moral defence'. According to Fairburn (1943), the infant or child faced with psychic frustration and deprivation will prefer to identify with the 'bad', that is see himself as the source of badness rather than locate this in his parents or caretakers. He or she does this on the assumption that 'it is better to be a sinner in a world ruled by God than to live in a world ruled by the Devil' (1943, pp66–7). Fairburn was not a Kleinian and did not hold that the structure of unconscious phantasy was 'given' at birth, but his account of the production of an internal world through various internalising manoeuvres results in a picture of this world that is remarkably congruent with that of later Kleinian thinkers.

Who's been doing what to whom? The indeterminacy of the social

The kinds of social processes and events with which I am concerned in this chapter are well documented in Elaine Showalter's (1997) *Hystories*, but this book does not engage very fully with the epistemological and ontological conundrums surrounding the ambiguous status of the processes described. They are typically highly affectively charged, and sites of considerable social conflict and contestation. The recent legitimation of the condition popularly known as ME as a medically recognised illness, following many years of scientific and public contestation, is a good example of the epistemological 'career' of one of these phenomena.

As already proposed, ambiguity, indeterminacy of meaning, and the frequent undecidability of the nature of the 'real event' are the stock in trade of the practising psychotherapist. However, the process by which a previously unrecognised, unnamed, or unknown social phenomenon that is a locus of psychic and/or social conflict achieves coherent *representation* in public discourse, will also inevitably be accompanied by epistemological uncertainties that mirror their contested ontological status. But the presence or absence of social contestation turns on the question of emotional conflict. In the private domain, represented by the privacy of the consulting room, this may be more or less all that is at stake (as if that were not enough). In the public domain much more may be at stake – reputation, professional legitimation, legality, positioning within configurations of power and structures of dominance/subordination and so on. All 'representions' are 'real', but a representation may make false or distorted claims about the status of what is denoted (as distinct from connoted) as represented. Equally what is 'real' may have no representation, and so belong in the realm of what Christopher Bollas (1987) calls the 'unthought known' or Bion 'beta elements' (1962).

The 'false memory' debates of recent years (Sandler and Fonagy, 1997) are among the most prominent moments of articulation between the consulting room and the domain of public affairs, extending to the courts. In Britain, their context was set by the Cleveland affair of 1987 when the mass diagnosis of child sexual abuse in Britain burst upon the social field, facing this society with a social crisis of epistemological undecidability. At the time, unless one was an active protagonist on one side or another of the contest, no-one knew what to think. I want to suggest we did not know what to think because:

First, there were no established epistemological categories with which to think about the claims being made. The claims were in various senses of the word 'unbelievable', not so unlike (but in the end distinct from) being asked to believe that a group of Martians had been discovered living in Middlesborough.

Second, the nature of our means of moving towards deciding on the 'believability' of the claims was missing. What *kinds* of evidence would we need? We could not know, because we did not really *know* what kind of phenomena sexual abuse was. In the absence of concrete medically verifiable damage, how were we to even begin reaching decisions? Hence the way in which so much came to depend upon the credibility or otherwise of the 'anal dilation' examination.

Third *if* something 'real' was in the process of being 'uncovered', (which it undoubtedly was) then obviously the questions of knowledge involved were structured by extremely powerful emotional forces seeking both 'disclosure' and 'repression'. Under these circumstances, the representational conditions for 'knowing about' the phenomena in question were subject to processes of distortion and displacement similar to those we encounter in the clinical psychoanalytic field, but at the level of the social.

However, as the 'crisis' itself unfolded there was little or no space for such dispassionate philosophical analysis. Events were powerfully shaped by the structuring force of phantasy relationships, as described by 'the drama triangle':

> ...what began as a triangle of 'victim' children, 'persecutor' parents and 'rescuer' doctors and social services rapidly shifted into 'victim' families, 'persecutor' doctors and 'rescuer' local MP and media, before swinging again into 'persecutor' media and MP, 'victim' doctors and social services and 'rescuer' official inquiry report. (Hughes and Pengelly, 1997, p111)

The rapid reversals of perspective described here are analogous to those found in dream life. When dreams are 'interpreted' via the subject's free associations in the context of clinical psychoanalysis they are taken (a) to contain or reveal multiple meanings but (b) these structures of meaning are taken to be organised around a determinate 'event' or constellation of events. Such events may be located primarily in external reality or internal reality, but are either way in principle empirically specifiable – the wish to murder a colleague, the anxiety that he was having murderous thoughts during yesterday's meeting. Out of the epistemological chaos occasioned by the surfacing into the public sphere of phenomena like child sexual abuse, the task is to forge epistemological order – categories for thinking – capable of both distinguishing between, but also retaining the connections between real events (internal or external) and our elaborations of these events in social phantasy.

The question becomes, what sociological tools do we have, and what do we need to develop, to satisfactorily approach such a terrain of analysis? As Hacking observes of the Cleveland affair, 'The case illustrates how the concept of child abuse craves objectivity' (2000, p150). So it is instructive to find that certain key passages of the Inquiry Report into the Cleveland affair (HMSO, 1988) are preoccupied with questions of epistemological clarification, that echo some of the distinctions and differences outlined in the present chapter. In the section of the report entitled 'Listening to the Child' Justice Butler Sloss comments:

> The concept of helping the child to tell (of sexual abuse) is recognised to have its uses in certain circumstances. When embarking on it for diagnostic purposes, it is important to remember at least three possible situations:
>
> 1. The abuse has occurred and the child is speaking of it.
> 2. The abuse has occurred and the child is unable to speak of it or is denying it.
> 3. The abuse has not occurred, and the child cannot speak of it.
>
> It is clearly a difficult matter of judgement to know whether the child is not telling because of some sort of pressure, such as fear of the consequences, or because there is nothing to tell. At the end of a session, the professionals may not know which of those two situations is the true position.
> (HMSO, 1988, pp206–7)

The space of 'undecidability', even if temporary, is key. In circumstances such as these, we require professional and social 'spaces' in which the reality of undecidability, ambiguity and the emergent nature of 'knowledge' of phenomena can be handled. As Butler Sloss indicates, this necessarily embraces the capacity 'not to know', to wait for meaning to emerge. The more the realm of conventional propositional and syllogistic logic asserts its claims, the further we will retreat from the possibility of knowledge:

> Dr Jones said: 'A fundamental problem of the "disclosure" approach is that it is inherent in the concept that there is *something* to disclose. The problem is highlighted by those professionals who consider that the child is either *disclosing* or *"in denial"*. The third, and crucial, alternative possibility, namely that the child has no sexual abuse to disclose, is not considered as a viable option...The premise that abuse has occurred, yet is hidden and shrouded from discovery, is inherent in the very term "disclosure work".'
> (HMSO, 1988, p206)

Legal positivism, and indeed all manifestations of positivism in the social sphere, inherently incline towards an epistemology of excluded middles, of binary logical choice, of reasoned determination of truth and falsity according to the evidence available (Cooper, 1999). Perhaps we fail to appreciate how necessary such constructs of truth and meaning are for the conduct of any form of rational social life. Yet, simultaneously, because we are captured by the elegant simplicities they proffer, we forget how necessarily unstable their grasp must be on the nature of actual social realities. Our world is simply not made up according to the rules and precepts of positivist logic. The disruptive character of the unconsciously generated character of social reality will make itself known. At such moments, epistemological confusion will organise the public sphere, because different realms of logic, truth and meaning are on a collision course.

We might say that the general questions thrown up equally by the Cleveland child sexual abuse affair, the public 'career' of chronic fatigue syndrome or Gulf War Syndrome, or many other contested psycho-social phenomena such as the struggle over the definition and legitimation of 'institutional racism', are:

> Does the phenomenon 'exist' at the level of empirically specifiable social relations, or is it the projection into the social sphere of

conflicts and anxieties which subsist only or primarily at the level of phantasy?

What are the criteria of decidability about existence or non-existence in the above sense?

How far does 'decidability' depend upon acceptance or rejection of particular varieties of 'knowledge', and conditions for establishing knowledge claims, as legitimate?

To what extent are conditions for establishing 'knowledge' a question of contestation resulting from relations of power and social positioning rather than more abstract epistemological relationships analysable independently of relations of power or social position?

Social theory as revelation

A social theory that presupposes the active ubiquity in social life of unconscious forces and thus an omnipresent inter-lacing of conscious and unconscious 'logic' in the production of social phenomena has barely started to be developed. One or two sociological thinkers have articulated the character of such a theory, and there are particular psychoanalytic clinicians whose theoretical work lends positive illumination to such a concept of social processes and formations. In the realm of knowledge about human affairs (that is human understanding directed towards human activity as distinct from towards the understanding of everything not in itself human), it is assumed in this chapter that the work of the unconscious is omnipresent, and that this renders futile all attempts to seek absolute closure in the empirical or theoretical study of social life. This does not imply that relations between representations and the represented are arbitrary. There *is* knowledge, but fragmentary, partial, 'won from the formless void and infinite' as Wilfred Bion (1967) put it. Waking consciousness and logic necessarily deals in 'separate' representations, with bounded identities that form the basis of the possibility of classical propositional logic with its 'law of the excluded middle'. But,

> Of the essential stuff of the unconscious, the representation, we can say practically nothing, if we confine ourselves to our customary logic ... The unconscious exists only as an indissociably representative/affective/intentional flux. (Castoriadis, 1997, p274)

And,

> Once we find ourselves within it, it is not so much the imaginary-representative magma of the unconscious that is the inexhaustible source of astonishment, but rather the schema of discreteness, the idea of identity, the relative effectiveness of the separation. (Ibid., p276)

In other words, for Castoriadis, the realm of bounded, logical phenomena, susceptible to the kind of reasoning that ordinarily governs social life is an inherently unstable, and in no sense privileged domain of being. A similar view, this time articulated by a clinical theorist, puts it thus:

> The unconscious is not 'subconscious'; it is an aspect of the indivisible totality of consciousness. Similarly, meaning (including unconscious meaning) is *in* the language being used, not under or behind it. (Freud [1915] believed the term 'subconscious' to be 'Incorrect and misleading since the Unconscious does not lie "under" consciousness.)'...Meaning is continuously in the process of becoming something new and in so doing, is continuously undoing itself (undercutting its own claims to certainty) (Ogden 1999, pp215–18)

Ogden's work is original and relevant to the project of elaborating a psychoanalytically informed social theory of the kind adumbrated in this chapter. His interest lies in the way the clinical encounter creates a new third object, what he calls 'the analytic third' out of the experiential and empirical 'field' constituted by the dyad of patient and analyst. The unconscious is not over there 'in the patient' or over here 'in the analyst' but subject to a process of co-evolution in the space, or field, between them. Part of his originality lies in his articulation of fresh ways of accessing or tuning in to the contents of this field through attention to the 'reverie' of the analyst. This suggests first, a view of the 'location' of the point of contact between conscious and unconscious life that is liminal, and available at a more everyday level than traditionally supposed; and second, a view of this relationship as productive, generative, rather than only problematic or pathogenic. Sociologically, it suggests that if equipped with the right sensibilities, we might be able to 'read' social processes for the evidence they contain of the interplay of unconscious and conscious forces. This is the project of social theory as primarily revelatory rather than explanatory or interpretive, which has been the broader concern of the present chapter.

However, for such a project to be genuinely sociological, and escape the reductive and psychologising tendencies implicit in much psychoanalytic sociology, it must take account of the structuring or delimiting action of social process on, as it were, 'what can be felt', as well as what can be known. Questions about what 'can be known' are very much the terrain of discourse theory and constructionist accounts of social relations. An implication of the position taken in this chapter is that they tend to be intellectually impoverished to the extent that they eschew interest in the emotional roots of our knowing relationship to social and personal reality. Perri 6 (2002) has developed an interesting account of the social structuring of feeling, arguing that,

> Emotions, like any other human activity, are of course made possible by the biological substrate, and no doubt the extent of the menu is subject to biological limitations. However, the menu is given its effective structure by the elemental forms of institutional social organisation which well up in different empirical forms in any society. (2002, p283).

Other perspectives take a more fluid view of the relationship between forms of psychic experience and social relations. Showalter, for example, suggests that 'A constant cultural negotiation goes on, of course, over both the symptom pool as a whole and then legitimacy of its contents' (1997, p15).

The present chapter has been concerned to re-assert the place of the emotionally 'real' in this complex schema, not by assigning it a privileged position, but certainly a determinate one – what happens happens, and once known cannot be in any final sense 'unknown'. The conditions shaping representability in society are what are at issue, and these are in turn crucially shaped by the capacity or otherwise of the social container to bear knowledge of emotional pain and conflict.

Notes

1 This chapter has also appeared in A Cooper and J Lousada, *Borderline Welfare*, London: Karnac Books, 2005

References

Bion WR, 1962. *Learning From Experience*. London: Karnac
Bion WR, 1967. *Second Thoughts*. London: Karnac

Bollas C, 1987. *The Shadow of the Object: Psychoanalysis of the Unthought Known*. London: Free Association Books

Castoriadis C, 1997. *The Imaginary Institution of Society*. Cambridge: Polity Press

Cooper A, 1999. With justice in mind: complexity, child welfare and the law. In King M (ed.), *Moral Agendas for Children's Welfare*. London: Routledge

Fairburn, WRD, 1943. The repression and return of bad objects. In *Psychoanalytic Studies of the Personality*. London: Routledge, 51–89

Freud S, 1896. *The Origins of Psycho-Analysis*. In Freud S (1953–73) *The Standard Edition of the Complete Psychological Works of Sigmund Freud*, Vol. 1. London: Hogarth Press

Hacking I, 2000. *The Social Construction of What?* London: Harvard University Press

Hinshelwood RD, 1994. *Clinical Klein*. London: Free Association Books

HMSO, 1988. *Report of the Inquiry into Child Abuse in Cleveland 1987*. London: Her Majesty's Stationery Office

Hughes L and Pengelly P, 1997. *Staff Supervision in a Turbulent Environment*. London: Jessica Kingsley

Isaacs S, 2003. The nature and function of phantasy. In *Unconscious Phantasy* (Steiner R. ed.). London: Karnac, 145–98

Janet P, 1925. *Psychological Healing*, Volume 1. London: Allen and Unwin

Karpman S, 1968. Fairy tales and script drama analysis. *Transactional Analysis Bulletin* 7.26, 39–44

Laplanche J and Pontalis JB, 1988. *The Language of Psychoanalysis*. London: Karnac Books

Ogden TH, 1999. *Reverie and Interpretation: Sensing Something Human*. London: Karnac

Sandler J and Fonagy P, eds, 1997. *Recovered Memories of Abuse: True or False?*. London: Karnac

Showalter E, 1997. *Hystories: Hysterical Epidemics and Modern Culture*. London: Picador

6 P (2002), What is there to feel? A neo-Durkheimian theory of the emotions. *European Journal of Psychotherapy, Counsellling & Health*, 5, 3, 263–90

7
Private Solutions to Public Problems? Psychoanalysis and the Emotions

Michael Rustin

Introduction

Psychoanalysis does not usually characterise itself as an investigation of the affects. Its object of study is not the emotions, but the unconscious mind, which is seen to have both cognitive and sentient dimensions, inseparably linked together. Indeed the refusal of the split between emotions and reason, as spheres requiring different modes of understanding, one belonging to the humanities, the other to the sciences, has been a challenge by psychoanalysis to the dominant academic conventions. Freud, as Schorske (1998) pointed out, was drawn powerfully both to the sciences – he was initially a doctor and a neurologist – and to the arts, and the hybrid form of investigation which he initiated draws on both the systematising and fact-gathering methods of the sciences and the imaginative and interpretative approaches of the humanities (Rustin, 2001).

The description, classification and explanation of states of feeling are nevertheless fundamental to psychoanalytic theory and practice. The human subjects of Freud's case studies are moved by passions, terrors and anxieties which they struggle to understand. Psychopathology is accompanied in the psychoanalytic view by unusual or extreme states of feeling, though it usually also involves abnormalities of perception and thought. Freud's account of affects was in some respects impoverished by presuppositions which he took over from psychological empiricism (a default appetite-aversion, pleasure-pain model of motivation and his early instinct-biologism) though it grew deeper as his work developed. Klein's revisions of Freud's theory, in her postulation of innate 'object-relations' (arising from the idea that human beings are related to other persons from birth onwards) opened the way to a more inclusive investigation of affective states. Klein's work elabora accounts of emotionally-valent ways of relating to others – love, hate, envy, jealousy, gratitude, reparation, for example – which propose theoretical explanations of feeling-states usually most searchingly explored in imaginative literature.

Psychoanalysis is a practice which has always mainly located itself in the private rather than the public sphere. The clinical practice from which most of its ideas derive takes place in consulting rooms, where individuals go to obtain help in understanding themselves better, often in order to alleviate their mental pain or unhappiness. Has psychoanalysis had any influence on the public sphere, during its century-long history? Should it have such influence today? Because psychoanalysis has developed such a formidably complex theory of the mind, and has such wide cultural currency, it seems that a consideration of the place of the affects in the public sphere has to take account of its contribution, or be radically incomplete.

Differences within psychoanalysis

The first thing to be noted is that even within the tradition founded by Freud, there is now not one psychoanalysis but many, though there remains common ground between them.[1] For this reason, in so far as psychoanalysts and their schools have espoused ideas or prescriptions which impact on the public sphere, they are often divergent from one another. Freud's (explicit) view of society differs from Klein's (more implicit) view, as we will see. Both are different from the perspective of American ego-psychology, and all three from Lacan's ideas. And the 'schizo-analysis' of Deleuze and Guattari (1977, 1988), which was constructed as a challenge to Freud's thinking, rejecting many of its canonical assumptions, generates a different engagement with the public sphere again. There is a complex interplay between these different forms of psychoanalytic thinking, and the societies and cultures in which they have taken root.

In this chapter, I am going to consider three moments in the development of psychoanalysis in Britain, and explore the relation that psychoanalysis has in each of them to the public sphere. These are Freud's own contribution, the work of the Kleinian School, and the post-Kleinians, continuing into the present. The questions I will be asking are how they are each shaped by the wider social context in which they emerged, and how do they seek to intervene in the broader public domain, to the extent that they do? The differences between these epochs of psychoanalysis in Britain are smaller than those between all of these 'naturalised British' traditions and the other tendencies of psychoanalysis referred to. But those more divergent tendencies are a topic for separate discussion. My contention is as follows. Although Freud, the Kleinians and the post-Kleinians were (or are) primarily occupied with the private sphere of individual psychoanalytic practice, they were (or are) all influenced by the public context in which they live. Reversing C Wright Mills' famous dictum, one could say that psychoanalysts and their patients seek private solutions to public problems. But in doing so, they necessarily find themselves having to attend to the effects of the public world on private lives. Psychoanalysts do not usually venture far from their consulting rooms into the public sphere to investigate such connections.[2] Psychoanalysts have had a mainly clinical formation, in professional associations, not an academic one in universities, and this has tended to keep their 'private' sphere of expertise cut off from the larger public domain. But in one way or another, psychoanalysts have been sensitive to these links, and their writings reflect their awareness of them. I will in turn explore how Freud, Klein and the post-Kleinian school have each represented their concerns about the problems which society generates for its individual members. And also how they have suggested that psychoanalytic insights, applied in the wider social domain, could alleviate these problems.

My argument, broadly speaking, is that Freud perceived society as excessively repressive, and that in his writing and practice he sought to create more space for individuals to choose and to pursue their own desires uninhibited by convention and conscience. Klein was concerned, by contrast, not with the excess of authority and constraint in her society, but with the precariousness of social relationships, and their vulnerability to destructive attack. The post-Kleinians, whose most influential figure was Wilfred Bion, were writing in a period when there was once again a reaction against social conformity, and the rise of a new individualism, characterised by recent social theorists (for instance Beck, 1992; Giddens, 1992) as 'individualisation'. Whereas the Kleinians gave normative emphasis to affective ties and moral responsibility in their account of the development of the self, the post-Kleinians have shifted attention towards an idea of 'reflectiveness' and the creation of a 'space for thinking' which allows for more uncertainty and turbulence than the previous Kleinian account, while retaining much of its theoretical architecture and implicit ethical preferences. One can sociologically account for these differences, to some extent, by noting that Freud (1856–1939) had his formation during what Arno Mayer (1981) has called the 'old regime' of pre-First World War Europe, while Klein (1882–1960) lived most of her life in the shadow of two World Wars, Nazism, and the Holocaust, but also saw and no doubt supported the inception of the post-Second World War welfare state. Bion (1897–1979) began his psychoanalytic career during the 1940s (his early work was with groups) and began his psychoanalytic writing in the 1950s, continuing into the 1970s. His psychoanalytic career starts in the 1940s, in the Second World War and the period of reconstruction, but between 1968 and 1979 (shortly before his death) he chose to live and practice in Los Angeles. Both of these cultural contexts left traces in his work.

Freud and society

Freud's ideas were formed in the last years of the 'old regime' of continental Europe, in which monarchy, aristocracy and church remained dominant forces, especially in the Austro-Hungarian Empire in whose capital city Freud lived. He identified with the transformative potential of science, and wished to see greater freedom of choice for individuals, at least among the educated. (He was as suspicious of the masses and those who sought to mobilise them politically as he was of traditional conservative elites). From his perspective, society was oppressive, authoritarian, and superstitious, and controlled its individual members as much through internalised inhibitions and feelings of guilt as through overt coercion. He thus defined the relationship between self and society as a largely negative and conflictual one. Greater autonomy for the individual required withdrawing the projected authority with which individuals invested gods, leaders, and fathers, and enabling them to choose for themselves, with fuller knowledge of their motives and of the likely consequences of their actions. Freud's life prescriptions of 'love and work' seem to be the watchwords of bourgeois man, the kind of man that Freud was himself.

Both the scientific empiricist tendency in his thinking which he drew from Britain, and its romantic and irrationalist tendency which derived (according to Schorske) from his passion for Parisian life and culture, share a focus on the individual as the primary locus of experience and meaning. Freud's ideas were thus allied to the claims of liberalism, against authoritarian and traditionalist aspects of the old regime, even though they were disruptive of some of the rationalist certitudes of the liberal world-view. Freud's individualism, and his critique of radical utopianism as an irrational projection, has made his ideas often as unpopular with the political left as with the right.[3] Psychoanalysis has flourished within authoritarian states of neither right nor left, but only in liberal political environments. Freud was 'modern' in another sense, in that he sought to ground his own authority and that of his new movement in an autonomous professional practice, which was dependent on fee-paying clients, on institutional self-regulation, and on the publication and influence of its ideas for its income and status. Many new professional callings emerged in the early part of the twentieth century, and have continued to do so. The profession Freud invented, that of psychoanalyst, sought to be a complement to that of medical doctor and rival to that of priest, in its offer to manage the problems of everyday life of modern citizens.

Freud's influence has been deemed comparable to that of Darwin and Marx in his undermining of traditional certainties, and in the de-centring of the idea of 'rational man' in the Western world-view. Freud, however, saw himself as enhancing, not undermining, the possibility of rational self-mastery, since he proposed to bring the passions and the unconscious within the sphere of rational understanding. What seemed 'modernist' at one moment, when a traditionalist social order was breaking down, has come to seem 'post-modernist' at a later one, as dominant 'modern' ideologies of industrial society, including that of science, became subjected to criticism and doubt. It seems that psychoanalytic ideas can be deployed in both directions, on the one hand making positive claims to new forms of understanding and legitimation, on the other hand undermining and discrediting old ones in a negative mode. Freud, in his own work, did both.

Ernest Gellner argued in a late paper (1995),[4] that Freud's diagnosis a century ago of the contradictions of high bourgeois life had proved highly influential. Gellner wrote that he was unpersuaded by Freud's account of the unconscious mind, and of his methods for revealing its secrets, but that he had been right to emphasise the irrationality and opacity of human action to its subjects. The importance of Freud's contribution was that he assigned the responsibility for deciding upon values and making choices to men and women themselves, not to gods or other transcendental forces. Gellner thus identified himself as a modernist, like Freud, sharing with him a courageous stoicism in the face of humans' inability to understand or control their own destiny, and also repudiating any supernatural sources of consolation. Freud thought that irrationality was made greater by an excess of sexual repression in society, whose prohibitions reinforced patriarchal authority both in its direct familial forms, and in its elaborations in broader forms of religious and political authority, and he sought to reduce the burden of this. His ideas have plainly had great cultural influence, far beyond those who have experienced psychoanalysis for themselves (Forrester, 1997). Deep social changes created a climate favourable to the influence of Freud's writings, which were available as resources of interpretation in a society in transition. These changes included greater equality of gender, connected to a long decline in family size, and the replacement of an ethic of sacrifice which was functional for a producer-oriented economy, by the hedonistic ethic necessary to consumer societies. (Marcuse, 1955, 1956). Freud's ideas thus contributed to the weakening of the bonds of authority and tradition, and to the achievement of greater freedoms in personal and cultural life. As Gellner pointed out, the lessening of repressive constraints has not brought about the dissolution of orderly social life that traditionalists feared it would. Rather it has helped to bring into being a gentler and more tolerant society.

Klein and social bonds

Klein belonged firmly in Freud's psychoanalytic movement, having been an analysand of both Ferenczi and Abraham, and having been invited to Britain in 1925 by Ernest Jones, Freud's great ally in Britain. Freud's writings were the starting point and organising framework for her own work, and remained important to her throughout her life. Nevertheless, she and her associates directly challenged Freud's teachings, on matters crucial to the development of her own theory.[5]

The difference between Freud and Klein[6] amounted to a disagreement about human nature, and it emerged in accounts which they respectively gave of the psychological attributes of the infant at the time of birth. Freud conceived infants as born into a state of primary narcissism, scarcely aware that their world was populated by other persons, and only slowly emerging into this realisation in their first months as consciousness developed. Klein by contrast presupposed a primary human relatedness, and an innate infantile knowledge of and attachment to parental figures.[7] Not only are human infants wholly reliant for their physical survival on the care of adults, but they also, according to Klein and her followers, depend for their mental and emotional development on their relationship to parents or care-givers. The development of the infant mind, according to this theory, proceeds through an initially symbiotic relationship to parental figures, whose role in processing and modulating the states of mind and feeling of the infant is essential in creating a sufficient state of mental equilibrium for the infant's mind to develop. The Kleinians held that such processes of introjective and projective identification were crucial to the development of the self.

Associated with Klein's insistence on object-relatedness from birth onwards, was her view that the development of what she called the internal world proceeded much more quickly than Freud had believed. She proposed that two contrasting patterns of object-relation emerged in the first year – the paranoid-schizoid and the depressive positions – and that the onset of the Oedipus Complex occurred in the first year of life, whereas Freud had located it later. She sought to demonstrate that it was possible to undertake psychoanalysis with children as young as three years, with her new 'analytical play technique'. (Klein, 1926)

Klein's concept of the depressive position assigned to infants, even in their first year of life, a capacity for recognition of the existence and concern for the well-being of another. The primary factors influencing mental life, and the growth of the personality, were the balance between the impulses of love and hate, which she saw as determined partly by innate disposition, and partly by the nurturing environment. While she followed Freud's view that the primitive conscience was the product of a persecuting superego, and in particular of Oedipal guilt, she differed from Freud in her belief in the importance to the growing personality of feelings of love and concern for the other, to which she linked feelings of reparation and gratitude. While Klein has been criticised for her emphasis on innate envy and destructiveness, what is just as notable in her work is her affirmation of the significance of love as the root of all social bonds, which she stated most eloquently in *Love, Guilt and Reparation*.[8]

She links this with the capacity for identification, writing that the 'capacity for identification with another person is a most important element in human relationships in general, and is also a condition for real and strong feelings of love. We are only able to disregard or to some extent sacrifice our own feelings and desires, and thus for a time to put the other person's interests and feelings first, if we have the capacity to identify ourselves with the loved person.' (Klein, 1937)

This represents a significant change of perspective from Freud's. Whereas Freud's individuals struggle to reconcile their pleasure-seeking desires with the demands of the superego and the reality-principle, Kleinian individuals are deeply identified, though in ambivalent and conflictual ways, with others. A moral sense is innate in them – she thinks that criminals are more likely to suffer from an excess of guilt, the effect of an early persecutory superego, than from its absence. Klein's subjects live in a social world, at risk from its destructiveness but innately capable of care and responsibility. For Freud, it seems that society is faced with the task of regulating impulses and instincts that are inherently anti-social. This was a major change of perspective. What explains how it came about? Was it merely the difference between highly gifted psychoanalytic writers of different generations? Or was it, as I will suggest, a response to and reflection of social and cultural changes in Britain, where it took place?

Kleinian women

The Kleinian development represented a notable 'feminisation' of the psychoanalytic field.[9] Melanie Klein was one of the few female figures to have been a major innovator and intellectual leader in the human sciences, during the period when she was working. Many of her leading associates[10] – notably Susan Isaacs, Joan Riviere, and Paula Heimann[11] – were women also, as were two of her most influential successors and advocates in British psychoanalysis, Hanna Segal and Betty Joseph. Klein shifted the focus of psychoanalytic interest from the unconscious struggle between father and son, for the possession of the mother, (and to a lesser extent of daughter and mother for possession of the father), to the dyadic relationship between mother and baby, of either sex. Although the Oedipus complex remains central in Klein's thought, there is a relocation of the focus of psychic action in her writing from the presence of the father to the formative role of the mother in infant development. The father becomes important in providing support for the emotional burdens of mothering, rather than merely as the looming, intrusive presence whose role is to displace the omnipotent infant – 'his majesty the baby' – from his omnipotent perch. Klein's thinking – her first publication was in 1921 and her work proceeded throughout the next 40 years – may thus be said to be one of the precursors of the broad change in the balance of gender power which has taken place in Western societies in this period. It is not 'feminist' work in the usual sense of attacking the enforced differentiation between male and female roles and entitlements. Kleinian psychoanalysis does not critique differences of gender, so much as insist on them, as separate sources of value and potency. Where the orthodox Freudian tradition made much of the envy of male power and potency – 'penis envy' – the Kleinians drew attention to another equally significant source of envy, namely that of the mother's capacity to make and bring forth babies.[12] The Kleinian commitment is neither to gender hierarchy, nor to the undoing of gender difference, but to 'equality in difference'.

Family and welfare

A second notable feature of Kleinian theory is its focus on the primary family of parents and children not only as a locus of unconscious conflict (though it is certainly that in Klein's account too) but also as the space within which the development of personality takes place. Donald Winnicott (1952) whose psychoanalytic ideas incorporated many of Klein's insights, while rejecting her emphasis on innate envy and destructiveness, wrote that 'there is no such thing as a baby'.[13] as a way of insisting on the essentially relational nature of the self in its earliest stages of development. Klein was the most important pioneer of the psychoanalysis of children, developing techniques which make use of play and drawing by child patients as forms of expression and interaction. From this followed the growth of interest within the Kleinian tradition on the development of infants in their family setting, and on the naturalistic observation of infant development in family settings, both as a means of training psychotherapists and as a means to enhance sensitivity to emotional life within families.

The programme of 'social reconstruction' initiated after the Second World War gave considerable emphasis to the family as a key building block of social solidarities perceived to have been damaged not only by the events of the war, but by the preceding period of class conflict, economic recession, poverty and unemployment. The value of a rhetoric of 'family' for an incoming Labour government in 1945 was that it enabled it to meld its commitments to the redress of inequalities with a commitment to familial values. It could thus pursue objectives which were based on acknowledged differences of class, in a language which nevertheless transcended class affiliations.

Thus emerged the idea of the 'welfare state', and its aim of providing decent conditions of life at each phase of the life-cycle. A good deal of the redistribution entailed by these policies aimed to even out 'life-cycle' rather than class inequalities, by attending to the unavoidable dependency needs of childhood, illness and old age. Much of the influential social science literature of this period, both empirical and sociological, focused on the importance of family relationships in maintaining social stability.[14] Although the idea of the welfare state won wide cross-party consensus during the 1940s and 1950s, critics in the Thatcherite era argued that other priorities should have been adopted.[15]

'Welfarism' and 'familism' provided a favourable climate for the new inflection to psychoanalytic ideas which were given by Klein and her followers.[16] Most of the support which psychoanalysis has received from the state in Britain has been in the context of family and child welfare, not in adult mental health services, though its relevance to the treatment of adult mental illness is considerable. The idea that families are crucial to the development of viable and ethically responsible personalities, and that supportive services should be in existence to support parental roles, has been widely endorsed in British welfare practice.[17]

While in some respects, this emphasis of British psychoanalysis on the indispensable nurturing role of families went with the grain of mainstream social thinking, whether in its conservative or social democratic inflection, in other ways it challenged conventional assumptions. This was in the attention it gave to the difficulties and complexities of family interactions, and to the need to face the realities of sexuality, negativity and potential violence, both emotional and physical, in early life. Only through giving more reflexive attention to emotional realities could problems arising from separation, loss and social turbulence be addressed. Moral injunction was seen to be no longer enough, especially in a society in which the authority of religion was in decline. But since the psychoanalysts and those allied to them held that families were vital institutions, that they depended on recognising differences in authority between generations, and that there were innate differences between genders, their teachings had some affinities with traditional pro-family habits of thought.

Destructiveness and violence

A third feature of Klein's writing was her emphasis on hatred, envy and destructiveness as innate aspects of human nature. This was a theme present in Freud's writing also, in his theory of the life and death instincts, especially following his response to the First World War, but this emphasis becomes stronger in Klein's work. Kleinian analysts account for the more severe kinds of psychopathology and developmental disorder through attention to unconscious hatred, envy and destructiveness, and their consequences for the development of the self, the mind, and the capacity to relate to others. It is this theoretical resource, and the therapeutic techniques which evolved with it, which has enabled the Kleinians to extend the range of psychoanalytically-treatable conditions. In child analysis, for example, where once 'ordinary neurotic' disturbances such as bed-wetting or school-refusal were the standard symptoms, child psychotherapists now routinely treat children who have been severely and multiply deprived, and whose character-structures – angry, without trust, and with a fragile sense of self – reflect these histories.

This attention to psychotic and 'borderline' states of mind which has characterised Kleinian psychoanalysis seems likely to have been a response to a broader social condition in which extremes of behaviour were hard to avoid or deny. The difference of a generation between Freud and Klein may be important. A rationalist optimism that seems part of Freud's formation, and of his great hopes for the new science of psychoanalysis[18] is much less evident in the writings of Klein and her group, whose work is rooted in everyday experiences of emotional pain, and is also more shadowed by the impact of war.[19] This divergence partly reflects differences of gender roles and perspectives – a different balance of interest between the public and private sphere than in Freud's work – but perhaps also takes up the deeper sense of the tragic evident in Freud's later writing.[20]

At any rate, one can draw parallels between the cultural attention given during Klein's working life to extremes of psychic desolation, sometimes directly related to War and the Holocaust – in the writings for example of Beckett and Adorno – and the states of mind explored in her and her contemporaries' psychoanalytic work. Whilst psychoanalysis in Britain has been able fully to absorb the Kleinian view of the extreme depth and violence of the unconscious, as has in France the comparable perspective of Lacan, both writers have remained marginal influences on psychoanalytic practice in the resolutely optimistic culture of the United States.[21]

Klein wrote mainly for a readership of psychoanalysts, and mainly on clinical and theoretical issues within psychoanalysis. She wrote only three papers intended for general readers, a few on applications of her ideas to settings beyond the family and consulting room – papers on schools and criminality, for example, and three papers on works of art and literature. But though, unlike Freud, she engaged little in her writing with wider questions, her analysands and close associates, such as Roger Money-Kyrle,[22] certainly did. Even though she did not assert the relevance of her psychoanalytic ideas to the condition of society in the way that Freud did, she and her circle were fully immersed in the experience of war and post-war reconstruction.[23] It does not seem far-fetched to see her ideas as offering a psychoanalytic dimension to the project of repairing and rebuilding a nurturing social environment against a background of disorganisation and destruction.

Post-Kleinian psychoanalysis[24]

Let us now turn to the development of psychoanalysis in Britain since Klein's death in 1960. Is there a distinct post-Kleinian theoretical position, and if so what connections can one make between it and the social context in which those ideas have evolved? Characterisation of such a position is made difficult by the fact that the principal post-Kleinian authors – for example Rosenfeld, Bion, Britton, Steiner – have been as reluctant to criticise Melanie Klein as she was herself to criticise Freud.[25] Furthermore they are Klein's undisputed successors, whereas Freud's own succession was contested, for example between Anna Freud and Klein.[26] The post-Kleinians did not need to insist on a break with Klein's ideas to establish their own standing.[27] This movement can even be said to have brought about some integration of psychoanalytic thinking in relation to its earlier tradition, by giving renewed attention to interests of Freud which had been somewhat eclipsed. I shall here consider three dimensions of post-Kleinian thinking. I will suggest that they reflect and respond to a changing social context.

Bion and the idea of containment

The most influential and charismatic figure of the post-Kleinian movement was Wilfred Bion. (Bion, 1962, 1963 1965, 1967, 1970) One of his main interests, derived from the analysis of patients suffering from psychotic disturbances, was in the development of the human capacity for thought, and what he called 'the mental apparatus'. He viewed the capacity for mental functioning as itself a developmental achievement, which depended on the processing of primitive states of feeling in the context of the earliest relationship between mother and infant. The psychotic patients he treated (Bion, 1967) lacked a capacity for coherent thought or communication in the consulting room in which he met them. Bion described phenomena of 'concrete thinking' (in which symbols could not be differentiated from what they were intended to represent) and the violent projection or 'evacuation' by patients of the intolerable contents of their minds. He thus extended Klein's idea of the splitting and fragmentation of mind inherent in the paranoid-schizoid position. He also developed Klein's idea, elaborated by Hanna Segal (1957), that the capacity for symbol formation was linked with the arrival of the depressive position, and the reduction of splitting between good and bad objects, and correlatively of the self, which accompanied this.

The over-arching conception which Bion developed to describe the processes leading to the development of mind was that of the relation of container and contained. Its prototypical form is the relationship between mother and infant, 'containment' being seen as an active psychic processing of emotion and anxiety by the mother on behalf of the infant. He saw the relationship between analyst and analytic patient in terms of this same 'containment' template. This idea has been applied to a range of settings in which a 'containing' presence of some kind serves to alleviate unconscious anxieties on the part of the 'contained'. The 'container' may be a person or an institution, the 'contained' may be an individual in some relationship of dependency, or a group or population. The idea is that reflection on such anxieties, which may be about learning, or illness, or guilt, or antagonism, by the 'container' creates 'space for thinking', in which change and development may become possible.

Questioning the normative in Klein

Although the capacity for symbolisation and thinking had a place in Klein's theory, (she held that an 'epistemophilic instinct' or desire for knowledge was innate, Klein, 1928, 1931), it was not its central focus.[28] Klein was more interested in the relational and moral capacities that ensued from development in infancy, which might be repaired through psychoanalysis, than in the processes of thinking per se. The titles given to some of her writings – for instance, *Love, Guilt, and Reparation* (1961), and *Envy and Gratitude* (1975), convey her interest in the moral and emotional aspects of relationships. She and her associates had a strong therapeutic commitment – perhaps this is one especially likely to be sustained by work with children. Critics of the Kleinians, even from within their circle, sometimes protested that in therapeutic practice their ideas could become all too normative, the paranoid-schizoid and the depressive positions becoming terms of moral judgement as much as clinical descriptions.

This 'normative' emphasis of Klein's ideas was qualified in another theoretical revision. Instead of the achievement of depressive states of mind being imagined as a once-and-for-all achievement, it has come to be viewed as just one aspect of creative mental functioning, one pole of a desirable oscillation between paranoid-schizoid and depressive states, as Bion first described this. Ronald Britton (1998) has argued that psychic development depends on the continuous re-formation of the self, in which the energy imparted by both libidinal and destructive impulses must have a place. He prefers the psychic turbulence which follows from the toleration of destructive and negative feelings as well as 'responsible' and other-regarding emotions, to the idea of an achieved state of 'maturity', which is likely to become complacently detached from emotional reality if psychic challenges and disturbances are refused.

'Borderline States' and the return of Oedipus

A third significant development is the increased salience in contemporary psychoanalytic work of states of mind described as 'borderline' between the paranoid-schizoid and depressive positions (Steiner, 1993).[29] Borderline patients are cut off from intense feelings, but, unlike psychotic patients, as able to survive and even prosper in their lives through splitting of their personality. A cool, rational part of the self enables them to function more-or-less normally even though their affective life is impoverished. One element of this state of mind is what Rosenfeld (1971) first recognised as 'destructive narcissism', the idealisation of a superior, denigrating part of the self, which creates a self-justification for indifference or hostility towards others. Such individuals hold other persons at a distance, and in their analysis seek to avoid emotion, preferring that they and their analyst should converse only as detached, rational beings. They try to keep out of their analysis the difficulties with intense feelings which have probably brought them into analysis in the first place.

Britton has explored a distinction made by Rosenfeld between 'thick-skinned' and 'thin-skinned' narcissists, from his clinical experience. The former try to keep feelings out of the analytic relationship, the latter thoughts. These opposite psychic strategies seem to map on to gender differences, in a way which corresponds to the socially-constructed norms of gender identity. Britton's hypothesis is that these forms of self-division are each defensive responses to the Oedipal situation, and express intolerance of the existence of the Oedipal triangle. In the Oedipal situation the self is confronted with the need to acknowledge the separate reality of two others, primarily its parents. The psychic strategy of affective merger denies thought – one may say it identifies exclusively with the maternal principle. The strategy of aloof, cerebral autonomy identifies conversely with an extreme paternal template.

Important to Britton's view of psychological development is the idea of 'triangular space', the possibility of reflection and thus individual development that is made possible only when a 'third perspective' on experience can be tolerated. Klein's view focused on the functions of the mother-baby dyad in development. In this she departed from Freud's earlier emphasis on the Oedipal triangle. Bion elaborated the 'containing' functions of this dyadic relationship, though noting that containment depended on the existence of concentric circles larger than the mother-baby couple. Britton and his colleagues have returned to the Oedipal situation as the necessary root of psychic development.

This intervention seems to represent a reassertion of male perspectives within a discourse that in the period of greatest influence of Melanie Klein was dominated by female analysts and those influenced by them. We could say that Freud was preoccupied with the struggle between fathers and sons, and Klein with that between mothers and babies. The more recent post-Kleinian development, perhaps the reflection of a partial equalisation of gender roles in society, reincorporates both parental figures into the drama of early psychic development. But where Freud saw the resolution of the Oedipus Complex primarily as a process of instinctual renunciation, probably also as the necessary reproduction of unambiguous gender identities, Britton's argument has another implication. The Oedipal triangle has for Britton the dynamic function of making possible the acceptance of difference, as a condition of mental growth. It is the space for reflection and choice that 'triangular space' makes possible that is most important in Britton's argument, not the reproduction of a particular parental template.

Sociological thoughts on post-Kleinian developments

The above describes some themes in post-Kleinian psychoanalytic thinking. How might one link them to changes in society and culture that have taken place since Klein's death in 1960?

One change that seems significant is the weakening of the post-war 'welfare settlement', and the consensus that underpinned it. Moral certitudes about 'human growth and development' and about families which seemed to carry conviction in the earlier post-war period, were subjected to challenge in the turbulence of the late 1960s and

1970s, from feminists among others. Psychoanalytic perspectives lost influence in one of their main fields of application, social work, in attacks both from managerialist behaviourists and rights-based collectivists.

Of course the problems of family pathology and social disorganisation which psychoanalysis addressed were far from diminished by 'individualising' social changes. Psychoanalysts responded to the situation by becoming less morally judgemental, but all the same retaining their commitment to integration and connectedness. Bion's concept of 'containment', and his emphasis on mental processing and 'space for thinking' were attractive ideas in this situation. Instead of insisting directly on the validity of their own moral discriminations the analysts focused instead on clarifying the conditions in which moral discriminations could be made by subjects. This led to more exploratory approaches by psychotherapists, not only in regard to directly ethical issues but also in regard to the varieties of gender, sexual and family forms which they now encountered in the more 'liberated' climate of the post-1960s period. Some convergence of thinking between different psychoanalytic schools has taken place in this climate. (Fonagy *et al.*, 2002; Fonagy and Target, 2003; Sandler, 1987a, 1987b)

At the same time, interest in 'pathological organisations' of the personality' enabled attention to be given to the more extreme consequences of greater social disorganisation. In the National Health Service, the largest area of growth was in child and family services, with child psychotherapists emerging as a new profession as numerous as the psychoanalysts. This happened in response to the increasing severity of presenting problems, with multiply-deprived and abused children becoming a large part of clinic caseloads. Substitute families replaced children's homes as the treatment of choice for children, and psychotherapists were called upon to provide out-patient support. The post-Kleinian attention to extreme destructive states of mind provided resources for working with emotional casualties among children and adolescents of a more 'individualised' age. (Boston and Szur, 1983; Williams, 1974)

In their work with adult patients, post-Kleinian analysts focused on another consequence of individualisation in their focus on 'borderline' or 'narcissistic' disorders. These may be adaptations to a competitive culture, in which individuals are encouraged to further their own interests without much regard to states of injury caused to others.[30] We may think of this as a manifestation of weakened social solidarity. The appearance of narcissistic disorders vindicates Marcuse's theory of 'repressive desublimation', his idea that the diminution of repression in a market society would lead to more sexual freedom but not to a greater sense of authenticity or fulfilment.[31]

Finally, we can note a 'cultural turn' in post-Kleinian thinking. The production of symbols and styles has become more salient in post-industrial society, and leads to emphasis on aesthetic discriminations. The idea of the sacred has migrated to some degree from religion to the arts.[32] The most influential of the post-Kleinians, Wilfred Bion, spent some years in analytic practice in California.[33] There is a 'mystical' dimension to his writing, in his insistence on the purity and autonomy of the analytic experience, and in his gestures towards an idea of the infinite, a kind of unknowable threshold of knowledge and experience, which he refers to as 'O'. (Bion, 1965, 1970) This 'Californian' tinge to Bion's ideas, further developed by some of his American disciples (Grotstein, 1981) marks a shift away from the more straightforwardly reparative moral and social agendas of the earlier Kleinians.[34]

I have described in this chapter the theories of emotion which have evolved in the British psychoanalytic school over the last century, focusing on Freud, Klein and the post-Kleinians. In each phase of development, I have suggested, analysts have taken note of the social context in which emotional life is constructed, and the problems which this social construction brings to both individuals and society. The British psychoanalytic tradition is a predominantly clinical one, and has been reluctant to engage in wider policy debate. Nevertheless, I have suggested that from its access to the painful emotional experiences of private life, it has presented implicit or explicit diagnoses of wider social problems, and developed theories and techniques which address them.

Notes

1 The idea of the unconscious, the significance of dream interpretation, the importance of the Oedipus Complex, are among these.

2 C Wright Mills proclaimed it as the task of sociology to find public solutions to private problems. (Mills, 1970, p248)

3 Raymond Williams, for example, made his lack of sympathy with the social assumptions of Freudian psychoanalysis clear in *Culture and Society* (1958).

4 This took a more positive view of Freud than his earlier critique, *The Psychoanalytic Movement* (1985).

5 Good overviews of Klein's writings are provided by Segal (1975), Likierman (2001), and, with a feminist inflection, Kristeva (2001).

6 These were set out in the 'Controversial Discussions' of 1944–45, after Freud's death. Freud's ideas were defended by Anna Freud, who had joined him in exile in London in 1939. (King and Steiner, 1991). A group of British

independent analysts (aligned neither with Anna Freud nor Klein) had the role of chorus in this struggle, and by their clear preference for clinical material and its interpretation over theoretical disputation, moved both camps in the direction of the 'clinical empiricism' which has subsequently become the dominant ethos of British psychoanalysis.

7 Disagreeing with Freud's theory of primary narcissism in which the libido is attached to the ego, Klein wrote:

> The analysis of very young children has taught me that there is no instinctual urge, no anxiety situation, no mental process, which does not involve objects, external or internal; in other words, object-relations are at the *centre* of emotional life. Furthermore, love and hatred, phantasies, anxieties, and defences are also operative from the beginning and are *ab initio* indivisibly linked with object relations. This insight showed me many phenomena in a new light. (Klein, 1952, p53)

8 I said before that feelings of love and gratitude arise directly and spontaneously in the baby in response to the love and care of his mother. The power of love – which is the manifestation of the forces which tend to preserve life – is there in the baby as well as the destructive forces, and finds its first fundamental expression in the baby's attachment to his mother's breast, which develops into love for her as a person. My psycho-analytic work has convinced me that when in the baby's mind the conflicts between love and hate arise, and the fears of losing the loved one become active, a very important step is made in development. These feelings of guilt and distress now enter as a new element into the emotion of love. They become an inherent part of love, and influence it profoundly both in quality and quantity.

Even in the small child we can observe a concern for the loved one which is not, as one might think, merely a sign of dependence upon a helpful and friendly person. Side by side with the destructive impulses in the unconscious mind both of the child and the adult, there exists a profound urge to make sacrifices, in order to help and put right loved people who in fantasy have been harmed or destroyed. In the depths of the mind the urge to make people happy is linked up with a strong feeling of responsibility and concern for them, which manifests itself as a genuine sympathy for other people and in the ability to understand them, as they are and as they feel. (Klein, 1937, p311).

9 Janet Sayers in *Mothering Psychoanalysis* (1991) describes the contribution of four major women psychoanalysts – Helen Deutsch, Karen Horney, Anna Freud, and Melanie Klein – in making the experience of mothering and the relationships of mother and infant central to modern psychoanalysis, in contradistinction to Freud's patriarchal perspective. Lisa Appignanesi and John Forrester (1992) in *Freud's Women* put forward a similar argument:

> Most importantly, Klein's work pioneered a slow and subtle shift, one, perhaps, that transformed psychoanalysis more than any other single factor: the reorientation of the understanding of the child's inner world around its relation to its mother. Mothers became models for the

profession of psychoanalysis, mothering provided descriptions of what psychoanalysts were supposed to be doing; via the mother, the normative life-story was introduced. (p454)

10   For the work of this group, see Klein, Heimann, Isaacs and Riviere (1952).

11   Heimann later parted company with the Kleinian group.

12   Discussing infantile envy, Klein wrote: 'The feminine desire to internalise the penis and receive a child from her father invariably precedes the wish to possess a penis of her own' (Klein, 1945 reprinted in Klein 1975, p419).

13   'If you show me a baby you certainly show me also someone caring for the baby, or at least a pram with someone's eyes and ears glued to it. One sees a "nursing couple"'. (Winnicott, 1952, p99)

14   Family solidarity was an important topic in the 'community studies' literature important to sociology in this period. (Bott, 1957; Klein J, 1967; Young and Willmott, 1957)

15   Corelli Barnett (1986) argued that Britain's economic competitiveness was sacrificed to this welfare priority, and Niall Ferguson (2004) has suggested that it unduly hastened the end of the British Empire. The former represents an economic liberalism which later had its moment in Thatcherism, the latter an attachment to an imperial vision closer to the perspectives of the landed aristocracy.

16   See Gerson (2004) for a good account of these links, focusing especially on 'middle group' analysts like Winnicott, rather than Klein. Also Rustin (2006) on Kleinian approaches.

17   That this is no universal commonplace can be seen from the different priorities of state socialist societies, and the extreme neglect of vulnerable or unwanted children that took place in some of them.

18   *Moses and Monotheism* (1939) reveals one of Freud's identifications and his sense of himself as the bringer of a new enlightenment.

19   Klein's child patient Richard, whose analysis is reported in detail in her *Narrative of a Child Analysis* (1961), is much preoccupied with the course of the war in his sessions.

20   For example, *Mourning and Melancholia* (1917) published when Freud was 61.

21   So far as Kleinian influence is concerned, there are some signs of change, for example in the work and influence of Thomas Ogden (1989). Lacanian ideas have greatly influenced post-structuralist cultural and literary studies in the United States.

22   He wrote a number of essays on the philosophical and ethical implications of Klein's ideas (Money-Kyrle, 1978), and co-edited with her and Paula Heimann a collection of papers (Klein, Heimann, Money-Kyrle, 1955) with a substantial 'applied' section.

23   Although Bowlby subsequently quarrelled with the Kleinian analysts, and went on to develop his attachment theory, he was associated with them for example in the establishment of the Tavistock Clinic within the NHS, from 1948 onwards, and helped them to start the new discipline of psychoanalytic child psychotherapy.

24   Ronald Britton (1998, p2) refers to 'the group of London analysts now generally known as post-Kleinians'.

25 An excellent introduction to the writings of this is the two volumes of Spillius (1988).

26 The most significant schism among the post-Kleinians took place in the withdrawal of the late Donald Meltzer, a prolific and gifted psychoanalytic writer, from the British Psychoanalytic Society. However he continued to be productive and no institutional division followed.

27 Most of the 'post-Kleinians' have remained members of the Kleinian Group of the British Psychoanalytical Society, and became its leaders through generational succession. Only Donald Meltzer broke away, leaving the Society altogether, but his departure did not lead to any broader institutional schism.

28 A valuable source for clarification of Kleinian psychoanalytic concepts is Hinshelwood (1989).

29 Part 4 'Pathological Organisations', of Spillius op. cit. (Vol. 1) provides a good introduction to this topic, reprinting several of the seminal papers.

30 An earlier argument about narcissism as a psycho-social state was developed by Christopher Lasch (1978). This drew on American psychoanalytic writings on narcissism by Kohut (1971, 1977) and Kernberg (1975). Kernberg's work has affinities with that of the British post-Kleinian analysts.

31 The classifications of disorders used by psychoanalyts to some extent reflect their clienteles. Child psychotherapists, working in the public sector, now encounter multiple disturbance in children. Adult therapists, working mainly privately, find patients able to work and thus pay for treatment, but unhappy about themselves and their relationships. The application of post-Kleinian ideas to adults with the most serious mental illness has been restricted by the lack of public sector psychoanalytic provision for adults.

32 Note the attention given by Britton (1998 and 2003) and Meltzer (Meltzer and Williams, 1988) to aesthetic creativity.

33 'Eschew memory and desire' was his famous adjurations to analysts approaching the consulting room.

34 'Independent' analysts, like Christopher Bollas (1993, 1995) and Adam Phillips (1995) take this further, arguing that the psychic destination of an analysis must always be open, and is the outcome of a process of narrative or poetic construction which should not be bound by prior psychoanalytic prescriptions or certitudes.

References

Appignanesi L and Forrester J, 1992. *Freud's Women*. London: Weidenfeld and Nicolson

Barnett C, 1986. *The Audit of War: The Illusion and Reality of Britain as a Great Nation*. London: Macmillan

Beck U, 1992. *Risk Society*. London: Sage

Bion WR, 1962. *Learning from Experience*. London: Heinemann

Bion WR, 1963. *Elements of Psychoanalysis*. London: Heinemann

Bion WR, 1965. *Transformations*. London: Heinemann

Bion WR, 1967. *Second Thoughts*. London: Heinemann

Bion WR, 1970. *Attention and Interpretation*. London: Heinemann

Bollas C, 1993. *Being a Character: Psychoanalysis and Self-Experience*. London: Routledge

Bollas C, 1995. *Cracking Up: The Work of Unconscious Experience.* London: Routledge

Boston M, and Szur R, eds, 1983. *Psychotherapy with Severely Deprived Children.* London: Routledge and Kegan Paul

Bott E, 1957. *Family and Social Network: Roles, Norms and External Relationships in Ordinary Urban Families.* London: Tavistock Publications

Britton R, 1998. *Belief and Imagination.* London: Routledge

Britton R, 2003. *Sex, Death and the Superego.* London: Karnac

Deleuze G and Guattari F, 1977. *Anti-Oedipus: Capitalism and Schizophrenia.* New York: Viking Press

Deleuze G and Guattari F, 1988. *A Thousand Plateaus: Capitalism and Schizophrenia.* London: Athlone Press

Ferguson N, 2004. *Colossus: The Rise and Fall of American Empire.* London: Allen Lane

Fonagy P, Gergeley G, Jurist EL and Target M, 2002. *Affect Regulation, Mentalisation and the Development of the Self.* New York: Other Press

Fonagy P and Target M, 2003. *Psychoanalytic Theories: Perspectives from Developmental Psychology.* London: Whurr

Forrester J, 1997. *Dispatches from the Freud Wars.* Cambridge: Cambridge University Press

Freud S, 1917. *Mourning and Melancholia.* In Freud S (1973) *The Standard Edition of the Complete Psychological Works of Sigmund Freud*, Vol. 14. London: Hogarth Press

Freud S, 1939. Moses and Monotheism. In Freud S (1973) *The Standard Edition of the Complete Psychological Works of Sigmund Freud*, Vol. 23. London: Hogarth Press

Gellner E, 1985. *The Psychoanalytic Movement.* London: Paladin

Gellner E, 1995. Freud's Social Contract, in *Anthropology and Politics: Revolutions in the Sacred Grove.* Oxford: Blackwell

Gerson G, 2004. Object Relations Psychoanalysis as Political Theory. *Political Psychology*, 25, 5

Giddens A, 1992. *The Transformation of Intimacy: Sexuality, Love and Eroticism in Modern Societies.* Cambridge: Polity

Grotstein JS, ed., 1981. *Do I dare disturb the universe? a memorial to W.R. Bion.* London: Karnac

Hinshelwood RD, 1989. *A Dictionary of Kleinian Thought.* London: Free Association Books

Kernberg OF, 1975. *Borderline Conditions and Pathological Narcissism.* New York: Jason Aronson

King P and Steiner R, eds, 1991. *The Freud-Klein Controversies 1941–45.* London: Routledge

Klein J, 1967. *Samples from English Cultures, Vols 1 and 2* (1967). London: Routledge and Kegan Paul

Klein M, 1926. The Psychological Principles of Early Analysis, Chapter 6 of *Love, Guilt and Reparation*, op. cit., 1975

Klein M, 1928. Early Stages of the Oedipus Complex, Chapter 9 of *Love, Guilt and Reparation*, op. cit., 1961

Klein M, 1931. A Contribution to the Theory of Intellectual Inhibition, Chapter 14 of *Love, Guilt and Reparation*, op. cit., 1961

Klein M, 1937. *Love, Guilt and Reparation*, Chapter 19 of *Love, Guilt and Reparation*, op. cit., 1975

Klein M, 1945. 'The Oedipus Complex in the Light of Early Anxieties', Chapter 21 of *Love, Guilt and Reparation*, op. cit., 1975

Klein M, 1952. The Origins of Transference, Chapter 4 of *Envy and Gratitude and other Works 1946–63*. London: Hogarth Press, 1975a

Klein M, 1961. *Narrative of a Child Analysis*. London: Hogarth Press

Klein M, 1961. *Love, Guilt and Reparation and other Works 1921–55*. London: Hogarth Press

Klein M, 1975. *Love, Guilt and Reparation and other Works 1921–45*. London: Hogarth Press

Klein M, 1975. *Envy and Gratitude and other Works 1946–63*. London: Hogarth Press

Klein M, Heimann P, Isaacs S and Riviere J, 1952. *Developments in Psychoanalysis*. London: Hogarth Press

Klein M, Heimann P and Money-Kyrle R (eds), 1955. *New Directions in Psychoanalysis*. London: Tavistock Publications

Kohut H, 1971. *The Analysis of the Self*. New York: International Universities Press

Kohut H, 1977. *The Restoration of the Self*. New York: International Universities Press

Kristeva J, 2001. *Melanie Klein*. New York: Columbia University Press

Lasch C, 1978. *The Culture of Narcissism: American Life in an Age of Diminishing Expectations*. New York: Norton

Likierman M, 2001. *Melanie Klein: Her Work in Context*. London: Continuum

Likierman M, 1989. The Clinical Significance of Aesthetic Experience. *International Review of Psychoanalysis*, 16, 2

Marcuse H, 1955. *Eros and Civilisation:* Boston: Beacon Press

Marcuse H, 1956. *Soviet Marxism*. New York: Columbia University Press

Mayer AJ, 1981. *The Persistence of the Old Regime: Europe to the Great War*. New York: Pantheon

Meltzer D and Williams MH, 1988. *The Apprehension of Beauty*. Perthshire: Clunie Press

Mills CW, 1970. *The Sociological Imagination*. Harmondsworth: Penguin

Money-Kyrle R, 1978. *The Collected Papers of Roger Money-Kyrle* (edited by D Meltzer) Perthshire: Clunie Press

Ogden, TH, 1989. *The Primitive Edge of Experience*. London: Karnac

Phillips A, 1995. *Terrors and Experts*. London: Faber and Faber

Rosenfeld H, 1971. A clinical approach to the psychoanalytic theory of the life and death instincts: an investigation into the aggressive aspects of narcissism. *International Journal of Psychoanalysis*, 52, 169–78

Rustin MJ, 2001. A Biographical Turn in Social Science? In M Rustin, *Reason and Unreason: Psychoanalysis, Science, Politics*. London: Continuum

Rustin MJ, 2006. Klein on Human Nature, in Jon Mills (ed.) *Other Banalities*. London: Routledge

Sandler J, 1987a. *From Safety to the Superego: Selected Papers of Joseph Sandler*. New York: Guildford Press

Sandler J, 1987b. *Projective Identification*. London: Karnac

Sayers J, 1991. *Mothering Psychoanalysis*. London: Hamish Hamilton

Schorske CE, 1998. To the Egyptian Dig: Explorations in the Passage to Modernism. In CE Schorske, *Thinking with History: Explorations in the Passage to Modernism*. Princeton: Princeton University Press

Segal H, 1975. *Introduction to the Work of Melanie Klein*. London: Heinemann

Segal H, 1957. Notes on Symbol Formation. *International Journal of Psychoanalysis*, 38, 291–7

Spillius E, 1988. *Melanie Klein Today: Vol. 1: Mainly Theory. Vol. 2: Mainly Practice*. London: Routledge

Steiner J, 1993. *Psychic Retreats: Pathological Organisations in Psychotic, Neurotic and Borderline Patients*. London: Routledge

Williams R, 1958. *Culture and Society*. London: Chatto and Windus

Williams G, 1974. Doubly Deprived. *Journal of Child Psychotherapy* Vol. 3, 4, reprinted as Double Deprivation in Williams G, *Internal Landscapes and Foreign Bodies: Eating Disorders and Other Pathologies*. London: Karnac Books, 1997

Winnicott DW, 1952. Anxiety associated with insecurity, Chapter 8 of *Through Pediatrics to Psycho-Analysis*. London: Hogarth Press, 1958

Young M and Willmott P, 1957. *Family and Kinship in East London*. London: Routledge and Kegan Paul

Part III
Cultural, Historical and Political Formations of Emotion

8
Theory and Affect: Undivided Worlds

Susannah Radstone

'(t)hinking starts with drives' (Caldwell, 1995, p25)

'...(t)he ideal of dispassionate inquiry is an impossible dream
...' (Jagger, 1997, p190)

'I simply indicate that I know it and thus *make myself known as
the one who knows.*' (Felman and Laub, 1992, p63 emphasis in
the original)

Introduction: theory versus feeling

This chapter extends the now routinised use of psychonalysis within
film and literary criticism to the analysis of theoretical discourse.[1] In
the critical practices of film and literary studies, psychoanalysis is
applied to the analysis of texts, as well as to the analysis of text/
spectator or text/reader relationships. In neither case are the findings
of such researches deemed to bear any direct relationship to a text's
author. In place of an auteurist approach to the relation between texts
and their authors, psychoanalytic textual analysis posits, rather that
'meanings ... are actually produced in and through the operations of ...
texts.' (Kuhn, 1994, p74). Psychoanalytic criticism argues, moreover,
that '... the meaning-production process is not always immediately
discernible ... The operation of the meaning-construction process has,
as it were, to be unearthed, for it is precisely the work of ideology to
conceal its own operations.' (Ibid.) As this account of psychoanalytic
criticism reveals, this approach to textual analysis has most usually
been deployed to unearth the production of hidden social *meanings*.
Psychoanalysis has less usually been deployed, that is, in the analysis

of affects and their relation to social meanings and world views. This is the aim of the following chapter.

In what follows, I make the argument that through the use of psychoanalytic criticism, the discourses of a particularly widely deployed and cited contemporary social theory, namely trauma theory[2] can be shown to reveal traces of aggressivity. This is not an argument that seeks to analyse the authors of trauma theory. Rather, it is informed by those traditions of psychoanalytic criticism described above, which ascribe an unconscious to discourses, texts, practices and culture. Discourses circulate within the public sphere, and organise and give meaning to the world. In tracing through the aggression that underlies trauma theory, this chapter seeks to integrate theory's affective dimensions into a discussion of the meanings, agency and politics of discourse.

Theory is commonly regarded as the antithesis of feeling and emotion. Reason and thought have long been prized for their capacities to achieve distance from – or even to reflect upon – the teeming and confusing world of feelings and the emotions. To adopt a thoughtful or philosophical attitude has commonly – but not always – [3] been associated with the distancing of the self from the potentially overwhelming immediacy of experiences of feeling in the present (Jagger, 1997, p188). While these commonsense understandings of the theory/feeling relation remain in place, the destabilisation of the opposition constructed in Western culture between the domain of the mind, or reason, on the one hand, and that of feelings and the emotions, on the other has long been attempted from within the academy. One aim shared by both feminist and deconstructionist theory, for instance, is the undoing of binaries such as reason/feeling.

The drive to problematise the reason/feeling binary is by no means limited to contemporary theory. The drive to establish the limits of objectivity can be associated, for instance, with the critiques of logical positivism (Kuhn, 1994). A number of more recent theoretical interventions have been associated, however, with the critique of the reason/feeling binary. Standpoint theory seeks to locate and acknowledge the position/s from which a researcher speaks and writes and values rather than denigrates the knowledge derived from such openly situated research. Autobiographical, or personal criticism begins from the acknowledgement and exploration of its author's subjectivity as it shapes their readings of texts. Both standpoint theorists and autobiographical critics openly avow their emotional and intellectual engagement with scholarship and research. Indeed, for many, that very distinction between the emotional and the intellectual may be regarded as false. Both standpoint theory and autobiographical criticism had their inception in second wave feminism, and most particularly, in that movement's contention that 'the personal is political'. The association that this statement constructed between two domains that had generally been regarded as opposed carried with it the implicit assumption that feelings – a constituent of the personal – ought not to be excluded from the spheres of the public and the political. In that feminism informed by poststructuralism and postmodernism, a critique of the conceptual apparatus that supported a patriarchal and phallocentric world view stressed the place of binaries within that apparatus. On this account, a set of binary oppositions operated in the interests of patriarchy by associating woman with the more negatively coded element in any pair. Woman, this approach argued, had historically been associated with the emotions rather than with reason, just as she has been associated with the body rather than with the mind, and with the domestic, rather than with the public domain.[4] Second wave feminism responded to woman's association with feeling rather than with reason in two ways. First, feminists proposed that women's capacity to reason was at least equal to that of men. But second, feminists also contended that this denigration of feelings and the emotions was but one aspect of patriarchy's disavowal of all that it associated with woman. The separation that its binary forced between reason and feeling emerges, on this account, as but one aspect of the violence of patriarchy's disavowal of that which it included within its paradigms of woman and the feminine. Alison Jagger's essay on emotion in feminist epistemology can stand, here, for the many feminist interventions (Lloyd, 1984) that have sought to deconstruct the binary opposition between reason and feeling. Jagger's opening contention is that emotions may be regarded as rational inasmuch as they contribute to survival. The 'derogatory Western attitude toward emotion' she argues, 'fails to recognise that emotion ... is necessary to human survival ... life without any emotion would be life without any meaning'. (Jagger, 1997, p190) Jagger's next move is to argue that modern epistemology itself 'may be viewed as an expression of certain emotions alleged to be especially characteristic of males in certain periods, such as separation anxiety and paranoia'. (Ibid., p190) Jagger continues by arguing that if modern positivist epistemology's opposition between reason and feeling can be shown to be rooted in ideology – in the denigration, that is, of those qualities and capacities that it ascribes to women, western epistemology, must 'rethink the relation between reason and emotion [and] construct conceptual models that demonstrate the mutually constitutive rather than oppositional relation between reason and emotion.' (Ibid.)

Jagger's essay goes on to construct an argument, rooted in standpoint theory, that 'the emotional responses of subordinate people in general and women in particular, are more likely to be appropriate than the emotional responses of the dominant class. That is, they are more likely to incorporate reliable appraisals of situations'. (Ibid., p192) This is not a move that seems to me easy to substantiate and neither is it a move that I wish to follow, but Jagger's previous statement concerning modern epistemology as the *expression* of certain emotions does not neccessitate this further move towards the celebration of the emotions of the subordinated. In what follows, then, I will develop and modify the idea of epistemology as the expression of emotion by arguing, rather, that this insight can be extended to the question of the feelings 'expressed', in Jagger's terms, by specific theories. Though Jagger does not herself make use of it, psychoanalysis has been deployed frequently by feminism's analyses of the cultural constructions sexual and gender differences. In what follows a psychoanalytic methodology will be deployed to demonstrate that certain theoretical discourses may be shaped by a set of feelings, or by affect, that mark those discourses in particular ways. Moreover, it will be proposed that even a theory which purports to be concerned with *understanding* a particular cluster of feelings might be better regarded as associated with, if not a direct consequence of, particular feelings or affects. The discourses to be addressed belong to the field of what is commonly referred to as 'trauma theory', which concerns itself with the impact of shocking and catastrophic events *on* feelings, memory and representation. This chapter will make use of psychoanalytic understandings of affect to argue that these discourses might be read not only for their concerns with feeling, but also as the bearers of particular unacknowledged feelings or affects. In what follows, then, I will be conceiving of trauma theory's discourses not as the direct expressions of emotion, but as the bearers of traces of unconscious affect. The project I undertake below is not equivalent to the 'diagnosing' of culture as though it were 'sick'. I start out from the assumption – commonsense within psychoanalysis – that the aggressive and sexual drives subtend all aspects of culture, just as they drive, at an unconscious level, the dreams, actions and reactions of subjects. But in acknowledging the particular and specific ways in which aggression subtends a particular theoretical discourse, my aim is first to demonstrate the particular way in which a theory – in this case trauma theory – may be at odds with itself, and second, to suggest how trauma theory's internal contradictions might relate to wider cultural tendencies in evidence today.

Psychoanalysis and affect

Psychoanalysts of all hues would concur, I think with Graham Music's view, that '(w)hat distinguishes a psychoanalytic "take" on the world of feelings and emotions is the idea that we are all in varying degrees unaware or unconscious of aspects of what we are feeling.' (Music, 2001, p3) Even where the idea of the unconscious may be held in doubt, Music argues that there has been 'an increasing body of research, both psychological and neuroscientific, to back up the idea of unconscious emotional states.' (Ibid., p7) Of all the theories available to the humanities and the social sciences, it is in psychoanalysis that the strongest case is made for the inseparability of affect or feeling from mind or intellect. As Music states, '(e)motions and feelings are very much tied up with belief systems and thought structures, and cannot be separated from them.' (Ibid., p26) The continuing commitment of psychoanalysis to this view is only strengthened by recent comments by the French psychoanalyst and theorist André Green. Green, who was originally associated with, but who later broke from the French psychoanalyst Jacques Lacan, now acknowledges his debt to the theorist and child analyst DW Winnicott (Caldwell, 1995, p15), whose work belongs to the British Independent tradition, and whose writings have had little influence, in general, on non-British European psychoanalysis. Green has written recently, indeed, that he considers that 'Winnicott is the greatest mind since Freud.' (Caldwell, 1995, p17) Notwithstanding these acknowledgements, Green argues that DW Winnicott's tendency to refer to all psychical development – 'apart from the intellectual functions' (Green, 1999, pxii) as emotional development 'is not without its dangers today in so far as it lends itself to a particular confusion, namely that psychoanalysis should confine itself to the affect, while the cognitive sciences should define their domain as that of the intellect, which is itself supposed to cover the whole of the psyche – except for the affects' (Ibid.). Though psychoanalysis strives still to track the relation *between* thought and affect, or even to propose, as Green appears to do, here, that from a psychoanalytical perspective, the binary thought/affect might be considered almost a mis-conception, psychoanalysis nevertheless embraces more than one understanding of the place, meanings, and roles within psychical life of what it variously refers to as the emotions, feelings and affect. These differences of understanding are even reflected in the terms used to describe their object. Though some, as the above quotes from Graham Music demonstrate, appear to deploy the terms 'emotions', 'affect' and 'feelings' almost interchangeably, choice of terms is usually a clear indication of a theorist's position. The terms 'feelings' and 'the emotions' are more usually found in the writings of the British independent and object-relations schools of psychoanalysis, both of which have their roots in the post-Kleinian works of Winnicott and others,[5] as well as in writings by US psychoanalytic thinkers also influenced by both ego-psychology and post-Kleinian object-relations.[6] The term 'affect' is found more often both in the writings of Deleuzian theorists (see the introduction to this volume) and in the writings of post-Freudian psychoanalytic theorists, whose work is less influenced by object-relations and for whom Freud's theory of the drives remains influential.

Though a detailed account of these complex debates is beyond the scope of this writer, and this chapter, the most important point to grasp is that the key difference between these two approaches hinges on what they each take to be primary in psychical life. While object relations foregrounds the significance of relations with others, arguing that it is these relations which shape the inner world from the earliest years, Freudians and post-Freudians emphasise, rather the primacy of the sexual and aggressive drives and their constitutive role in the formation of the psyche. André Green is the best known of those psychoanalytic theorists, particularly in France, whose work is less influenced either by object relations theory,[7] or by contemporary ego psychology[8] than it is by recent revisions of classical Freudian theory: speaking for French psychoanalysis in general, Green wrote recently indeed, that '[our] interest in theory also comes from our belief in Freud ... we can read papers we have read thirty times before and still find something new.' (Caldwell, 1995, p17) A more extended summary of the different approaches to affect found within psychoanalysis will now follow.

Object relations, which originated in the work of Melanie Klein[9] emphasises the innate sociality of the child and the influence of early 'object relations', or, crudely, relations with others, as they are perceived and taken in, on the shaping of the inner world from the earliest moments of infancy. Ego psychology builds on Freud's second topography of the psyche, which identified its constituent elements as 'id', 'ego' and 'super-ego'. It is, then, a version of psychoanalytical structural theory, but in its more recent developments, particularly in the US, it has tended to focus on the ego and its development and adaptation, to the detriment, perhaps, of a continuing attention to the id, in particular. Both ego psychology and object relations theory – schools of psychoanalytic thought which are not entirely separate from each other – attend closely to the presentations of emotions or feelings by patients, as well as to the ways in which feelings and emotions are transferred and transmitted between analyst and patient in the consulting room. While both contemporary ego psychology and object relations theory have arguably contributed a wealth of insights concerning the complex textures of emotionality that arise in the moment-by-moment work of analysis, this attention to the psychical surface,[10] to ego adaptation, or to a phenomenology of feeling-states, arguably threatens to lose sight of what is, for André Green, at least, the founding insight of psychoanalysis: its emphasis on the drives. For Green, indeed, the study of affect is significantly what I'll call the royal road to the drives. In a recent interview, Green, who has himself published a book titled *The Fabric of Affect in the Psychoanalytic Discourse* (Green, 1999) goes so far as to caution against the over-use of the term affect, since it can lead, he argues, to a separating out of what he regards as the inseparable elements of thinking and feeling: (I)n my opinion, Green argues, 'the use of "affect" becomes an abuse because now we fall into the trap of posing the cognitive and the affective ... I think the real unity is the drive which combines the representation of the affect. This *is* the psychic ...' (Caldwell, 1995, p25). For Green, the key insight of psychoanalysis concerning the affect, is that it is rooted in the sexual and aggressive drives. Thus, he argues that '(t)his locus of the affect cannot be anywhere other than in the sexual, aggressive affect. This is the price that has to be paid if psychoanalytic theory is to preserve its specificity.' (Green, 1999, p72) For Green, then, '(t)he greatest danger facing psychoanalytic research ... is to slide into phenomenology, which can only lead to a surruptitious return to the psychology of consciousness.' (Green, 1999, p347)

Nancy Chodorow's recent *The Power of Feelings: Personal Meaning in Psychoanalysis, Gender and Culture* (Chodorow, 1999), might perhaps be taken to represent just such a 'slide into phenomenology'. Chodorow's account of transference,[11] which constitutes, for her, '*the root psychoanalytic discovery*' (Ibid., p26, emphasis in the original), emphasises that it is 'continually created and transformed. It is fed by infantile sources but also by many sources in daily life – by the moment-to-moment animating of the world and investing it with subjective meaning ...'

(Ibid., p32). If Green's approach is to trace the relationship between the affects and their association with sexual and aggressive drives, Chodorow's aim is to attend closely to the moment-by-moment flux of affect and to link it to those processes of transference and meaning-making in the present through which 'self-stories' (Ibid., p31) are made and re-made. That Chodorow's book was published in the same year that André Green's book on affect, originally written in 1973, first appeared in English demonstrates the current interest in affect within psychoanalysis as well as its present divisions, for aside from a shared interest in the work of DW Winnicott, Green and Chodorow arguably represent two opposed poles of a complex continuum. Divisions notwithstanding, both Chodorow and Green emphasise the falseness of the division between affect, on the one hand and cognition and the capacity to reason and learn on the other – a division that continues to mark much work within the discipline of psychology. Unsurprisingly, Chodorow mobilises her critique of a theoretical division between reason and affect through the concept of transference, which, she argues 'is not just an obstacle to clear thinking or a resistance. By invoking the concept of transference', she goes on, 'psychoanalytic theorists argue that emotion is always intertwined with cognition ...' (Ibid., p27). On Chodorow's terms, then, it would be through the operation of transference that affect would be associated with, for instance, a set of ideas or a particular thinker. As we have already seen, a position informed by André Green's writings on affect would also critique any theoretical division between intellect and affect. But Green's position would suggest that this is a false division not because transference will always blur the boundaries between thought and feeling, but on the basis, rather, that conscious thought is made up of mental representations and all such conscious representations are related to the psychical representations of the drive, which have affective and ideational components: '(t)he drive, though unknowable' argues Green, 'is [affect's] reference. The affect is one of the two elements of the psychical representations of the drive. It denotes the element of energy in this representation, endowed with a quantity and quality, linked to the ideational representative, but capable of being dissociated in the unconscious.' (Green, 1999, p70)

If for Green, the specificity of psychoanalysis's view of affect resides in its association with aggression and sexuality, and therefore with the drives, my own sense of the significance of this view concerns the importance of retaining an emphasis on the ultimate waywardness and unbiddability of psychical life. That self-knowledge and self-government are thus fated to be at best partial and inevitably incomplete is one lesson taught by this version of psychoanalysis. These disquieting ideas arguably appear in slightly tamer, or more domesticated form in those versions of psychoanalysis which aim to produce narrative reconstructions of the past to explain present transferences. Even where those narratives are accepted as constructions in the present which may bear only a tenuous relation to the past, they do provide a sense of something which can be known in a once and for all manner, which is not the case with drive theory. That the version of the self bequeathed to us by this version of psychoanalysis is a deeply unsettling one is beyond dispute and is a point to which this chapter will be returning.

In a recent essay tellingly entitled 'The Other Inside' (Antze, 2003) Paul Antze borrows from the French psychoanalyst Jean Laplanche the term *étrangèreté* to capture that aspect of psychical life which is at risk of being domesticated in many current understandings of psychoanalysis. Elaborating on this term, Antze explains that Laplanche 'equates it with what he takes to be truly revolutionary in psychoanalysis, the "Copernican" idea of a subject whose centre of gravity lies elsewhere, outside consciousness'. (Antze, 2003, pp102–3) As I have already suggested, in my view, the retention of drive theory constitutes one defence against this process of domestication, since that theory postulates forces that literally 'drive' the subject in ways that can neither be fully known, nor brought under the subject's conscious control. In this sense, the subject of psychoanalysis is always, to an extent, beside her/himself. Antze's essay goes on to critique the development, under the imperative of anchoring psychoanalysis more firmly in science, of a new school of neuro-psychoanalysis. The influence of this school can be seen in Graham Music's reference to 'an increasing body of research, both psychological and *neuroscientific*, to back up the idea of unconscious emotional states' (Music, 2001, p7, emphasis added), which I quoted earlier and which appears in the volume on Affect in the introductory texts series 'Ideas in Psychoanalysis'. Antze proposes that the understanding of memory developed by this school is particularly vulnerable to the charge of domestication since they propose an 'encoding' of memories into neural sytems, and forget the complex processes of symbol formation that were 'absolutely central to Freud' (Antze, 2003, p100).

While I find Antze's account of the current domestication of psychoanalysis convincing, his suggestion that this has arisen primarily as a consequence of psychoanalysis' attempts to align itself more closely with science leaves aside broader questions of the cultural and theoretical contexts within which this version of psychoanalysis has gained ground. In the next section I want to move on to suggest that though this 'domestication' of psychoanalysis might be associated, in part, with the imperative to align psychoanalysis with science it might be interpretable, also, and paradoxically, in relation to particular affects that are screened, or repressed by those discourses which purport to take affect, and the workings of the psyche more generally, as their explicit subject matter.

Trauma theory and affect

Discourses are components of the public sphere that circulate in, mark and give meaning to the world. To speak of a discourse's unconscious affective freight is to suggest that psychoanalysis can illuminate less evident aspects of those circulations, markings and meanings. Yet the project of tracing affect in discourse is fraught with difficulties. André Green responded to his own question '(c)an one speak of the affect?' in the following terms: '(D)oes not what one says about it concern the periphery of the phenomenon, mere ripples at the furthest remove from the centre, which remains unknown to us?' (Green, 1999, p3). The difficulty of 'knowing' affect is compounded by the risk of the projection of the researcher's own affects onto the object of study. (Ibid.) Before offering some thoughts of my own about affect and trauma theory, it is important to be clear about what I am not doing in what follows. First, as I have already stated, the tracing of affect in discourse is by no means equivalent to the analysis of a text's author/s. This would be to undertake the sort of psychobiography which I consider to be a version of 'wild' psychoanalysis (Freud, 1910) that is, psychoanalysis undertaken without due rigour and outside the consulting room. It is important to acknowledge that the academic psychoanalysis of the sort practiced by literary, film, media and cultural theorists has no access to the unconscious of authors, and certainly not to a consulting room. It has access, rather, to texts, to discourses and to cultural processes and practices. The analysis of these objects is not equivalent, moreover, to the analysis of 'culture', or 'the public sphere'. Nancy Chodorow's proposal that '(c)ulture ... can help make some emotions more salient consciously and also, as it were, invest these emotions with emotional and fantasy meaning, thus shaping how they are experienced' (Chodorow, 1999, p186) is a helpful one. But to speak of culture or, by extension, the public sphere, in these terms is by no means equivalent to asserting that culture actually 'feels' or 'possesses' emotions. 'Culture', in the broadest terms, does not 'feel' or 'suffer'. Even where 'culture' designates a group of individuals, it would still not be possible to undertake an adequate psychoanalytic analysis of that group's feelings, outside of the context of group analysis, for this would be yet another version of 'wild' analysis. What can be essayed, however, is the more modest enterprise of the psychoanalysis of discourses and texts and in what follows, I want to suggest that we might extend those practices of textual analysis to which I referred earlier to the analysis of theoretical and scholarly texts, and to the analysis of the affects that they screen, repress or symptomatically represent.

Trauma discourses and the affects

I choose to focus on trauma theory for several reasons. First, trauma theory is *itself* explicitly concerned with the analysis of the cultural scars of traumatic affect. Second, due to its concern with unspeakable suffering, trauma theory has the power to elicit powerful feelings in its readers. For these reasons the particular and specific affective dimensions of trauma theory itself are of particular interest.

The rise of trauma theory in the Humanities is now well documented.[12] Trauma theory is associated with attempts to move beyond postmodernist and poststructuralist doubts concerning the referential status of representations (Elsaesser, 2001). These doubts were prompted, in part at least, by the Holocaust and its aftermath (Freidlander, 1992), and trauma theory is itself linked with the theorisation of the experiences of traumatised groups and individuals, including, most particularly, Holocaust survivors (Felman and Laub, 1992) and the survivors of sexual and extreme physical abuse (Herman, 1992). Its most profound impact has arguably been felt, however, within literary and to a slightly lesser extent media and film studies, where attention falls on the analysis of '[traumatic] memory and its – politically enforced, patriarchally inflicted – gaps, absences and traceless traces'. (Elsaesser, 2001, p194)

Though the term 'trauma theory' arguably unifies a diverse field of discourses, its broad contours share in the attempt to overcome a series of theoretical impasses concerning referentiality and the representation of the unrepresentable. In short, trauma theory promises to revise theories of referentiality through the production of a theory that testifies to the tracelessness of the traces left upon texts by (traumatic) history.

Unsurprisingly, though problematically, trauma theory tends to take as its objects of study only those texts that are explicitly concerned with catastrophe and suffering (Radstone, forthcoming) (though the types of suffering it concerns itself with may range from the truly catastrophic to the less exceptional experiences of, for instance, childbirth). As I have argued elsewhere, this is a project that demands respect. (Radstone, 2001, p62) Yet, notwithstanding trauma theory's important contributions to debates concerning referentiality, history and memory, its analyses of testimony, photographs and other discourses and texts are limited by their capacity to countenance only their potential proffering of witness to, and empathic identification with, unrepresentable sufferings. Given that its objects of study allude to abuses of many kinds, the absence of any theorisation, in trauma theory, of the potential for identification with perpetration is striking. (Radstone, 2001)[13] In place of the psychoanalytic account of the subject as driven by sexuality and aggression in ways that will always exceed, in part, the capacity either for full self-knowledge or self-government, trauma theory delivers us a subject who is either the innocent victim of, or the guilty perpetrator of abuse. Not even trauma theory's to my mind almost self-evident associations with, at its mildest, the indignation of the witness/analyst or the resentment[14] or rage of the victim (Wood, 1998) are much discussed or acknowledged by trauma theory, even though, in the words of the writer WG Sebald, 'Few emotions are more difficult to repress than resentment.' (Sebald quoted in Phillips, 2003) and even though the latter has been discussed by approaches to trauma informed by alternative psychoanalytic perspectives.[15]

Trauma discourses are thus fully consonant with contemporary preoccupation with social movements of survivorhood (Showalter, 1997), and with their tendency to designate as traumatic a wide range of experiences, ranging from the catastrophic to the more everyday – a tendency which has been deemed to debase the term. (Leys, 2000, p2) These social movements have been associated with a 'current fascination … with the allocation of responsibility and the politics of blame'. (Antze and Lambek, pxxi) These are social movements and tendencies which are founded upon a certain Manicheanism (Radstone, 2001) in which that which is threatening and bad is positioned in the other, or perpetrator, while that which is good and ethically pure is located within the innocent, suffering one who is 'done to' by that other. In these discourses, the potential for ethical equivocation or for the designation of a subjective position capable of 'doing' and being 'done to', and with the potential for feelings that can encompass (simultaneously, perhaps) aggression and love disappears from view.

In this book, our concern is more with the consequences of certain feelings, or affects for public life, than it is with tracing the causes, or origins of those feelings themselves. My concern, here then, is to provide some indications of the ways in which unconscious affect may be leaving its traces on trauma theory – to suggest, that is, the ways in which trauma theory might be seen as *arising from* unconscious affect.

Trauma theory concerns itself with the sufferings of others and with terrible events that come from the outside. It is a theory concerned with tracing the marks left by these events in the texts and speech that are its objects of study. What is most striking about this theory, apart from the Manicheanism to which I have already referred, is first, the capacity to discern trauma's traceless traces that it invests in the analyst of trauma, and second the extent of the unspeakable sufferings that trauma theory locates in its chosen texts and subjects. Trauma theory is concerned with what the traumatised cannot know, and feel, and with what the trauma theorist can know and feel. My examples will be drawn from trauma theory's most seminal text within the Humanities, Felman and Laub's *Testimony* (Felman and Laub, 1992).

In his essay 'Bearing Witness', Dori Laub describes the processes of witnessing and listening required of an analyst working with survivors of trauma. In the order of their appearance, he identifies these as, first, coming to look for 'something that is in fact nonexistent; a record that has yet to be made.' (Ibid., p57) 'The emergence of the narrative which is being listened to – and heard – is, therefore, the process and the place wherein the ... "knowing" of the event is given birth to' (Ibid.). Second, Laub suggests that in listening, the listener comes to 'partially experience trauma in himself', a process that is complicated by the listener's own feelings (pp57–8). Third, Laub proposes that the listener must be fully aware and sensitised to the effects of trauma: 'The listener must know all this and more.' (p58) Laub's essay discusses the case of a woman who witnessed the uprising at Auschwitz,[16] a woman who, he surmises, was a member of the 'Canada commando' who dealt with the belongings of the recently murdered. Laub explains, however, that though he had access to this knowledge, the woman did not herself know that she had been a member of this exact group: 'I had probed the limits of her knowledge and decided to back off; to respect, that is, the silence out of which this testimony spoke.' (p60) Though 'Bearing Witness' presents an empathic and moving account of testimony to terrible sufferings, what I am struck by here is the knowledge and power it invests in the analyst, though it is also true that Laub acknowledges, too, the limits of his own knowledge – he acknowledges, that is, that he never knew that the Jewish inmates who took part in the uprising were betrayed by Poles (Ibid., p61). Yet even where what is not known is acknowledged, this is followed by a statement that resituates the analyst as the one who knows: '(o)f course it is by no means ignorance that I espouse. The listener must be quite well informed if he is able to hear – to be able to pick up cues.' (Ibid.) Further on in the essay the knowledge that the analyst can glean from this testimony is compared favourably with that to which historians had access 'The historians could not hear, I thought, the way in which her silence was itself part of the testimony.' (p62) As the essay proceeds, its emphasis on the analyst's knowledge – albeit a fluctuating knowledge – is made yet more explicit, for instance, '(i)t has happened to me many times that thinking back to a psychoanalytic session with a patient, I suddenly realise that I have understood it ... At times, when I lose myself in such deliberations, the melody is gone ... At other times, I seize upon it and echo it in my response. I simply indicate that I know it and thus *make myself known as the one who knows*' (p63; emphasis in the original). And, in another example, talking of the joint acceptance of Holocaust reality that is the primary stage of psychoanalytic trauma therapy, Laub writes, 'The analyst must often be there first, ahead of his patient, ... must wait with patience and readiness for the latter to join him in that place.' (p69) Again, Laub stresses the power vested in the analyst: 'Testimonies are not monologues;' he states, 'they cannot take place in solitude. The witnesses are talking to *somebody*: to somebody they have been waiting for for a long time.' (p71; emphasis in the original) In another passage he describes the listener's/analyst's roles in the following terms: '(P)aradoxically enough, the interviewer has to be, thus, both unobtrusive, nondirective, and yet imminently present, active, in the lead ... he has to move quietly and decisively in bringing things together ...' (p71).

I have dwelt on this example of trauma theory at some length in order to draw out the features of that discourse that I now want to discuss in relation to unconscious affect. In the discussion which follows, I want to focus particularly both on the satisfactions or pleasures offered by trauma theory to its readers and practitioners, and on what those pleasures might screen.

One question literary and cultural theorists ask of texts concerns the satisfactions and pleasures that they offer their readers. This may seem an inappropriate, or even an insensitive question to pose of trauma theories, given their concern with the most appalling sufferings of others, yet the apparently oxymoronic 'popularity' of trauma theory (Radstone, 2001a, p189) invites some consideration of the reasons for that popularity. This is a theory which has, after all, established an almost astonishing dominance across the Humanities, in a relatively short space of time.[17] What I have tried to show in the preceding examples, is that trauma theory offers the reader/practitioner an identification that oscillates between the sufferings of the traumatised testifier and the knowledge and assurance of the analyst. Though the ego-syntonic aspects of the latter position would suggest that it might dominate over the former, an identification with the sufferings of another do function to *locate* suffering in that other, rather than in the self. Both positions in this oscillation arguably shield the reader, then, from the anxiety that might be posed by the suggestion of an encounter with *their own* vulnerability to unknown and unpredictable suffering. These positions arguably share more, however, than this 'shielding' effect. Though identifications with the quasi-omnipotence of the analyst – the 'one who knows' – and the innocent and 'done-to' victim may appear to occupy rather different psychical territory, common to both is the denial and displacement of aggression (Radstone, 2001, p70). An identification with the control and being 'in the lead' (Felman and Laub, 1992, p71) of the analyst of trauma offer the reader an identification with a position that has 'achieved total mastery and "evacuated" all "badness" or aggression from itself.' (Radstone, 2001, p71),[18] while an identification with victimhood offers the reader an identification in which all aggression is located with the perpetrator and firmly outside the self. (Ibid.) What is screened, then, is any potential identification with aggression. This is an aspect of trauma theory that has been foregrounded by Ruth Leys' trenchant critique of the work of Cathy Caruth, whose reading of Freud's *Moses and Monotheism*, argues Leys, converts 'the Israelites who murdered Moses into passive victims of the trauma of an accidental "separation" ...' (Leys, 2000, p294).

Yet if the identifications offered by trauma theory *appear* to offer pleasures associated with a narcissistic view of the self as 'pure' and 'good' they also betray, in telling ways, the aggressivity that they screen. In a recent essay prompted by listening to holocaust testimony (Ball, 2003) Karyn Ball explores, from the perspective of feminist studies, the 'unconscious value of women's Holocaust testimony as an object of feminist inquiry. 'What would it mean', Ball goes on to ask, 'to view this testimony not only as a focus of feminist scholarship, but also as a voyeuristic venue of fantasy and repressed desire?' (Ibid., p22). Ball's essay then goes to respond bravely to her own question by examining the potential for voyeuristic and fetishistic pleasure that she discerned in her own responses to hearing the testimony of a woman Holocaust survivor:

> My imagination gags on these images, which seem at once to crystallise and seduce my sense of horror; it is nevertheless driven to return to them again and again. This compulsive repetition speaks against desensitisation by betraying a voyeuristic side to my attempts to assimilate the traumatic significance of the Holocaust through its imagery of death and destruction. (Ibid., p38)

That voyeurism is associated with aggressivity is a psychoanalytic truism. Voyeurism constitutes an attack at a distance, as it were, against a perceived threat, which is conceived of, in Freudian terms, as the threat of castration. If the aggressivity that subtends an identification with the knowingness and control of the one who listens to testimony is relatively easy to discern, the aggression at stake in the identification with victimhood is perhaps less evident. The adoption of the position of having been 'done to', of being the victim involves the location, or, in psychoanalytic terms, the displacement of all aggression into the other. Yet an identification solely with victimhood is, as Gillian Rose has so tellingly described it, an identification with the position of 'the ultimate predator' whose position is so utterly invincible that it precludes the requirement for an identification with the predation of others (Rose, 1998, p246).[19]

What are we to make of the 'screening' or disavowal of aggressivity by trauma theory? If psychoanalytic drive theory is right, and agressivity is one of the two primary forces that drive the psyche and through and by means of which all representations, meanings and relations are, in part, forged, we should hardly be surprised to find its traces here, even where what is ostensibly at stake is the theoretical elaboration of empathic witnessing of another's pain. Yet there are questions to be asked, perhaps, about the popularity of this theory, now, given its disavowal of and yet its address to the aggressive drives of readers and practitioners. Are there specific conditions that render the containment and acknowledgement of aggression within and by the self harder, such that it vents itself where it is least (and perhaps, therefore, from a psychoanalytic perspective, most) to be expected? To ask such questions is to ask not only whether specific historical conjunctures have their own particular affective character, but to question, also, whether specific theories are likely to be marked by that character.

A number of recent speculative psycho-social analyses of contemporary western society offer accounts that suggest where the origins of this other-oriented aggressivity may lie. One approach identifies a contemporary hysteria that results from a common inability to acknowledge ordinary human fallibility, depression, and rage and that leads, therefore, to an increase in other-directed aggressivity and fear (Showalter, 1997). Another set of approaches suggests that a contemporary difficulty identifying obvious social authority or threat leads to a break-down of super-ego re-inforcement and of the inability to contain aggression within the self (Craib, 1994; Salecl, 2004). In such circumstances, one appeal of trauma theory and therapy may lie in the clear distinctions that it constructs between benign authority and threat, and in the clear directions that it carves out, therefore, for the venting of aggression. Yet, as we have seen, aggressivity continues to circulate and reveal itself in ways that do not accord tidily with trauma theory's Manicheanism – it marks, that is, what appear to be empathetic listening and reading relations with sufferers as well with perpetrators. Psychoanalysis teaches us to expect this 'ordinary' waywardness of the unconscious but trauma theory's consolingly Manichean discourses have arguably emerged into public scholarly life at a time when such expectations are arguably particularly hard to countenance.

I have argued, then, that trauma theory is driven, at an unconscious level, by a certain aggressivity. This is an aggressivity which is domesticated by trauma theory itself. In locating trauma in a specific event and in the acts of locatable 'others' it wards off any acknowledgement of aggression's ubiquitous, unpredictable and unbiddable presence amongst all human beings. This may be a reality that is hard to acknowledge under the social conditions described by Showalter, Craib and Salecl.

Arguments concerning the affective character of epochs or conjunctures invite charges of generalisation and homogenisation. Specific case-studies of particular groups, domains and discourses would no doubt produce a far more nuanced and variegated map of the affective character of a conjuncture than these theories would allow. My argument is therefore of a far more limited scope. Trauma theory is explicitly concerned with the empathic witnessing of the unspeakable sufferings of others. It is an ethically driven theory that seeks to redeem those sufferings by bringing them to language and to the light.

But theory is never affect-free; thinking, that is, 'starts with drives' (Caldwell, 1995, p23). Judith Butler reminds us that morality and violence are inevitably linked since, according to Freud, the strength of conscience is nourished precisely by the aggression that it forbids (Butler, 1997, p70). But forbidden aggression leaves its marks on trauma theory, the explicit aims of which are woven through with unconscious drives. Trauma theory is a consequence both of acts of violence and aggression that it seeks to redeem, and of unconscious aggressivity that it unconsciously vents. The public salience of this theory cannot be understood without reference to both these aspects of the theory.

Notes

1 For an introduction to psychoanalytic film criticism see Lapsley and Westlake, 1988, pp67–104 and for an introduction to psychoanalytic literary criticism see Vice, 1996.
2 For accounts of what is meant by and included by the term 'trauma theory' see (Elsaesser, 2001; Leys, 2000; Radstone, 2000, esp. pp85–91)
3 As Alison Jagger reminds us, Plato's *Phaedrus* viewed the emotions 'as needing direction by reason ... the split between reason and emotion was not absolute, therefore, for the Greeks.' (Jagger, 1997, p188).
4 An emphasis on the place of binary oppositions such as these in the construction of woman is associated with feminisms of many hues, but most particularly with what has been termed 'new French feminism' (Marks and de Courtivron, 1981).
5 For an introduction to the work of Melanie Klein see Hinshelwood *et al.* (1999) and Mitchell (1986); for an introduction to DW Winnicott see Phillips (1988); Abram (1997).
6 See especially Nancy Chodorow's recent *The Power of Feelings* (Chodorow, 1999) which makes a strong case for a post-Kleinian, object-relations theory of the emotions.
7 André Green's acknowledgement of his debt to Winnicott notwithstanding.
8 See note 10 below.
9 For an introduction to the work of Melanie Klein see Robert Hinshelwood, *Introducing Melanie Klein* (Hinshelwood, 2006) and Robert Hinshelwood *Dictionary of Kleinian Thought* (Hinshelwood, 1988)
10 For a longer discussion of ego psychology see http://eseries.ipa.org.uk/ prev/newsletter/98–2/blum.htm
11 The term transference refers to that process in which qualities associated with figures associated with one's past – typically parents – are unconsciously transferred onto others in the present. For instance, one might respond to an adult in a position of authority in the present, as though they were one's father or mother.
12 Key texts include Felman and Laub's *Testimony* (Felman and Laub, 1992), Cathy Caruth's (ed.) *Trauma: Explorations in Memory* (Caruth, 1995), Cathy Caruth *Unclaimed Experience: Trauma Narrative and History* (Caruth, 1996). For an alternative view of trauma theory, including a trenchant critique of

Caruth's work, see Ruth Leys, *Trauma: A Genealogy* (Leys, 2000). Several journals have dedicated special issues or sections to trauma and testimony including *Cultural Values* (5, 1, 2001), *Screen* (42, 2, 2001) which includes a dossier edited by myself, *Screen* (44, 2, 2003) and *Paragraph* (forthcoming, 2007). The international conference on trauma (Manchester Metropolitan University, November 2005) testifies to ongoing interest in trauma theory.

13 Martha Minow is amongst those who, writing from a position outside trauma theory, has remarked on the possibility for such identifications: 'even more disturbing may be moments when listeners identify with bystanders and even with perpetrators (Minow, 1998, p74). Likewise, writing of Daniel Goldhagen's book *Hitler's Willing Executioners*, Nancy Wood quotes Liliane Kandel who argues that its descriptions of Holocaust atrocities 'permit a vicarious identification with the perpetrators' perverse pleasures – the book authorises each reader to put him/herself in the exact position of the executioner ... and yet virtuously deny that any such identification has taken place.' (Wood, 1999, p91) If historical accounts of atrocity offer the possibility for identification with perpetration, then the question of that possibility being offered through witnessing testimony, or through reading accounts or theories of such witnessing should also be countenanced.

14 The question of trauma theory's relation to what Nietzsche termed *resentiment* is too large to be taken up here, but deserves to be more fully debated. Wendy Brown summarises Nietzsche's description of resentiment in *Genealogy of Morals* in the following terms: 'It produces an affect (rage, righteousness) that overwhelms the hurt; it produces a culprit responsible for the hurt; it produces a site of revenge to displace the hurt (a place to inflict hurt as the sufferer has been hurt). Together these operations both ameliorate and externalise what is otherwise unendurable (Brown, 1995, p68). 'Starkly accountable yet dramatically impotent' she goes on, 'the late modern liberal subject quite literally seethes with resentiment.' (Ibid., p69)

15 Caroline Garland's object relations approach to trauma, for instance, argues that rage has an important function for the survivor of trauma: 'The broken down fragments of the ego can reorganise themselves around a convincing state of rage, and give some semblance of coherence to a very damaged personality'. (Garland, 2002, pp210–11)

16 For an alternative commentary on Laub's account of this woman's Auschwitz testimony that emphasises the distinctions Laub makes between historical and emotional knowledge, see Walker (2001).

17 See Hodgkin and Radstone (2003), pp97–103.

18 My previous analysis to which I refer here was informed by Ian Craib's illuminating book *The Importance of Disappointment* (Craib, 1994).

19 For a slightly longer discussion of this point see Radstone, 2001, p66.

References

Abram J, 1997. *The Language of Winnicott: A Dictionary and Guide to Understanding his Work*. London: Karnac Books

Antze P and Lambek M (eds), 1996. 'Introduction: Forecasting Memory' in *Tense Past: Cultural Essays in Trauma and Memory*. New York and London: Routledge

Antze P, 2003. 'The Other Inside: Memory as Metaphor in Psychoanalysis' in S Radstone and K Hodgkin (eds), *Regimes of Memory*. London and New York: Routledge

Ball K, 2003. 'Unspeakable differences, obscene pleasures: The holocaust as an object of desire'. *Women in German Yearbook* 19

Brown W, 1995. *States of Injury: Power and Freedom in Late Modernity*. Princeton: Princeton University Press

Butler J, 1997. *The Psychic Life of Power*. Stanford: Stanford University Press

Caldwell L, 1995. 'Interview with André Green'. *New Formations* 26, Autumn, 15–35

Caruth C, ed., 1995. *Trauma: Explorations in Memory*. Baltimore: Johns Hopkins University Press

Caruth C, 1996. *Unclaimed Experience: Trauma, Narrative and History*. Baltimore: Johns Hopkins University Press

Chodorow N, 1999. *The Power of Feelings*. New Haven and London: Yale University Press

Craib I, 1994. *The Importance of Disappointment*. London: Routledge

Elsaesser T, 2001. 'Postmodernism as Mourning Work'. *Screen* 42: 2, Summer, 193–201

Felman S and Laub D, 1992. *Testimony: Crises of Witnessing in Literature, Psychoanalysis and History*. New York and London: Routledge

Friedlander S (ed.), 1992. *Probing the Limits of Representation*. Cambridge MA: Harvard University Press

Freud S, 2001 [1910]. '"Wild" Psychoanalysis' *The Standard Edition of the Complete Psychological Works of Sigmund Freud*, vol. 12. London: Vintage, 219–27

Garland C, 2002. 'Action, Identification and Thought in Post-traumatic States', in C Garland, ed., *Understanding Trauma: A Psychoanalytic Approach* (2nd enlarged edition). London: Duckworth

Green A, 1999 [1973]. *The Fabric of Affect in the Psychoanalytic Discourse*. London and New York: Routledge

Herman J, 1992. *Trauma and Recovery*. New York: Basic Books

Hinshelwood R, 1988. *A Dictionary of Kleinian Thought*, London: Free Association Books

Hinshelwood R, Robinson S and Zarate O, ed., Richard Appignanesi, 1999. *Introducing Melanie Klein*. Duxford: Icon

Hinshelwood R, 2006. *Introducing Melanie Klein*. Cambridge: Icon Books

Hodgkin K and Radstone S, 2003. 'Remembering suffering: trauma and history: Introduction', in K Hodgkin and S Radstone, eds, *Contested Pasts: The Politics of Memory*. New York and London: Routledge

Jagger A, 1997 [1989]. 'Love and Knowledge: Emotion in Feminist Epistemology', in S Kemp and J Squires, eds, *Feminisms*. Oxford and New York: Oxford University Press, orginally published in *Inquiry* 32, 1989, 151–72

Kuhn A, 1994 [1982]. *Women's Pictures: Feminism and Cinema*. London and New York: Verso

Lapsley R and Westlake M, 1988. *Film Theory, An Introduction*. Manchester: Manchester University Press

Leys R, 2000. *Trauma: A Genealogy*. Chicago: University of Chicago Press

Lloyd G, 1984. *The Man of Reason: Male and Female in Western Philosophy*. Minneapolis: Minnesota University Press

Marks E and de Courtivron I, eds, 1981. *New French Feminisms*. Brighton: Harvester

Minow M, 1998. *Between Vengeance and Forgiveness*. Boston: Beacon Press

Mitchell J, 1986. *The Selected Melanie Klein*. Harmondsworth: Penguin

Music G, 2001. *Affect and Emotion*. Cambridge: Icon Books

Phillips A, 1988. *Winnicott*. London: Fontana

Phillips A, 2003. 'The truth, the whole truth', review of WG Sebald, *On The Natural History of Destruction*, *Observer* review section, 17

Radstone S, 2000. 'Screening Trauma: *Forrest Gump*, Film and Memory' in S Radstone, ed., *Memory and Methodology*. Oxford and New York: Berg, 79–107

Radstone S, 2001. 'Social Bonds and Psychical Order: Testimonies'. *Cultural Values* vol. 5 no. 1 January, 59–78

Radstone S, 2001a. 'Trauma and Screen Studies: opening the debate'. *Screen* vol. 42, no 2, Summer, pp188–93

Radstone S, forthcoming. 'Trauma theory: contexts, politics, ethics'. *Paragraph*

Rose G, 1998. 'Beginnings of the day: Fascism and representation' in B Cheyette and L Marcus, eds, *Modernity, Culture and 'The Jew'*. Cambridge: Polity

Salecl R, 2004. *On Anxiety*. London and New York: Routledge

Showalter E, 1997. *Hystories: Hysterical Epidemics and Modern Media*. New York: Columbia University Press

Vice S, ed., 1996. *Psychoanalytic Criticism, A Reader*. Cambridge: Polity

Walker J, 2001. 'Trauma cinema: false memories and true experience'. *Screen* vol. 42, no. 2, Summer, 211–16

Wood N, 1998. 'The victim's resentments', in B Cheyette and L Marcus, eds, *Modernity, Culture and 'The Jew'*. Cambridge: Polity

Wood N, 1999. *Vectors of Memory: Legacies of Trauma in Postwar Europe*. New York and Oxford: Berg

9
Feeling Entitled: HIV, Entitlement Feelings and Citizenship

Corinne Squire

Introduction: public emotions, entitlement and HIV

We live with a sense of being continually immersed in, even assailed by, publically performed emotions. Popular commentators and social theorists compete in dating this tendency to a variety of beginnings – enlightenment individualism; liberal humanism; discourses of the self in the late nineteenth century and onward; postwar mass mediatising of the emotions; the postmodern relativising of representation; the late-modern breakdown in social and political organisation or the globalising of emotional and other economies (Baudrillard, 1995; Bauman, 2000; Craib, 1994; Furedi, 2004; Giddens, 1991; Himmelfarb, 1996; Lasch, 1991; Lyotard, 1984; MacIntyre, 1984). These explanatory trajectories often value their endpoint negatively, as the banalisation and even the destruction of the public realm; or occasionally, positively, as indicating an expansion, even a democratisation, of culture. In this chapter, I want to look not at the value of the public culture of feelings or where it comes from, but at the social consequences of one particular public feeling, that of entitlement, when it is expressed in public and quasi-public contexts by or on behalf of a particular social group: people in the UK who define themselves as HIV positive.[1] I am going to argue that this public feeling does indeed have 'positive' consequences: it tends to promote a kind of HIV citizenship within a frame of social inclusion and at times, social justice.[2] I am also going to suggest that these consequences are specific to the feeling, the group that feels it, and the context in which it is felt. One can, indeed, see the limits of HIV entitlement's socially 'good' consequences being tested in some of the representations discussed here, which seem to ask for something less or different from social inclusion, cohesion and justice, or which fundamentally break with such notions by demanding everything, or nothing. I shall suggest, therefore, that accounts of public emotions should occupy themselves first with the particularity of such emotions, their objects and subjects, and the ways in which we define their 'effects'. Public articulations of for instance 'anxiety' or 'fear' are never so homologous with their individual versions, that we can apply individual theories of them. Lack of attention to such particularity can lead to 'sociologies' of emotions that are sociological only in name, based on generalising theories of individual emotions.

First, we need to examine entitlement as a feeling. Is an individual who feels 'entitled' really expressing an emotion, rather than simply staking a claim to certain goods or rights? I would suggest that expressing your entitlement *feelings* is at present a required medium for many entitlement claims, particularly those based on membership of socially disempowered groups. We live in social and historical conditions where 'subjects' have increasingly become defined as psychological beings who make moral and political judgements on the basis of individualised emotions (MacIntyre, 1984; Rose, 1996; see also Squire, 2000). Representations of emotions thus convey political and ethical arguments as well as personal opinions. Interior monologues, interpersonal communications and public statements elide with each other; personal preferences become indices of right and wrong. This condition, which MacIntyre (1984, pp11–12, 1989, 1991) calls emotivism, governs resistant and marginal articulations of entitlement, as much as entitlement representations within the mainstream. For MacIntyre, 'emotivism' unacceptably simplifies and constrains moral, political and social judgements. However, I shall argue that in the case of HIV entitlement, there are some *emotionalised*, if not emotivist, (Squire, 2000) public articulations, signifying emotionality in specific and complex ways, that work to include the social realities of HIV within the space of citizenship.

Entitlement is a particularly interesting 'emotion' to examine: strongly felt and represented as such, yet also connoting discourses and practices, for instance in law, that are not necessarily emotion-laden, but whose increasing entanglement with affect often makes them strong candidates for MacIntyre's 'emotivism' category. The term 'entitlement' works both to signify a personal sense of ownership, something which you claim in your own name and about which you can say, 'I feel entitled to it'; and to indicate a legitimate, named or titled place in the social body, the synecdoche for which is 'entitlement' in its older sense: a property that is attained at adulthood or on meeting other citizenship conditions. When you express a feeling of 'entitle-ment', it is both a claim on objects, and, indirectly, a claim to belong to and be included in the group to whom those objects accrue – a group that may vary in type from family, work, or community, to local, national, or international citizenship. Entitlement is a concept that morphs interestingly between 'psychological' and 'social' fields, and in the process plays out the co-construction of these fields.

Entitlement also has considerable contemporary political currency. It was used in early UK government discourse on identity documents or 'entitlement cards', which were intended to combat crime, access benefits and services and – in a move that clearly emotionalised citi-zenship – signify as well as prove 'identity'. Entitlement cards' useful-ness should be judged, then-Home Secretary David Blunkett suggested, both on their daily usefulness for people, and as means of 'affirming their identity' – a formulation that foregrounded 'identity's' conflation of emotionalised individuality with legal rights. The term 'entitlement' also appears in charters, codes of practice and agree-ments that are formulated emotionally, as statements of personal expectations and responsibilities, in public, public and voluntary sectors – for example, in the signed commitments by teachers, parents and children that make up 'home-school agreements'. In popular discourse, too, 'being' or 'feeling' entitled is a common phrase, indicating a personalised claim to specific rights that does not need further justification. Entitlement is thus a term that fits closely with contemporary representations of social and political relations as emotional states. It is a lesson in the disputed significance of such emotionalised representations.

As a feeling, entitlement that does not belong to the menu of primary or secondary emotions drawn up by evolutionary, cognitive and social psychologists, or to the categories used by sociologists inter-ested in the emotional correlates of social formations. Nor is it a widely acknowledged everyday emotion, like 'anger' or 'depression'. It is, rather, one of many feelings – probably the majority – that seem to have a variable existence historically and socially. This variability points us towards the historical and social specificity, and the constitu-tion in and through representation, of many, perhaps all, 'emotions', which are not, on that account, the less strongly held. While what we commonly call emotion clearly has a level of embodied reality, this chapter takes a 'constructionist' position that assumes little particular-ity in physiological emotional arousal. Instead, it explores the social shape of one contemporary form of emotionality – entitlement –

through some of its symbolic articulations – as Malik (2000) and Schweder (1991) for example do for other emotional constellations. The approach is also congruent with Ahmed's (2004a, b) description of feelings as generated by an economy of movement between signifiers which often becomes 'sticky' in a fetishistic way. However, this chapter suggests that points of affective and symbolic fixity can sometimes undo other such fixities. In this case, the insistence of HIV entitlement feelings can mobilise previously-entrenched and exclusionary representations of citizenship.

Public articulations of 'feeling entitled' are particularly interesting because such representations often seem closely linked to social change. To articulate a feeling of entitlement is not the same as obtaining that entitlement or even making your claim heard. But the process of making such representations is often an important step in pursuing an entitlement claim; that pursuit will not happen if the claim remains implicit and unrepresented.[3] Such a representation, couched in emotionalised terms, may at least contribute towards social inclusion, viewed within a frame not simply of economic participation or community membership but of citizenship and social justice (Lister, 2000). Even if the representation seems ineffective, it may establish a kind of dissident (Sparks in Lister, 2000) or equivalent (Mouffe, 1993, p84) citizenship – an identification that does not obliterate difference – for those who make it.

The representation of entitlement feelings by people who are HIV positive has a specially strong potential to work as 'emotional capital' (Williams, 1998), to perform social inclusion and to claim citizenship rights. HIV is a condition with a high likelihood of fatality, strong associations with transgressive behaviours especially of a sexualised kind, and materially disempowering effects on health, employment and social relations. People who are HIV positive are thus susceptible to social exclusion and sometimes to the reduction or deprivation of their citizenship rights.

HIV does, however, carry emotional freight besides that of entitlement or its absence. It confronts you with the sadness of a potentially curtailed life; possible losses of relationships, children, work and sexuality; fear of illness and death; anger, shame, uncertainty; and also, at least in the west, with some pleasures and hopes associated with coming to terms with the condition and living relatively healthily with it, perhaps for many years (Watney, 2000). HIV entitlement 'feelings' are themselves variable, shaped by changing medical expertise about the condition, shifting epidemiological patterns, conflicting entitlement claims from other interest groups, people with HIV's multiple identifications, social stigma, and the general difficulties of representing sexuality and death. Nevertheless, I want to argue that entitlement feelings have played and continue to play a particularly significant role in public representations of HIV, because they contest social exclusion more directly than other forms of public emotionality around this condition.

Some of the most iconic public representations of HIV clearly demonstrate this convergence of emotionality and entitlement claims. In the US, at the height of the epidemic, Silence=Death, the ACT UP (AIDS Coalition to Unleash Power) slogan emblazoned on stickers, flyposted on medial and religious institutions and shouted in the streets, was an early example of HIV activism's loud and affect-laden insistence on the public, citizenly place to which HIV positive people were entitled. The 'die-ins' staged by ACT UP in New York City certainly represented grief, rage and fear, but their most immediate effect was to reverse HIV's social invisibility and exclusion through people's insistence on being heard and seen as HIV positive citizens in public spaces. Similarly, the Names Project, the quilt memorialising those who have died from AIDS, undid the silence of funeral and obituary representations of AIDS as 'leukaemia' or 'a long illness,' drawing on a craft tradition associated both with American 'pioneers' and with resistance to slavery, to inscribe citizens with HIV into the national fabric. Rose and Novas (2004) cite such actions to exemplify new modes of biological citizenship in which subjects negotiate with regulatory authorities around the biological rights that constitute their subjecthood. As Foucault himself described, the techniques of 'anatamo- and bio-politics' (1979, p141) developed in the eighteenth century, now operate within a set of regulatory apparatuses where issues of 'life', rather than law, are the objects of political struggle (1979, pp141–5). HIV 'citizenship' provides pertinent instances of this shift.

HIV acts, then, as a limit case of the social inscription of entitlement feelings, which are in its case intensely 'emotional' but also clearly 'political'. In the overdeveloped world, to live with HIV is to live with powerful emotions, biological uncertainty and social exclusion, while at the same time negotiating a range of services, ranging from traditional and alternative medicine through dedicated insurance provision, to counselling, home help and befriending. Living with HIV in this context also means living, not just with people 'like' you but with people who may be, aside from their HIV status, very unlike you. In the HIV 'nation' of clinics, support groups, drop-in centres and crèches, you meet people of different genders, sexualities, ages, socio-economic groups, ethnic and national backgrounds, health and HIV statuses. You will also encounter a transnational HIV world in which there are even more striking differences – notably, at present, in access to HIV treatment. In the HIV 'nation' and 'world', therefore, you have to live alongside differences that you recognise and respect but do not always understand. Such convergences and confrontations are, for writers such as Stanley Aronovitz (1995), Simon Watney (1994, 2000) and Jeffrey Weeks (1995), producing new notions of entitlement and new forms of social inclusion and citizenship, embodied in the activism of, for instance, ACT UP and the Names Project, and more recently, TASO in Uganda, South Africa's Treatment Action Campaign, and their diasporas of support. It is hard to imagine entitlement feelings more wedded to public expression and effectiveness than the ones involved in these movements.

HIV entitlement in mainstream and HIV institutions

I am going to look briefly at current representations of HIV entitlement, and then in more detail at how 'feeling entitled' was addressed in two recent HIV awareness campaigns, and in the talk of people with HIV in research interviews.

58300 people are living with HIV in the UK, of whom a third do not know their status.[4] Death rates from AIDS have fallen to around 450 a year, a quarter the rate in 1995, after which relatively effective drug therapies became available through the NHS. However, new diagnosis rates have also been rising, up from 3800 in 2000 to 7300 in 2004. Of those newly diagnosed, roughly two-thirds were infected heterosexually, mostly outside the UK, predominantly in Africa, mainly women; around one-third are men infected through sex with other men. Given such changing rates and demographics, it is perhaps not surprising that representations of HIV entitlement are shifting.

After considerable discrimination and political neglect early in the epidemic, UK citizens living with HIV are now entitled to legal protection from discrimination; free medical and social services; and rights under disability legislation. There is a raft of policy and practice guidelines operating in the fields of employment, education, health, housing and insurance. And there is a popular-cultural commitment to normalising western HIV as a chronic illness – the Mark Fowler character's longstanding role in the TV soap *EastEnders* was an obvious example – that is a dramatic advance on earlier media pathologisations. Others include the early 1990s *Observer* columns and subsequent book *PWA* by Oscar Moore; the film, drama and art work of Derek Jarman, Neil Bartlett and – more controversially – Gilbert and George; the high UK profile of the Elton John AIDS Foundation – though its work is now concentrated in the developing world – and the yearly Crusaid 'Walk For Life'. At times, then, HIV entitlement achieves both policy presence, and a broadly sympathetic popular emotional significance. This entitlement is specific to the condition, yet also part of the general, socially inclusive field of citizenly entitlement, where both 'feeling' entitled and obtaining practical entitlements are enabled. Non-HIV positive citizens are positioned in a relation of equivalence (Mouffe, 1993), understanding the HIV positive as citizens 'like' them, yet with some particularities – for instance, entitlements to specific medical and social service care, legal protection, and confidentiality and acceptance in interpersonal and social relationships.

However, the present framework of HIV entitlement has a low political and cultural profile compared to, for example, the early 1990s, and is contested. Following late-1990s treatment success and death rate declines, HIV services were cut and consolidated, targeted towards 'men who have sex with men', 'young' gay men[5] and people of recent African origin living in the UK. People living with HIV and other infectious diseases can now face prosecution if they knowingly pass on the illness to others, as with the case of HIV positive Mohammed Dica, eventually sentenced to four and a half years on the grounds of 'biological' grievous bodily harm caused by 'reckless' transmission.[6] Tabloid representations of this case revisited earlier media polarisations between the HIV guilty and innocent, counterposing the 'AIDS assassin', a Somali 'immigrant', to his 'victims', respectable women, UK citizens and mothers. In the absence of other strong contemporary discourses of HIV entitlement, these representations reinforced a developing exclusionary cultural trope of a 'non-entitled' set of HIV positive people in the UK, often presented as a subset of 'asylum seekers', who are to be feared, disliked and excluded. This representation is coming to occupy a distinct political, cultural and emotional space between two other HIV representations: the first, of developed-world HIV as a managed 'post-AIDS' condition that turns those living with the virus into sympathetic people 'just like us', working, non-illegal drug using (even if chemically maintained) and monogamous (whatever their sexuality); and the second, of developing-world HIV, fatal, tragic, inspiring sorrow and pity – but, crucially, somewhere else.[7] Whether by pathologising, normalising or exoticising, these representations all remove HIV from the space of emotional and political entitlement that could confer equivalent citizenship.

What of entitlement representations within the HIV sector? This sector's voluntary organisations have, as we have seen, a strong history of making highly emotionalised entitlement claims that, though sometimes criticised for lightweight, 'MTV' activism, have had powerful effects on social inclusion (Boffin and Gupta, 1991; Crimp, 1989; Crimp and Ralston, 1990; Oppenheimer and Reckitt, 1997; Patton, 1991, 2002; Watney, 1994, 2000; Weeks, 1995). In the US and Europe, HIV service organisations started by gay men and lesbians, mounted effective claims for HIV positive people's social inclusion through non-discrimination and treatment rights. Those organisations' entitlement claims shifted with the epidemic, now including the right to refuse treatment or to use alternative treatments, and attention to side-effects; specific service provision for gay men, women, drug users, hemophiliacs, people of African origin, youth, the newly and long-term diagnosed; targetted, local and non-acute services; support for people with HIV who return to work and for those who cannot; opposition to stigma and discrimination; rights for what is increasingly perceived as a poor, usually non-citizen HIV underclass; and a re-establishment of education projects aimed at the general population.

As with mainstream representations, the HIV sector does not provide a single agreed picture of feeling HIV-entitled, but continually debates HIV entitlement's political and personal boundaries. In relation to the Dica case, some argued that the judgement criminalised all people with HIV, and that HIV prevention is the responsibility of the HIV negative as much as the HIV positive. Others saw the judgement as a reasonable attribution of responsibility in a situation of willed infantilism, 'knowing and lying, knowing and *not caring*'.[8] Across such debates, however, the institutional and emotional entitlements of an equivalent, 'normal' yet distinctly HIV positive citizen are consistently asserted. There seem, though, to be more qualifications of such assertions now in this sector than previously, partly because of medical and demographic shifts in the epidemic, partly because the sector has in organisational terms 'grown up' – become more managed, and 'professional'. We might expect, then, that the emotionalised demands for social inclusion made by HIV-sector representations will be weaker than those expressed earlier in the epidemic, although that might not be true of entitlement representations produced by people with HIV themselves.

I want to examine two recent representations of 'feeling entitled' in the HIV sector, before going on to examine some accounts of 'feeling entitled' produced by HIV positive people.

Representing entitlement feelings indirectly: 'Are *you* HIV prejudiced?'

Throughout 2003, the National AIDS Trust, the UK's largest HIV policy and advocacy organisation, ran an 'Are *you* HIV prejudiced?' campaign.[9] The campaign, funded by the Department of Health and Levi-Strauss, was directed at government and council departments, HIV organisations, students and popular media. It aimed to support the formal and emotional entitlements of HIV positive people, and pursued this by dealing in emotions as well as facts. Its 'information pack' for instance included not only 'factsheets' on stigma, discrimination and their effects on different groups affected by HIV, what can be done to reduce stigma and discrimination and what prejudice is; but also vignettes of HIV positive people's experiences of stigma and discrimination and an invitation to contribute more; an 'are you HIV prejudiced?' quiz; a participatory workshop guide and suggestions for how you yourself can help reduce stigma and discrimination.[10]

The campaign had wide media and organisational reach, and made a strong attempt to inscribe HIV entitlement on grounds of general citizenship, both political and emotional, that nevertheless left space for the distinct and diverse nature of 'living with HIV'. Its confrontational title invoked not just the shaming possibility of prejudice about HIV – a kind of twin to HIV stigma that brings people of HIV negative or unknown status into the same frame as people who are HIV positive – but also, subtextually, the possibility of another, status-based affinity. For the question almost inevitably brings up another uncertainty: 'Are *you* HIV positive?' The poster and website images of well-looking people of varying ages and ethnicities, looking out at the viewers, connoting interpersonal, subject-to-subject connection through naturalistic, individualised photo-portraiture, exploit these ambiguities. Are these people HIV prejudiced or not, HIV positive or not, and would different answers make us feel differently about them? Since no-one looks ill and there is no other related content, these ambiguities remain unresolvable.

ARE YOU HIV PREJUDICED?

REGISTER FOR NEWS   EMAIL A FRIEND TELEPHONE HELPLINES   CONTACT US   SITEMAP

BY ENDING IGNORANCE, WE'LL END PREJUDICE
Find out the facts about HIV

THE IMPACT OF HIV/AIDS STIGMA AND DISCRIMINATION
Read and download our stigma and discrimination fact sheets.

TRUE STORIES
Read about people's experiences of HIV discrimination.

THE CAMPAIGN
Click here to listen to our tv and radio ads and view the other campaign materials

The campaign's triple assault on prejudice through factsheet reason and discussion, the images and stories of HIV positive people's reported experience, and its call for workshops and a consideration of 'what you can do', calls up spaces of thought, feeling and action around HIV that associate those of negative or unknown status with the HIV positive. Nevertheless we might note the distinction such a campaign now draws between an audience assumed to be HIV negative or of unknown status, feeling and thinking HIV entitlement by monitoring and correcting its own 'prejudice'; and the declaredly HIV positive, whose 'feeling entitled' is offered up through brief personal stories 'told' about entitlements refused or gained, situated halfway through the website and resource pack.[11]

Here, then, HIV entitlement discourse demands social inclusion by focusing on the democratic citizenship of the non-HIV positive and bracketing off, to some degree, people who are HIV positive themselves. The effects of what I am calling emotionalism, the emotional weighting of representations, are therefore weakened by an indirect and in the case of the stories and portraits – abbreviated, 'emotivist' voice. This is not to indict the campaign, which may have fulfilled its remit well, but rather to mark the limited address, to the non-HIV positive, and the consequent limits to social inclusion and citizenship, within which many 'public' expressions of 'feeling entitled' in relation to HIV now operate.

Distancing entitlement feelings: 'HIV/AIDS/POVERTY/ SKINT/NO MONEY'

A year on, and the organisation Crusaid marked World AIDS Day 2003 with a new poster campaign on the London Underground, addressing HIV and poverty. Three near-monochrome images showed a white bearded man at the bottom of the frame, a large metallic spindryer in the background; a black man huddled to the side and bottom of the image, in a blurry white empty space; and a white baby, eyes closed, lying across the bottom of the picture, with a woman cradling it against her torso. The figures are looking to the side or down, not at the camera and viewers. Each poster carries short descriptive phrases about the person, in capitalised white typewriter text,[12] and information about Crusaid's report on HIV and poverty in the UK.

As with the National AIDS Trust campaign, these are images that engage their viewers in interpersonal emotionality. They are life-size pictures, displayed at eye level in tube stations. Yet their textual and imagic austerity, recalling conventional 'charity advertising', may shape this emotionality into pathos. The texts, with the terseness and shape of medical or social service notes, indicate the abjection as well as the otherness of HIV. Perhaps the picture of mother and baby, which encompasses the whole poster and is softer in tone and contours, works more inclusively, against the differentiating hardness of the words, and despite the anonymized, abstracted 'mother' image. In the context of shifting demographics, welfare provision and political discourse around HIV, these ads were said to picture an HIV underclass (Cairns, 2004)[13] of 'victims', shorn of entitlement and reclaiming it mutely, presented for 'us', the HIV negative, to learn about; sympathise with; dread, perhaps; give to, certainly, and thus restore to their institutional and emotional entitlements.[14]

Again, I am not criticising Crusaid's campaign, which may have been highly effective for the organisation's objective: raising money for people with HIV who need help. Its Chief Executive argued that to accuse the images of victimology, is to heighten the stigma and discrimination with which positive people still live (http://www.ukcoalition.org/discuss/messages/62/135.html?1085683295, accessed December 2005). The images remain, however, indications of the present muted state of public HIV entitlement claims. Here again, a claim is made for HIV entitlement in an 'emotivist' visual and verbal vocabulary that also marginalises that entitlement – in this case, by calling for the 'inclusion' of HIV positive subjects while also partly exiling them within the space of citizenship by representing them through passivity, silence and abjection.

Representing HIV entitlement feelings' complexity

If the inclusive effects of current public representations of HIV entitle-ment are limited, what of people with HIV's own representations? I want to look now at a quasi-public instance of these representations: HIV positive people's talk about feeling or being entitled, in research interviews about HIV support conducted since 1993. Research inter-views can of course contain many kinds of representation. But with the 'support' topic, HIV positive people get to speak about a highly emotion-laden personal and public issue as experts, they are assured confidentiality and anonymity, and they are aware of having a poten-tial academic, policy, and HIV-affected audience for what they say. This situation generates talk that is both highly politicised and highly personal; that represents speakers as HIV positive, members of other social groups, and general citizens; and that offers indications of how 'feeling HIV entitled' can work in everyday representations to construct an inclusive though highly differentiated social world.

I want to examine the transitive nature of 'being/feeling entitled' in these representations, that is, the specificity of who feels entitled to what, and how parameters of feeling HIV-entitled overlap with repre-sentations of entitlement based on for instance drug use, sexuality, age, class, gender, and non-British national origin. I also want to look at the occasionally intransitive nature of representations of feeling HIV-entitled to everything – or nothing. I'll be suggesting that these repre-sentations of HIV entitlement set up a world characterised by what I'll call neighbourliness, a form of elective and effective, but also condi-tional and pragmatic entitlement that criss-cross nations, cities and local communities – a minimal, everyday version of the new political citizenships identified early by Aronowitz (1995), Watney (1994) and Weeks (1995) in the HIV-affected world and described more generally by Mouffe (1993) as equivalent citizenship.

The interviews I am writing about were conducted between 1993 and 2002 with 55 people affected or infected by HIV, most of whom were interviewed two or more times (Squire, 1997, 1999). The interviews were semistructured, and addressed expectations of support, and experiences of it.[15] Interviewees in the study all seemed familiar with the term 'support', and used it to mean practical, informational, social and emotional help. They formulated their relation to support very frequently in terms of what they felt entitled to.

I shall discuss first the provisional entitlements that interviewees talked about, in which entitlement was calibrated, so that they felt or did not feel entitled to some things and not to others.

Feeling lucky

A common term in these calibrations was 'feeling lucky', a phrase used to mean not an internal quality of 'luck', but a positively judged and felt relation to HIV entitlement. Interviewees often said they felt lucky, even in conditions that looked distinctly unfortunate. They felt lucky because they knew their status, were well, *felt* well, had access to drugs, had a drug regime that worked for them, or had support from partners, families and friends. Sometimes they were 'lucky' because they had good relationships with their doctors, social workers or voluntary organisations; because they had savings, a pension or an employer that understood HIV issues; because they were a man rather than a woman with HIV, a white European rather than an African migrant, a parent, or a non-parent. For some, HIV itself was a form of luck, spurring them to give up drugs, become more interested in spirituality, or really think about how they wanted to live. Chris, a white man in his sixties, for instance, living with HIV for over 20 years, said,

> To me, it's a blessing in disguise...I'm lucky to be HIV (positive), because I'm in these circumstances where I had a working career, I would have retired, and I would probably have been like any other old cabbage, where now, I've got the urge to live ... it's the learning and the seeing, and the finding out of different things.

This sense of feeling lucky, feeling that entitlements had been met or even superceded, could be interpreted as a conventional response bias towards optimism and satisfaction, however incongruous in the HIV context, or an unconscious identification with pathologising mainstream discourses of HIV, or an expiation of survivor guilt. However, many interviewees commented on the incongruity explicitly, fully aware of the irony of feeling HIV-related 'luck', and all of them measured out such luck against particular criteria, rather than swooning gratefully under the generalised weight of it. They told stories of feeling luckier than specific others because they were entitled to specific services those others did not get. They were luckier than those who had died – but even this was represented as a provisional luck, based on not yet having a difficult-to-treat condition or encountering drug resistance or problematic side-effects, and still having good quality of life. Chris for instance prefaced his story with a list of less 'lucky' HIV positive people:

> (They) are less fortunate than me, they don't have a pension or home, they're struggling ... and now they're faced with living a long time without a good income.

Later he suggested that given resource shortages, treatment should be available to others, not him:

> We're talking about a lot of money, at least £10,000 a year, and I think that I don't want to be wasting that amount of money on me at my age, when that money could be helping a child with HIV ... a younger person.

'Feeling lucky' was also articulated within broader frames of citizenly entitlement. Urwin, a young white man who contracted HIV around six months before the interview and was currently recovering from illness, praised his local support organisation and noted his luck in having it available to him, but also specified the time limits to which that luck could extend without him feeling overentitled:

> ... they're very friendly ... this is not going to be my last stopping point or anything like that, I mean it's just an introduction to sort of like the lifestyle, you make a few friends you know, it's local for me as well you know I can walk, twenty minutes, some people don't have that kind of privilege um but it is, it's kind of a refuge, like shelter for when you're going through problems and rough times.

Charles, a recent African migrant in his thirties whose asylum case was pending, located his 'luck' in his good health and treatment access, and restricted his further entitlement to times of future illness within a frame of citizenly autonomy and non-dependency:

> If I stay strong, which is what I am, I don't think there's much I will need from outside ... I will try to work on my own to get what I want without anything from the outside, I won't go for welfare unless I was weak and couldn't work on my own.

Many interviewees throughout the study also represented 'feeling lucky' within a discourse of citizenly responsibility, feeling impelled to 'give back' for the luck from which they had benefited, particularly within the voluntary sector. As Ursula, a white woman HIV positive for over a decade, put it,

> (The HIV service organisation) say(s), 'You've done enough,' but to me it's about thanking them, I don't believe I would be here without their support, they've done a lot for me and I don't think I've paid back enough yet.

In interviews after 1996, the relative success of new 'highly active' or 'combination' antiretroviral treatments, intensified transnational analyses of luck. Feelings of 'luck' were qualified not only by the recognised provisionality of treatment success, but also by frequent representations of the drugs' inaccessibility outside the developed world, and by increasing diasporic and activist connections between the UK and the wider HIV 'world' in which interviewees lived.

'Luck' is thus in these interviewees' representations a transitive feeling that assesses entitlement, who is entitled to what, rather than an objectless internal attribution. It gives entitlement an explicit textual object, something specific which is due to the subject. This specificity means that interviewees have complex and disputed relationships to 'entitlement' which they are always evaluating. The relationships are emotionalised, morally and publically freighted with emotion, but here emotionalism does not rely on the simplified 'emotivist' lexicons of negative and positive HIV status and feeling purveyed in the media representations discussed earlier. Instead, emotionalism produces shifting pictures of the terrain of citizenship and interviewees' place within it: included, but nevertheless differentiated from those without HIV, and from many other people with HIV also.

Feeling disadvantaged

The potential of representations of 'feeling lucky' to articulate both complex entitlements and an analysis of HIV citizenship, was borne out by interviewees' parallel emotionalised 'complaint' discourse about 'feeling disadvantaged', which specified their failures to receive entitlements. In the 1997 and 2001 interviews, many participants noted declining and negative media coverage, and strongly resented social services giving them no or reduced help, despite symptoms, because they were working or healthier, or due to general cutbacks. As Teresa, a young woman of African origin, said,

> It was awful when they said I don't need (the social worker), they stopped the service ... I used to have home help and things, yes, which I don't have any more ... I used to get help (with the children) but then it all stopped. ... they thought I didn't need it due to my health improving. I could manage alright, which is not so bad. But ... There are some days when you really don't need to get up to anything you feel tired and with the drug side effects, sometimes you have a drop ... and your feet is all aching.

Interviewees in all years reported instances of social or medical discrimination ranging from family members or strangers physically attacking them, to doctors doing HIV tests without consent, underestimating the significance of drug side-effects, and generally neglecting the HIV patient voice. Morag, a white woman, HIV positive for many years, said of her doctor,

> My quality of life doesn't mean anything to him, he just wants my T cells up and viral load down and he doesn't really care that I have a rash, and it's very attractive isn't it?. He just says, 'what's your choices, what's your options, it's a rash. Or your T cells disappear.' He's not being horrible, it's a fact of life isn't it? But...I don't think that many of them take (the side effects) on, if you're going to dig a bit deeper, you know?/mm/It's like 'we'll cross that bridge when we come to it.' I think, the first sign of a hump and these pills are down the toilet, what can he say to that? But I mean would you want a hump and big tits and no, no backside? It's horrendous.

Many interviewees also criticised HIV services they felt excluded them because they were oriented towards groups to which they did not

belong: gay men; women; African people; people with or without children; people who were ill or well; people who were or weren't working;
the newly diagnosed or long-term survivors; people for whom antiretroviral combination therapy works, or doesn't; the middle class. As
Ursula put it, considering HIV organisations' address to women,

> Our needs are not the same as gay men. You and we're all what I've
> said right from the very very beginning we're all different we've all
> got different needs erm and we should be treated differently but
> sometimes you know you tend to be all clumped together and then
> they put labels on you.

As with 'feeling lucky', emotionalised representations of feeling disadvantaged therefore situated interviewees within a specific but contested nexus of who was entitled to what. They allowed interviewees
to claim the kind of citizenly entitlements that anyone, HIV positive
or not, should get, though differentiating these claims by HIV status
and by other factors. Teresa is asking for some social service help,
though not as much as previously; Morag is asking for a negotiated, if
imperfect, doctor-patient relationship; Ursula is arguing that some
but not all HIV needs are demographically distinct. These representations are more specific, nuanced and persuasive than are the claims
made by the short, decontextualised texts and images of disenfranchisement and exclusion in the public campaigns. Indeed, interviewees' articulations of feeling disadvantaged were often associated
with explicit representations of how to claim entitlement – most generally, through informed and determined negotiations with doctors.
By 2001, all interviewees reported such negotiations as part of their
entitlement repertoire. Again, then, as with 'feeling lucky', representations of 'feeling disadvantaged' were cast in emotionalised terms
that would make them hearable within mainstream cultural formations, but were not as emotionally simplified as the media representations discussed earlier.

This complex interplay of 'feeling lucky' and 'feeling disadvantaged'
as particular kinds of HIV subjects in relation to specific entitlements,
thus generated a map of types and extents of HIV entitlement, and their
likely limits, on the general ground of citizenly inclusion. Talk about
luck and misfortune was usually transitive, situating the emotions in
relation to precise objects of entitlement. At the same time, there was a
degree to which emotions did not accede to this particularity or stay on
this ground.

Intransitive entitlements

HIV is not a condition that can be dealt with in an entirely explicable way. The powerful and inchoate emotions associated with illness, death, transgressive sexualities and other pleasures, and their linked social stigmatisations, cannot be managed entirely by accounts of transitive entitlement. Sometimes their abjection seemed to rip holes in the general emotionalised fabric of the interviews (Kristeva, 1982, p141). At such times, 'feeling entitled' shifted from its transitive meanings negotiated between the personal and the social, to connote something intransitive – a complete absence of entitlement, or an entitlement to everything – and HIV entitlement emotions jettisoned the web of citizenly ascriptions and limitations described above.

Vivien, for instance, a white British woman, describes herself after diagnosis:

I mean basically I've been through um a crisis either through diagnosis or just through how it affects your life. It's quite comprehensive, in turning your whole world upside down, you know, you have to, you know, you feel so uprooted on so many levels that it, the kind of problems you have go right across the board of life as you find it. Because you might of cut yourself off from your friends, your family, all the normal support systems.

Helana, a white European heterosexual woman in her twenties, was one of several interviewees who represented this post-diagnosis dissociation as rendering her as for a while already dead, outside the realm of entitlement. For the first year, 'I never went anywhere, I don't talk with no-one ... I told myself I don't need to buy clothes, you know, because I will die.' Such representations of feeling outside entitlement echo the powerfully excluding social imaginary of AIDS panic (Squire, 1997) – closely connected with homophobic and xenophobic representations and acts – that allows people who are HIV positive or affected by HIV to be ostracised and disenfranchised, the term 'AIDS' to operate as an insult, and, at the more acceptable end of this representational pathologisation, people living with HIV to be presented emotivistically, as arguably happens in the Crusaid images, as 'victims'.

HIV is also sometimes represented as bestowing on its doomed bearers an absolute entitlement, a complete and horrific freedom: to infect the blood supply; have dangerous sex and milk the social, health and immigration services dry (Garrett, 1995; Shilts, 1987; Squire,

1997). Feelings of such absolute intransitive entitlement, characterised by one interviewee, Carl, a man diagnosed with HIV for many years, as the 'I have AIDS, you owe me' syndrome, appeared rarely in interviews. One research participant, however, Rachel, a white woman with serious HIV illness, was interviewed once before she returned to her home city in another European country, and in that interview produced a continual stream of complaints so angry and encompassing that they constituted a kind of total claim: nothing was not due to this interviewee. In her story, family, friends, social workers, medical services and AIDS service organisations had all failed to deliver her entitlements, which increasingly assumed an objectless, fantastic character, taking in everything.[16]

This is a feeling that, in allowing HIV to define you entirely, is always on the edge of a reversal that will comprehensively refuse HIV. 'I'm fed up, I'm sick of this honestly', Rachel also said. 'I wish I could forget altogether, you know. Oh God, it's just driving me nuts, it really does.' Andy, a white British heterosexual man in his thirties, presented the most dramatic examples of such foreclosures of HIV entitlement, in two interviews in which he often refused to allow HIV any significance whatsoever, in contrast to spirituality, which had interested him long before HIV:

> I have had various sorts of things done to me over the years, various kinds of therapies, and I've always done periodically mediations ... it's been that way for, oh it's gotta be coming up twenty years now ... physical existence, well I mean it's all illusion at the end of the day ... the permanency of myself as (it) is with everyone else is, you know, a physical coil.

Such absolute refusals of HIV act as strong emotional claims to social inclusion as, simply, 'citizens', irrespective of HIV status. This claim is similar to the emotivist entitlement discourse of the National AIDS Trust campaign described earlier. Representing us, as subjects, as 'all the same', it excludes the important specific entitlements of HIV positive status.

But the research participants were never as caught up in the fantasy realm of complete entitlement, or its absence, as short interview quotes might suggest. The moments of abjection that broke up representations of transitive entitlements did not disrupt those representations entirely; the representations always returned to transitive, negotiable forms of entitlement. Helana's withdrawal from entitlement was turned around, for example, by her narrative of a subsequent coming out of seclusion and into an entitlement to treatment and life. Rachel's interview contained moments when some transitive forms of entitlement were claimed, as when she described meeting someone who shared some of her symptoms and whose health had improved, or discussed her hopes about faith healing, her trust in some doctors, and the different, happy person she became in her country of origin. Andy's interviews produced the curious sound of two distinct stories, often in conflict, but unavoidably related: one, detailed and pragmatic, about how to live with HIV; the other, idealised and totalising, about a spiritual transcendence that seemed to erase all HIV entitlements. Sometimes the interviews linked such transitive and intransitive accounts of 'feeling entitled' – when, for instance, Andy wondered whether he would have reformulated his life so quickly and committedly without the virus, and thus turned HIV itself into a kind of privileged route to spirituality:

> It all happened rather wonderfully, sounds a bit macabre, and I'm actually very pleased I got diagnosed and have actually got something to work on, you know, as opposed to a sort of drifting life.

Usually, interviewees' representations of their HIV entitlements moved in and out of abjection more smoothly, giving intransitive aspects of HIV feelings some expression while still allowing emotionalism to operate in a more effective, transitive way. John, a white gay man in his forties, told stories in 2001 that, like Morag's account of the 'horrendous' bodies of women she had seen, frequently expressed with the abjection of the new combination-therapy HIV body, living and 'healthy' in medical terms, but marked as 'other' by HIV and now also, the drugs' side effects. Despite John's emotional acceptance of his state, he still wants his 'own', painfree, attractive, 'normal' body back, although this desire can sometimes only be represented indirectly, through ironic laughter:

> The pain (from neuropathy) is like most pain really. They give me (painkillers), which helps a little bit to take for it, but mainly you just get used to it. It's there all the time. But as I say, you just, you just live with it really (laughs). There's not much you can do about it. And they say 'we can't do much more.' So that's the answer. It's part of the thing really but if you're still alive I suppose (laughs). It's a pretty small price to pay … I had a good run at looking good, you know, for a couple of decades … which a lot of

people won't so (laughs) ... But I don't let it bother me too much. Just get on with life, really. And if people, you know, the gay beach notice, well so they notice and that's that. And nobody says anything and nobody's awkward about it and you see other people in the same situation (laughs) ... probably I'm as bad as it gets, to be honest with you, as far as sticking-out veins and, you know, loss of fat on my arms and legs. I've not seen many people much worse than I am (laughs), so ...

Morag similarly spells out a trade-off: the monstrosity of rashes, perpetual diarrhoea and shape change that leads her to envisage a potentially dangerous drugs 'holiday' – 'I would rather die than have a hump thank you very much' – versus the privilege of relative health offered by the drugs: 'women (are) dying in Africa and all over the world, and here we are concerned about our body shape.' In both Morag's and John's accounts then, as in more obviously intransitive examples, there is a repeated emotionalised insistence on HIV entitlements that go beyond what is currently possible, within narratives that otherwise make more qualified emotional claims about HIV.

This registering of the intransitive impossibilities of HIV makes explicit some ultimately insoluble difficulties of including HIV within the social body. The popular representations considered earlier either ignore these difficulties, or respond to them with tendencies to pathologise or exclude the HIV positive citizen, but these more contextualised representations manage to register them, while still continuing to negotiate an HIV positive citizenship.

There are, of course, unclear historical, medical and social boundaries between transitive and intransitive HIV entitlement in many areas. In 1993, a decision to buy no more clothes and max out on your credit cards after an AIDS-defining illness was comprehensible in a way that it is not now, with relatively successful drug regimes leading many HIV positive people to contemplate near-normal life spans. Feeling suicidal after diagnosis, when you are asymptomatic, may seem an understandable but temporary response; feeling suicidal in the course of fatal illness often looks like sanity. People infected or affected by HIV thus live with 'borderline' senses of entitlement, unsure whether they are being paranoid, greedy or realistic about their requirements. These ambiguities were often present in the interviews. There were, too, signs throughout the interviews of movement in and out of representations of HIV entitlement, when people came to terms with a positive diagnosis, or encountered new health problems, or had to deal with multiple deaths of friends. At times, all the interviewees simply wanted to get away from HIV, to stop it ruling or even being part of their lives. Yet such apparently erratic senses of HIV entitlement were accompanied by a strong commitment to the continuity of entitlement. Interviewees maintained some principles of entitlement for the generalised HIV other even when they were not themselves 'feeling entitled'. Most represented HIV entitlements as needing to endure, just as the intransitive, nonnegotiable stigma of HIV seems to. 'Feeling entitled' even when you do not need that entitlement operates as a kind of resistance to the almost inevitable failures of such representations to guarantee your social place.

HIV entitlement and neigbourliness

I have tried to describe interviewees' representations of 'feeling entitled' as operating as a kind of analysis or map of citizenship possibilities. These representations sketch out a debate about who is entitled to what, and indicate too the limits of this debate, moments when HIV becomes the condition of absolute entitlement or total disestablishment. I am suggesting that these representations of entitlement emotions are themselves theories of HIV citizenship, which help enable that citizenship to be maintained.

The interviews suggest that 'feeling entitled' as an HIV positive person does not map onto a single mode of citizenly inclusion. There are powerful differences between feelings of HIV entitlement, and in how people of different HIV statuses feel 'entitled,' that render 'citizenship' an overgeneral description. HIV entitlement also includes claims for a flexibility of entitlement that falls outside the boundaries of conventional citizenship conceptions. People move into and out of the social and personal correlates of seropositivity; they do not always want to 'be' HIV positive citizens and they are not positioned as such in all circumstances. People can, though, listen to and respect other inhabitants in and outside the HIV 'nation' who encounter citizenship differently, and can convey the information and experiences they have. This is a pragmatic, variable form of citizenship, based on what Mouffe (1993) calls equivalence rather than identity, and Michael Walzer (1992) calls critical associationalism, and limited in its range. Its salience depends on the importance of HIV identities in a particular situation or time, and the degree of HIV-related or other commonalities between people who are HIV infected or affected. These equivalent representations of 'feeling entitled' will also at times lead to unbounded claims for an Arendtian 'free city' (Derrida, 2001) of emotional, cultural and political entitlements that cannot be met, but that are an unavoidable correlate of the drive to citizenly inclusion (Stewart, 2000), and a persistent and useful reminder of its limits (Mouffe, 1993). Such utopian claims do not derail the pragmatist project, rather they are a part of it (West, 1989).

We could better describe 'feeling entitled' in the HIV context as a demand not for citizenship, but for neighbourliness, a changeable form of sociality that is harder to formalise or generalise about. This interpretation originated with an interviewee who formulated his relation with other HIV-infected or affected people precisely in these terms, as that of neighbours who might – as in the tv soap opera theme tune – 'become friends' (Squire, 1999). Many other participants also discussed the variable levels of commonalities between themselves and other HIV positive and negative people. Neighbourliness usually refers to geography; here though I am using the term to refer to relationships that are both assigned and chosen, between people living with and alongside HIV; and to refer to the limits and changeability of the relationships as well as their contingent intimacy. Neighbours can quite usefully remain neighbours. They do not need to enter the state of friendship, with its own, impossible-to-formulate set of entitlements (Derrida, 1997). Neighbours do things for each other: they may be different from each other and even dislike aspects of each other's behaviour, but they have some mutual, time-limited goals and responsibilities. This flexible, plural and partial involvement fits well with interviewees' stories of entitlement as a conditional matter, something to be negotiated and changed.

Neighbourliness is a social articulation of the uncertain and changeable entitlement feelings that accompany living with HIV. It is not clear whether it can extend across all the divides in the realities and fantasies of entitlement discussed above. But the many interviewees who exchanged their emotionalised articulations of HIV entitlement across such divides, for instance between HIV positive gay white British men, heterosexual white European women, and African-origin women and men living in Britain, were testing this out in their quasi-public articulations of emotionalised HIV entitlement.

Can such articulations of neighbourly HIV citizenship achieve wider currency? It would seem from the interviews that HIV entitlement can achieve emotionalised and quasi-public articulations that are complexly contextualised and effective, within the realms of the social networks of people infected or affected by HIV. In a national situation where HIV is of relatively low prevalence and no longer an untreatable condition, it is unlikely that such representations will achieve the wider public articulations through forms of activism that they did with ACT UP and the Names Project in the US and Europe in the late 1980s, or that they reach now through similar organisations in high-prevalence countries such as Uganda and South Africa. Nevertheless it is notable that current UK media representations, even when they derive from the HIV advocacy and voluntary sector, such as those presented earlier in the chapter, do not match the interviews' levels of emotionalised complexity in their expressions of HIV entitlement.

Of course, interviews are more complicated and modulated events than poster campaigns, but there are many precedents for popular versions of such complexity, like the activist instances just mentioned, or the South African constellation of *Soul City* tv and radio programmes, magazines and clubs (http://www.soulcity.org.za/ accessed December 2005).[17] Even in the relatively low HIV-prevalence situation of the UK, the Mark Fowler character in the soap opera *East Enders* lived with HIV for over a decade. Interviewees often discussed Fowler's representation, sometimes critically but never dismissively. For despite the constraints of the medium and the genre this representation included, at least until its disputed end,[18] realistically complicated emotional claims on HIV entitlements of many kinds, including the entitlement to identities not defined by HIV.

The emotional representation of HIV entitlements, either in 'emotivist' simplicity that can have exclusionary effects, or in more complex 'emotionalised' forms that claim social inclusion and achieve a kind of theorisation of HIV citizenship or neigbourliness, are similar to patterns of representation of other disenfranchised conditions that claim entitlement, both in health and social fields – for instance, of other chronic health conditions, breast cancer, and disability. While western HIV representational activism partly modelled itself on the emotionalised forms of for instance lesbian and gay activism, civil rights, and feminist and peace activism, it quickly became a model itself for similar emotionalised entitlement campaigns, especially in the fields of health and sexuality. Perhaps it is particularly around conditions of embodied social stigma such as HIV that emotionalised public entitlement claims have their strongest potential excluding – or including – effects. However, it may be that a similar pattern of complex, differentiated and socially including public emotionality, rather than simplified, exclusionary public emotivism, can be discerned and pursued more broadly, outside those conditions, in contemporary entitlement claims made across a range of states of disenfranchisement, and to a variety of audiences. The current state of the UK HIV epidemic, involving rising HIV diagnoses; continuing treatment difficulties; significant shifts in epidemic demographics, particularly in relation to citizenship status; and increasing social, economic and political connections to the broader pandemic, demonstrates how far we are from being in a 'post-AIDS' state. At such a time, public translations of the complexities of HIV into entitlement feelings, similar to those produced by the interviewees, but reaching beyond local social networks, can usefully promote social inclusion and more precise and differentiated concepts of HIV citizenship and neigbourliness. Complex representation of 'feeling HIV entitled' may not be the only means to these ends, but in the contemporary western context they can have particularly powerful and modulated effects.

Notes

1   I am referring here not to people tested HIV positive but people who declare their HIV positive status to themselves and usually others, generally but not always after testing.

2   The concept of social inclusion is controversial, too often based on a notion of 'common life', measured through simple economic participation or community membership, aimed at social cohesion rather than social justice (Gray, 2000, pp22–3; Lister, 2000). Straightforward measures such as technology access can be more complexly articulated (see for instance Warschauer, 2003), but still tend to base 'social inclusion' on strong communities that support individual agency.

3   The material significance of representations and of 'speaking' versus 'silence' has been extensively debated within considerations of many forms of 'identity politics'. It can also been argued that 'representation' must supplement the 'represented' in situations where interest groups such as people living with HIV in the developed world are claiming entitlements (Laclau, 1996). 'Representation' in its linguistic or symbolic sense, can be an important part of this supplementation.

4   All figures come from the 2005 Health Protection Agency report and data tables to end 2005; figures in the latter are liable to rise. See http://www.hpa.org.uk, accessed June 2006.

5   Watney (2000) discusses the problems of such categories.

6   This application of the Crimes against the Person Act now has precedent in England and Wales. There have been other cases: in early 2004, Feston Konazi was jailed for 10 years on GBH for infecting three women with HIV (Cole, 2004, p20). The same activity was prosecuted in 2001 as culpable and reckless behaviour under Scottish common law. This case involved the use of a police warrant to obtain confidential information from a research study. Such cases are much debated and unlikely to become numerous (Cole, 2004).

7 These representations coincide roughly with Patton's (2002, pp47–50) two 'epidemiological' (cure-related, time-based, narrated like a detective story) and 'tropical' (diaspora-related, space-based, narrated in melodrama) discourses of HIV.

8 Bernard Forbes of the UK Coalition of People Living with HIV and AIDS promotes HIV positive status disclosure, however emotionally risky, as a sign that people with HIV 'respect ourselves and our partners' and can manage with rejection – have, in summary, grown up. However, a Terrence Higgins Trust (THT) spokesperson commented, 'The question is how this case will impact on the vast majority of people living with HIV in the UK today, who may be discouraged from being open about their HIV status with people for fear of a backlash. We must work toward a society in which people with HIV can talk about their diagnoses without fear of stigma or rejection.' Lisa Power, THT's Director of Policy and Communications, said, 'I am not surprised at the length of Dica's (original) sentence, especially because there is a long history of ethnic minorities getting longer sentences'. (*Positive Nation* 97–8, December 2003) The message board of the UK Coalition provided a similar split response, as did published letters to *Positive Nation,* the magazine associated with the Coalition.

9 This programme was in ideological synch with the UNAIDS-supported International Federation of the Red Cross and Red Crescent's longer-term anti-stigma campaign. Saatchi and Saatchi helped formulate it. Many thanks to the National AIDS Trust for permission to reprint this image.

10 The workshop guide itself mixes facts and emotion-eliciting activities, advising a discussion of human rights, using quotes from people with HIV about stigma and discrimination, and asking workshop participants to think about comparable experiences of their own.

11 Examples of such tales include:

Bryn
Having been diagnosed HIV positive, the hardest thing was the fact that I had to build a new family from the friends that had stayed by my side. My family just shut me out and pretended that I was gone and out of the way.

Julie
I was diagnosed HIV positive in 1991 aged 24 at the time I was at collage, but working as a cook/nanny in the holidays. Despite fear, shock and the lack of awareness, my friends supported me.
(see http://www.areyouhivprejudiced.org, accessed December 2005)

12 MARK, 43:
HIV/AIDS/INCONTINENCE/
DIRTY SHEETS/POVERTY/
HUMILIATION

ALEX, 20:
HIV/AIDS/BEATEN UP/
OSTRACISED
/SKINT/HOMELESS

RACHEL, 32:
HIV/AIDS/CAN'T BREASTFEED/
NO MONEY/BABY INFECTED

13   Discussions on the UK Coalition of People Living With HIV and AIDS message board give similar interpretations though are also concerned about the use of models rather than 'real' HIV positive people and with Crusaid's perceived current bias away from funding gay men. The magazine *Positive Nation* has also rehearsed these arguments in an article on the campaign (Issue 100, March 2004).

14   Early western HIV activists called for 'no representation without context', (Crimp, 1989) – it is type as well as amount of context that is at stake.

15   Although 'support' is a problematic concept (Green, 1993), social support is often cited as important for psychological and even physiological wellbeing for people with HIV and other long-term serious illness.

16   See Squire, 1997, 1999, 2003, for other accounts of such abjection. Such a totalising representation of entitlement also appeared occasionally in the interviews at secondhand, in stories of healthy people pretending to be HIV positive to gain the imagined benefits, or of HIV service organisations cleaned out by clients who ran up taxi bills and stole supplies.

17   MacIntyre (1984) describes moral discourses as transmitted through community narratives. Such discourses may be emotion-laden, but they are not 'emotivist'. However I am not arguing as he does that interpersonal social media are intrinsically better than broadcast cultural media for the transmission of publically effective affect.

18   Cairns in *Positive Nation*. 'Realism' here may not mean statistical representativeness, so much as the presentation of a span of HIV-related experiences, and consultation with HIV service organisations and organisations run by people with HIV. (http://uk.gay.com/article/1647, accessed December 2005)

References

Ahmed S, 2004a. *The Cultural Politics of Emotion*. Edinburgh and New York: Edinburgh University Press and Routledge

Ahmed S, 2004b. Affective economies. *Social Text*, 22, 2, 121–39

Aronowitz S, 1995. Against the liberal state: ACT-UP and the politics of pleasure. In L Nicholson and S Seidman, eds, *Social Postmodernism: Beyond Identity*. Cambridge: Cambridge University Press, 357–83

Baudrillard J, 1995. *Simulacra and Simulation*. New York: UMP

Bauman Z, 2000. *Liquid Modernity*. London: Polity

Boffin T and Gupta S, eds, 1991. *Ecstatic Antibodies*. London: River's Oram Press

Cole S, 2004. Crimes of passion? *Positive Nation*, June, 102, 20–2

Craib I, 1994. *The Importance of Disappointment*. London: Routledge

Crimp D, ed., 1989. *AIDS: Cultural Analysis/Cultural Activism*. Cambridge, Massachusetts: MIT Press

Crimp D and Ralston A, 1990. *AIDS DemoGraphics*. Seattle, Washington: Bay Press

Derrida J, 1997. *The Politics of Friendship*. London: Verso

Derrida J, 2001. *On Cosmopolitanism and Forgiveness*. London and New York: Routledge

Foucault M, 1979. *History of Sexuality Volume 1*. London: Allen Lane

Furedi F, 2004. *Therapeutic Culture*. London: Routledge

Garrett L, 1995. *The Coming Plague*. New York: Farrar, Straus and Giroux

Giddens A, 1991. *Modernity and Self-Identity*. San Francisco, California: Stanford University Press

Gray J, 2000. Inclusion: a radical critique. In P Askonas and A Stewart, eds, *Social Inclusion: Possibilities and Tension*. Basingstoke: Macmillan Press, 19–36

Green G, 1993. Social support and HIV. *AIDS Care* 5, 87–104

Himmelfarb G, 1996. *The De-Moralisation of Society*. New York: Vintage

Kristeva J, 1982. *Powers of Horror*. New York: Columbia University Press

Laclau E, 1996. Deconstruction, pragmatism, hegemony. In C Mouffe (ed.) *Deconstruction and Pragmatism*. London: Routledge

Lasch C, 1991. *True and Only Heaven*. New York: Norton

Lister R, 2000. Strategies for social inclusion: Promoting social cohesion or social justice? In P Askonas and A Stewart, eds, *Social Inclusion: Possibilities and Tensions*. Basingstoke: Macmillan Press, 37–54

Lyotard J-F, 1984. *The Postmodern Condition*. Manchester: Manchester University Press

Malik R, 2000. Culture and emotions: depression among Pakistanis. In C Squire, ed., *Culture in Psychology*. London: Psychology Press, 147–62

MacIntyre A, 1984. *After Virtue*. Notre Dame, Indiana: Notre Dame University Press

MacIntyre A, 1989. *Whose Justice? Which Rationality?* Notre Dame, Indiana: Notre Dame University Press

MacIntyre A, 1991. *Three Rival Versions of Moral Inquiry*. Notre Dame, Indiana: Notre Dame University Press

Mouffe C, 1993. *The Return of the Political*. London: Verso

Oppenheimer J and Reckitt, H, eds, 1997. *Acting on AIDS*. London: Serpent's Tail

Patton C, 1991. *Inventing AIDS*. London: Routledge

Patton C, 2002. *Globalising AIDS*. Minneapolis, Minnesota: University of Minnesota Press

Rose N, 1996. *Inventing Our Selves*. Cambridge: Cambridge University Press

Rose N and Novas C, 2004. Biological citizenship. In A Ong, S Collier and S Blackwell, eds, *Global Assemblages: Technology, Politics, and Ethics as Anthropological Problems*. Oxford: Blackwell, 439–63

Schweder R, 1991. *Thinking Through Cultures*. Boston, Massachusetts: Harvard University Press

Shilts R, 1987. *And the Band Played On*. New York: St Martin's Press

Squire C, 1997. AIDS panic. In Jane Ussher, ed., *Body Talk*. London: Routledge, 50–69

Squire C, 1999. 'Neighbours who might become friends': Selves, genres and citizenship in narratives of HIV. *The Sociological Quarterly*, 40, 1, 109–37

Squire C, 2000. The public life of emotions. *International Journal of Critical Psychology*, 1

Squire C, 2003. Can an HIV positive woman find true love? Romance in the stories of women living with HIV. *Feminism and Psychology*, 13, 1, 73–100

Stewart A, 2000. Social inclusion: A radical agenda? In P Askonas and A Stewart, eds, *Social Inclusion: Possibilities and Tensions*. Basingstoke: Macmillan Press, 293–6

Walzer M, 1992. The civil society argument. In C Mouffe, ed., *Dimensions of Radical Democracy*. London: Verso, 89–107

Warschauer M, 2003. *Technology and Social Inclusion*. Cambridge, Massachusetts: MIT Press

Watney S, 1991. Representing AIDS. In T Boffin and S Gupta, eds, *Ecstatic Antibodies*. London: River's Oram Press, 165–92

Watney S, 1994. *Practices of Freedom*. London: Rivers Oram

Watney S, 2000. *Imagine Hope*. London: Routledge

Weeks J, 1995. *Invented Moralities: Sexual Values in the Age of Uncertainty*. London: Polity Press

West C, 1989. *The American Evasion of Philosophy*. Madison, Wisconsin: University of Wisconsin Press

Williams S, 1998. 'Capitalising' on emotions? Rethinking the inequalities in health debate. *Sociology*, 32, 1, 121–39

10

The Future is Not There for the Making: Enduring Colonialism, Shame and Silence

Amal Treacher

In his memoir *Out of Place* (2000), Edward Said writes of a walk that he took with his father when he was a young child:

> I scampered along behind him, while he pressed on with his
> hands behind his back at a resolute pace. When I stumbled
> and fell forward, scratching my hands and knees badly,
> I instinctively called out to him 'Daddy...please', at which
> he stopped and turned around slowly toward me. He paused
> like that for a couple of seconds, then turned back, resuming
> his walk without a word. That was all. It was also how he died,
> turning his face to the wall, without a sound. Had he, I wonder,
> ever really wanted to say more than he actually did
> (Said, 2000, p79).

In Said's account, his father was powerful, authoritarian, bullish, noisy in his demands and in his silence. My Egyptian father was also stubbornly quiet, proud, resolute in his determination to succeed, and silent. These two successful and powerful fathers were reserved, taciturn, mute almost about their political and historical formations. This essay is an exploration of this silence and of the necessary forgetting of what the meanings and consequences of having been formed as a colonised subject.

Egypt is a talking society, talking is a national pastime as all 'sorts of topics are subject to detailed discussion, evaluation, comment' (Danielson, 1997, p5). This talking society, which dissects politics endlessly and incessantly discusses everything that is happening or not, is guarded on a particular matter – the breakdown of the Egyptian Revolution of 1952. This revolution (led by a small group of Army

Officers – named the Free Officers), which began full of drive, commitment and idealism, has not led Egypt to a more coherent, democratic,
or materially prosperous society. Nevertheless, the fiftieth year anniversary celebrations were full of the discourses of triumph, liberation and
progression. While the media was full of this rhetoric, in private something else altogether was going on. My father was desolate over the
failure of the revolution (in our home we had to call it a coup), and I
discovered that many Egyptian men of a certain class, age and
influence were profoundly depressed about how their dreams had
crumbled and evaporated and were wretched over how corrosive corruption had won out as opposed to the social law of collective good.
Egypt at this moment in time (2004) is in a desperate economic and
political state and this essay is a partial exploration of how a dream
turned to dust, of how a brief period of optimism and zeal turned into
pessimism and passivity. It shares a concern with Galal Amin's essays
Whatever Happened to the Egyptians? (2000), but while his collection is a
lively series of short takes on aspects of everyday life, this essay is
concerned with the disintegration of a political dream and with how
colonialism endures and lives on inexorably in the Egyptian present.

Colonialism haunts, it does not inhabit only the past but continues to
be a serious presence in people's lived experience, in psychic lives, in
matters of globalisation and the local, and in material relations.
The inscriptions of the past can be glimpsed, sensed, felt profoundly not
only through the continuing matters of aid, fiscal treatment of third
world countries, but also through emotions such as anxiety, uncertainty
and diffidence. These marks are there whether known, understood or
not. Like a palimpsest, successive layers of history co-exist within
the present; despite attempts to erase the past, 'all present experiences
contain ineradicable traces of the past which remain part of the constitution of the present' (Aschroft *et al.*, 2003, p174).

Colonialism persists and rather like the repressed it will not disappear. As Elliott, argues a society's present always risks 'becoming
haunted by what is excluded. And the more rigid the position, the
greater the ghost, the more threatening it is in some way' (Elliott,
2002, p153). In short, the past is inescapable and cannot be sloughed
off – either by discovering and telling another narrative or by focusing
on acts of resistance. This chapter is an exploration of how a colonised
past inextricably lived in the present has hindered the development of
a different political society. I concentrate on the political domain and
on masculinity. It is important to say that in the social and cultural
spheres, Egyptian life is not moribund but full of lively and creative

activity. In its theatre, films, literature and music much dynamic work is being undertaken and appreciated. Similarly, a project in Egypt – Creative Women in the Shadow – is exploring with women their creative possibilities and is opening up spaces for different means of expression. Women have been actively involved in political life, and they fight for women *and* the nation and their participation should not be ignored.[1]

In this essay I focus on masculinity, emotion and post colonialism in the Egyptian context. Masculinity barely features in current debates on gender in the Arab region and because, crudely, it was, and remains the case, that men are in power and have influence. A recent edited collection *Imagined Masculinities* (Ghoussoub and Sinclair-Webb, 2000) has produced a unique attempt to understand masculinity and the experience of male gender in Arab regions. It stands as a worthy example of an understanding of masculinity in what is otherwise a dearth of theorisations of men and masculinity in the Arab region, and the impact of masculinity on the political domain. Little, if any, work has been undertaken on the vexed subject of the consequences of colonisation and on emotional and public life. Similar to the West no theoretical understandings have been elaborated on emotions and their effects on political life.

It is unclear quite why so little work, if any, has been undertaken on Egyptian masculinity or a different approach to the political situation tackled. One possible reason for the absence of studies of Egyptian masculinity is that the authority of Arab men was not to be questioned when some Arab countries were under colonial rule. This historical legacy of maintaining the illusion of power is imprinted on the present. Men's role is as responsible providers of material and spiritual sustenance. Men are not to be questioned; indeed the Law of the Father predominates. It has to be acknowledged that the Middle East remains a seat of contested but powerfully felt patriarchy. It is on matters of the nation and nationalism that men make their presence felt powerfully. At the same time, masculinity was severely challenged and dented by the continuing experience of colonisation and the systematic incapacity to unify and establish Arab societies into a powerful force once more. Now, masculinity and patriarchy are in possible crisis in Egypt as it has become more difficult for men to provide materially for their families, and this cuts across the class spectrum. This is a huge point of shame and impotence for Egyptian men (more so than in the West). In this context, erosion of the role of material provider coincides with political impotence.

The political background: 1952 and beyond

In Egypt, from the 1920s a profoundly nationalistic movement had taken hold and there were growing demands for the removal of the political powers and hold of the British and French on Egyptian political life. Growing radicalisation and political involvement derived from frustration. Much talk centred on justice to Egypt and the restoration of a glorious Egypt. Embedded in these beliefs in the possibility of recovering greatness were prevalent anti-British views that cut across the political spectrum as students and young revolutionaries attacked the old political structures, the Wafd political party (the ruling party during the 1930s and 1940s) and the monarchy.

Nasser (an army officer who was one of the leading group that led the revolution) and his generation came from either the petit bourgeoisie or the lower classes, and were brought up under the conservative rule of the monarchy and the Wafd party. They, along with many other members of the populace, were radicalised by alienation, fury and frustration at the levels of bribery and corruption in the government and higher echelons of society. Many Egyptian peoples felt dispossessed and crushed by economic and social difficulties.

The Free Officers inherited a history of radical politics that had built up from the early 1920s onwards. They seized power in July 1952 and King Farouq, Egypt's reigning monarch, was exiled to Italy – after being allowed a spectacular farewell from Alexandria – never to return. His complicit and corrupt entourage was denied power and never regained its position of influence. The Wafd party never regained their foothold on Egyptian politics. The fatherly and popular Mohamed Naguib was the first figurehead of the new government and was in fact the first Egyptian President before he was ousted due to his adherence to the monarchy and conservatism. Following a distasteful removal – Naguib was under house arrest for many years but never tried nor sentenced – Nasser took over as President and remained in power until his death in 1970.

From the beginning of 1953 democracy was not followed through and Egypt became, and remains, a single party state. Egyptian governments have used the law of emergency rule in order to stop any opposition and interventions from other political groups – from the Communist Party to the Muslim Brotherhood. Division and diversity have been squashed – sometimes successfully, sometimes not – but Egypt has seen resistance and vehement disagreements against all Egyptian governments from 1952 to the present day. Political opposition ranges from the secular left, the secular right and from those who adhere to a conservative version of Islamic politics. These various factions, except for the Muslim Brotherhood, have struggled with little impact.

In the early days of this revolution many of Nasser's comrades and government ministers were coming to grips with their ministerial positions, and while there was diversity of thinking and experience in abundance, Nasser's ideas prevailed and his thinking became adopted policy. As Aburish points out, Nasser turned his colleagues into complaint and complicit yes-men.[2] It can be difficult, if not impossible, to discover anything about the influence of the Cabinet and of Government Ministers during this time. Nasser was the dominant figure as President, as the leading figure of the Cabinet, and in the popular imagination (both in the Arab region and in the West). Arrests and torture of those who dissented occurred throughout the 1950s onwards. While the early 1960s saw the formation of a new cabinet, a new constitution and a new revolutionary council and the organisation of local legislative assemblies in all villages and cities, the idea of a new revolution assumed neither importance nor urgency.

The important military success of Nasser in 1956 over the Suez Canal (known in Egypt as the Tripartite War due to the involvement of Britain, Israel and France) was heralded rightly as the defeat of imperialist nations and specifically England. The war was over whether or not to nationalise the Canal. Nasser wanted the Suez Canal to be directly and exclusively under Egyptian control; Britain, France and Israel disagreed due to its important geo-political position and their military attacked Egypt despite much international outrage. America disagreed with the tripartite action for it was not a major player, as yet, in the Middle East and was just beginning to exert its power in that region. According to Aburish (2004, p96), Nasser held two contradictory beliefs about England – he thought England would never listen to him unless he shouted and kicked, while simultaneously he believed in the British sense of fair play. His bold political move to defy the English and outrage Anthony Eden was greeted with the hope, and profound belief that this would be the beginning of the Arab region's ascendancy.

This hope was reinforced by Nasser's own speeches and an analysis of his speeches reveal that his most oft-used words were honour, glory, dignity and pride (Aburish 2004, p112). Nasser represented hope and was a defiant, living symbol of the Egyptian peoples' desires and will. Nasser was a charismatic speaker and his speeches aimed to stir the people and certainly did so. Full of pleas for 'dignity and unity', 'strength and purpose' and anti-imperialist oratory, Nasser's rhetoric was devoid of policy and an actual vision of how these aims were to be achieved. As Aburish states it, '[T]he Free Officers possessed an attitude, but they had no practical plan, just a six-point program' (Aburish, 2004, p44). The six-point reform plan was created in 1962, and included importantly land reform in which land ownership was restricted. This plan was spoken about, and referred to, but never instituted.

The years (from approximately 1958 until 1967) were spent with Nasser concentrating on attempting to fend off interventions in the Middle East by America and Britain. Much effort was made to establish a coherent Arab Region that had power and influence. Internal affairs were neglected and social, cultural and political structures and institutions that would have ensured the social welfare of the Egyptian peoples were not put in place. In short, Nasser and his government failed to create either the structures that would have given their ideas content or the action necessary for their realisation.

Meanwhile, there was serious involvement in the affairs of other Arab states, for example Syria and Yemen and this participation did nothing other than drain the economy. The serious defeat of Egypt in 1967 during the six-day war (which also put Israel on the map as a nation to be taken seriously) and the scars of this military and political rout live on.[3] Following defeat, Egyptian morale plummeted and the thinness of the pan-Arab nationalist project became apparent and known to all. Optimism was replaced by anger and bitterness. Since 1967 no one speaks of pride, dignity or unity of purpose.

I am profoundly puzzled by the emotional responses and their consequences on this particular political history, and remain bewildered as to why a different political future could not be made. Before discussing these emotions further, it is worth considering the difficulties inherent in any exploration of a society's emotions and their relation to a particular political history. The exploration of an emotional tenor risks pathologising a nation or its leaders, reinforcing a whole set of preconceptions and perhaps, most vexed of all, reifying and simplifying that which is complex and elusive. Alongside these risks lies the problem of how to understand, indeed know, what feelings exist (and this matter troubles the whole of this book) and to analyse how these feelings may impact or not on the public polity without resort to loose analogies between the personal and the political, the individual and the collective, the familial and the public sphere. While working on this essay I was haunted by a sense that I am thinking within at best the tendentious and at worst, within clunky clichés that foreclose on the nuances of being human and living a political life. It is a vexed, if not impossible endeavour to locate and trace through issues of emotion in public life especially, perhaps, when focusing on a Middle Eastern country and its history. This project risks coming close to reinforcing dominant Western perceptions of Arab masculinity as that of excess and simultaneously that of lack. It is all too easy to reinforce a view of the Arab region as inhabiting a culture of oppression or misery and thereby to miss issues of resistance, power, commitment and enjoyment of life. To echo a troubling question of Edward Said's 'can so utterly indecisive and so deeply undermined a history ever be written? In what language, and with what sort of vocabulary?' (Said 2003, p55). In short, how can we think through the matters concerned without recourse to reductionism, reinforcement, or concretising the complex?

The attempt to understand the relation between political history and masculine emotions is simultaneously impossible and a worthwhile pursuit as the attempt to think through the partial collapse of a society that is under duress can open up hitherto unimagined theoretical arenas of possibilities, theoretical understandings and political actions. This requires learning to live and think 'without consoling fictions, for in the death of such numbing and dangerous fantasies lies our only hope' (Rose, 2003a, p68). These thoughts about Nasser and his generation, Egyptian men who started full of zeal and optimism and failed are not meant to encourage liberal pity, empty guilt, or anxious vulnerability for the most respect that can be given to the other human being is that of a robust engagement, where the other is seen as a nuanced and complex subject (Fanon, 1992). This is a much more radical quest than granting or demanding self-esteem, self-worth or pride and calls for stringent thought and exploration. One way in which Western representations, by both the left and the right of the Western political spectrum, rob Egyptian (if not all men of colour) of their humanity is to deny them interiority. This chapter is an attempt to restore a degree of interiority to these men that I grew up with and am attached to, not by celebrating their achievements, but rather by focusing on painful aspects of their political lives.

Shame, thinking and mourning

As the above brief account illustrates this post-colonised society could not shape a better social order – corruption, high and ever-increasing unemployment, galloping inflation remain as profound corrosions.

There are many valid ways to analyse this situation and I have chosen to focus on shame and mourning as two partial but important factors that have led to the perpetuation of this impoverished situation. I am not suggesting that Egyptian men are the only men who experience shame, or indeed that Egypt is the only post-colonised society to be in such a desperate state, rather I am speculating that Egypt can be taken as *one* specific example of how a society which had opportunities to create something anew for a brief period could not manage this endeavour. Shame, I am suggesting, led to a paralysis of thought about what it means to have been a post-colonised subject inhabiting a post-colonised society; about what it means to be 'overdetermined from without' (Bhabha quoting Fanon, 1993, p115). For these Egyptian men, for my father and his father before him, silence may be the only option.

It is apposite to draw on Hannah Arendt's focus on matters of will, judgement and thought, capacities that for Arendt are indispensable for a functioning ethical and political life (1998). For Arendt, it is through persistent thought and judgement and exploration of public life that political life can be recovered. A political life of the mind in this account, though Arendt died before she could formulate it fully, centres on responsibility and being a morally accountable agent. I am suggesting, and it is provocative but not meant to be offensive, that previous histories of colonisations (it has to be remembered that these Egyptian men were the first Egyptians to rule Egypt for centuries) hindered stringent thought about how to create a different society. Authority could not be inhabited with integrity. The only power known was that of exploitation, corruption and subjection. It remains a problem, however, to trace through how conscious and 'unconscious inheritance – histories, individual and collective, are moulded and passed down' (Rose, 1998, p42).

An enduring theoretical and political matter refuses to disappear and this focuses on how we can recognise our inheritance and how to do so responsibly. Recognition calls for judgement, and judgement for Arendt is never final, but always and by necessity, has to be woven back into action and woven back into thought. Arendt viewed humans as multiple, fragmented and suffering beings and believed that thinking is always divided; but it is our consciousness of others and the public polity that we inhabit, that sees, has to see us, through. The difficulty though is how to know the extent to which Egyptian masculinity has been formed through and within colonisation, when colonisation and its effects are precisely what cannot be thought through, has to be triumphed over. Focusing on absence and silence of discourses and narratives is one route to a fuller exploration of colonised experiences but it remains frustratingly intangible and unsatisfactory. Colonisation and its effects are elusive and can be understood as what Toni Morrison 'sometimes just calls *the thing*, the sedimented conditions that constitute what is in place in the first place' (Gordon, 1997, p4). Colonisation endures because as Gordon puts it, it 'makes its mark by being there and not there at the same time' (1997, p6); when without a doubt that which 'appears absent can indeed be a seething presence' (Gordon, 1997, p17). It is difficult enough to write retrospectively of the emotional and thinking conditions that existed, let alone inhabiting this political and emotional context.

The dilemma is how to think about this without arousing more immense shame, or reinforcing shame. For Kaufman to 'live with shame is to feel alienated and defeated, never quite good enough to belong. And secretly we feel to blame. The deficiency lies within us alone. Shame is without parallel a sickness of the soul, to echo Silvan Tomkins' (Kaufman, 1992, p12). Shame is an intensely painful experience and emotion and it evokes and is provoked by other emotions – humiliation, retaliation, mortification, helplessness and ridicule. Humiliation is precisely one of the tropes of colonisation – colonised, taken over and made to feel as if they cannot and should not rule, Egyptian men were rendered helpless. Lord Cromer (the British Governor) infamously humiliated through contempt Egyptian men and made public his views of disdain and ridicule. This scorn and continual humiliation despite resistance had effects on Egyptian men's capacities to rule and to take authority.

Anxiety and depression can follow and be interlinked with the experience of shame. As Kaufman poignantly expresses it, contained in the 'experience of shame is the piercing awareness of ourselves as fundamentally deficient in some vital way as a human being. To live with shame is to experience the very essence or heart of the self as wanting' (Kaufman, 1992, p9). To compound the adversity, this experience is itself shaming. Shame is experienced when we 'are the targets of actual or anticipated contempt of others' (Ben-Ze'ev, 2000, p525). Shame is not just an internal and visceral emotion as it expresses 'our deepest values and commitments; freeing ourselves from shame implies unloading these values and commitments' (Ben-Ze'ev, 2000, p514). Alongside the emotions generated when we are done to, shame occurs when we do, or indeed do not act. Shame, indeed, strengthens bonds and enables us to be cognisant of our relationships and obligations to others.

Thinking about shame is challenging as in a paradox, to think about a shaming event causes shame to occur. Frequently, shame is not thought about – the event forgotten – or interpreted differently. Shame shuts down on thought for it cannot bear to be known and the conditions that brought it about elucidated and explored. As Jacqueline Rose argues '[S]hame is very precious, but in a strange tautology, it also seems to be ashamed of itself' (Rose, 2003, p1). Shame is about exposure of self to the other, or the nation to the other nation, yet it is felt as a profoundly visceral feeling. Shame is tautological for how can the conditions that brought it about be known and recognised when exposure 'is what it hates most, and most militantly struggles against' (Rose, 2003, p1). There is always an act of cruelty with shame for it always evokes and recalls the most primitive infantile rage (Rose, 2003, p3). Shame, I am suggesting is one of the emotions and states of mind through which Egyptians could not, cannot, think about their situation. Shame is felt about the past, about colonisation and its legacy, about the social, political and emotional conditions of life. For, [T]hought stalls on an event it cannot bear to contemplate, can go no further. Shame and rage spell the end of mental freedom' (Rose, 2003, p7). But how can we think about shame when as Rose points out we would 'rather die'. Shame is dreadful – full of dread – not just the emotion itself, but the knowledge of the consequences of what one has done, or not, that has led to shame.

Facing up to the past, to responsibilities, to how one has been formed is never easy nor straightforward, for as Bhabha expresses it '[R]emembering is never a quiet act of introspection or retrospection. It is a painful re-membering, a putting together of the dismembered past to make sense of the trauma of the present' (Bhabha, 1993, p121). Here Homi Bhabha is exploring the issue of memory through the work of Frantz Fanon and the intricacy, if not impossibility, of remembering colonisation itself. It could be argued that one issue for Egyptians is to remember and re-claim their colonised past, but personal memories of political and social history are not spoken about. Instead, jokes are made about King Farouq (the disposed king), the Suez War is recalled with pride, but otherwise what emerges is a noisy silence. Shame leads to a paralysis of thinking and to denial. The responsibility for the shameful situation is shunted elsewhere to another, to the event, to the situations. Shame can be paradoxical, for it can be felt acutely and painfully and simultaneously denied with a vengeance. Shame can lead to a profound forgetting – for in that situation these men had to act, and become the first Egyptians to rule for centuries, in doing so they reproduced 'not as memory but as an action; we repeat without knowing we are repeating' (Phillips, 1994). In short, when we are in the event we cannot remember and to act we have to forget.

It is perhaps ill-advised to call on remembering as a solution to political ills as it seems to suggest a psychological solution to a political problem, and as if retrospection and interiority will deliver a different political future. In any case remembering and forgetting are closely intertwined. Luisa Passerini's essay 'Memories Between Silence and Oblivion' (2003) explores the difficulties of remembering, silence and forgetting. For Passerini the profound impediment is that to remember something you and others have to know that something is absent, forgotten even. In a further twist – to forget something, you have to forget that you have even forgotten (Rose, 2003, p7). To produce a different political future, these Egyptian men had to, just had to, believe and know that the future was there for the making and the past could not, should not, have mattered. The tragedy is that through that denial the past became endlessly reiterated – the Egyptian government of 1952 and beyond did not shake off the shackles of imperialism and did not access and use the rich range of political, social and material resources to make a society anew. Forgetting the effects of being colonised is one aspect, and these Egyptian men knew, and know, about being subject to the power and agency of others, but 'being subject to their own experience' (Lambek, 2002, p25) is disavowed. I am speculating that the knowledge of having been formed as a subject in the shadow of the other is an intolerable knowledge has had to be dismissed profoundly.

Shame and the experience of colonialism can weaken the ego, precisely at the time when the ego is most urgently needed. The problem is how to forge a political future anew when the ego is most needed and yet paradoxically at its most fragile. Locked in profound shame about the past, about what has been inherited and perpetuated, the ego can only 'come to believe in its own supremacy by blocking the shades and layers of former identifications out of which it has in fact been made' (Rose, 1998, p12). What could not, cannot, be acknowledged (and Egyptian political leaders are certainly not alone in this) is the extent to which matters of authority and leadership are shot through with fantasy, unconscious desires and fears, with longings for power and triumph. Fantasy as Jacqueline Rose points out 'fuels, or at least plays its part in, the forging of the collective will' (Rose, 1998, p3)

for it is not just private but is a part of, active in, the social and political domains. The initial success of the Suez war, of the beginnings of
the establishment of a strong Arab union, of a more equal economic
society evaporated and were never repeated and the difficulty is that
when nations imagined that 'they have made it, that it is all in (their)
grasp, there for the possession, that everything starts to go so terribly
wrong' (Rose, 1998, p47). One way that it 'went terribly wrong' was the
denial of the internalisation of colonisation – that we are all peopled
and burdened by connections and bonds that we would rather not
have within us – emotionally, socially and politically. It is under these
conditions of pressure that thinking cannot occur, for where is there to
go when you are the first Egyptians to rule for centuries? Where do you
go to think about authority, moral leadership, political integrity, when
your only inheritance and experience is that of having been colonised,
by cruel, aggressive and patronising colonisers?

Shame cannot be thought about not just because to survive the experience, shame itself has to be denied and our subjection forgotten but
also because shame is that which binds people together. Shame occurs
and is felt not just due to solipsistic concerns, but also as the expression of a moral obligation that has not been fulfilled. The dilemmas
and conflicts that these failures of obligations to others bring about are
perhaps best illustrated by drawing on Jacqueline Rose's example of
Winnie Mandela. Rose writes of the impossibility of Winnie Mandela's
position at the Truth and Reconciliation Commission, for '[T]he
essence of this hearing was the collision of two cultures alive in
the black community. The culture of human responsibility, human
virtue and guilt; and the culture of clan honour and shame [...] if she
admits to wrongdoing, she dishonours them all' (Rose, 2003, p3). For
Egyptians to think about their political distress means not just bringing
shame on their own selves, but also on others. Shaming another is
shameful; it cannot and should not occur. It cuts across the strong
ethical code of social, emotional and political cultures. Another, or an
external event, is blamed – it is the coloniser, the colonising situation.
It is all out there. This perpetuates the very situation itself. For as
Nandy poignantly argues, colonisation is internalised, the external
coloniser is blamed, but the external coloniser is also exploited to legit-
imise and perpetuate internal divisions, corruption, social and political
failures. Then in a final twist of an endless, vicious cycle – colonisation
is internalised again (Nandy, 1983). Authority is relinquished and
mimicry with the coloniser is perhaps the only option. Homi Bhabha
following Fanon argues that the person of colour can only ever imitate,

never identify and writes '[I]t is imitation ... when the child holds the newspaper like his father. It is identification when the child learns to read' (1993, p120). In this situation of mimicry and a lack of political authority thought cannot take place, again and again.

The ethical obligations to another can take priority even at the risk of failure and disappointment. To shame can be cruel and to think about the issues concerned can feel impossible. For example, I could not speak with my father about what he could have done differently – it felt impossible. I felt silenced and complicit. Complicit with a view that the responsibility and blame was all out there – with Nasser, with the Free Officers, with the British, with history, with whatever as long as it did not touch those in the room. My post-revolutionary generation shrug our shoulders and declare with resignation – what can we expect? At the risk of returning the responsibility back to colonialism and in a different but none the less powerful way robbing Egyptians of their agency, it cannot be stated strongly enough how colonisation colonised minds and this has led to 'the lost capacity to define what it means to be human, to have knowledge ... effective colonisation cuts out from under the colonised all conceptual ground for critique. It leaves no space to claim that things might (or should be otherwise)' (West-Newman, 2004, p192).

Shame is a persistent reminder of obligations to others and this ethical imperative can lead to silence as it binds people to one another, to an ideal and to the nation. Like love shame is a binding emotion. The Egyptian people loved Nasser as he filled a void, he represented hope, and hope after all is essential when there has been little optimism around. Nasser was a 'defiant, living symbol of their hopes, will, and desires' (Aburish, 2004, p121). Shame and love bind as emotions that point to the importance of ethical relationships but they can also bind to the past, to that which cannot be, to facing up to truths and to mourning that which has passed and a dream that turned to dust.

The politics of mourning can serve a number of necessary processes – it can enable a community to know its ties to itself, it can allow obligations and promises to be known, acted on and thought about and it is essential in enabling the shadow of the past to dissipate. I am here adhering to the necessary distinction between mourning and melancholia. For Freud, melancholia is unashamed of its depression – it endlessly repeats, cannot allow movement or different thoughts and emotions to occur. In melancholia, as Kristeva expresses it, 'affect is the thing. The Thing is inscribed in us without memory, the buried accomplice of our unspeakable anguishes' (Kristeva, 1989, p14). Mourning in the psychoanalytic account is not a drowning in sorrow or in melancholic refrains (there is enough of that as it is) but rather to mourn is a different and more difficult process altogether. Mourning, however, can allow a different stance to be occupied, if 'one accepts that by the loss one undergoes one will be changed possibly forever. Perhaps mourning has to do with agreeing to undergo a transformation (perhaps one should say submitting to a transformation) the full result of which one cannot know in advance' (Butler, 2004, p21). Loss in the Egyptian context I would argue is the loss of a specifically nuanced fantasy of wholeness, of triumph over the future, triumph over the colonial past and of a loss of a dream. Egyptians have much to mourn, not in order to be depoliticised, anything but. Rather so that grief 'can furnish a sense of political community of a complex order, and it does this first of all by bringing to the fore the relational ties that have implications for theorising fundamental dependency and ethical responsibility' (Butler, 2004, p22). For as Arendt reminded us we are nothing without our promise to the other, without our obligations, and without giving ourselves over to an idea, an ideal, to the body politic. Mourning and remembrance I am suggesting are two possible ways forward to a different ethical future with more optimistic political possibilities. Thinking the political past anew would have to focus on that which occurred and also as Avery Gordon argues that which eludes, the 'hauntings, ghosts and gaps, seething absences, and muted presences' (Gordon, 1997, p21); and that which evades 'representation and naming' (Kristeva, 1989, p14). This requires stringent and careful thought, and a continual revisiting of what has been, and what is in the present. Resignation of thought and passive complicitness are perhaps two states of mind (individual and collective), which lead to stagnation and perpetuation and above all hinder, if not paralyse, 'movement outside of one's primary place, to a new location from which the self, and its others, are seen in a different light' (Bollas, 2003, p8).

Notes

1   Women's political activism has a history in Egypt and a careful account of secular women's activism is Nadje Al-Ali's book *Secularism, Gender and the State* (2000).
2   To repeat a commonplace Egyptian joke, Anwar al-Sadat (later President of Egypt 1970–1979) was known as Colonel Yes-Yes.
3   This six-day war as it is generally referred to in the West occurred in 1967. A series of small but significant incidents culminated in an attack by Egypt on

Israel and a spectacular and speedy defeat. The incidents centred on Israel and Syria and disagreements over land. It is unquestionable that Nasser was ill-advised to militarily attack Israel. The defeat was unexpected, stunning, and soul destroying and will be remembered as the greatest defeat of the Arabs in the twentieth century (Aburish, 2004, p249).

References

Aburish S, 2004. *Nasser – The Last Arab*. London: Duckworth

Amin G, 2000. *Whatever Happened to the Egyptians*. Cairo: The American University in Cairo Press

Al-Ali N, 2000. *Secularism, Gender and the State: The Egyptian Women's Movement*. Cambridge: Cambridge University Press

Arendt H, 1998. *The Human Condition*. Chicago: Chicago University Press

Aschroft B, Griffin G and Tiffin H, 2003. *Post-colonial Studies: The Key Concepts*. London: Routledge

Ben-Ze'ev A, 2000. *The Subtlety of Emotions*. Massachusetts: Massachusetts Institute of Technology Press

Bhabha H, 1993. Remembering Fanon: Self, Psyche and the Colonial Condition. In P Williams and L Christman, eds, *Colonial Discourse and Post-Colonial Theory: A Reader*. Hemel Hempstead: Harvester Wheatsheaf

Bollas C, 2003. *Introduction to Freud and the Non-European*. London: Verso

Butler J, 2004. *Precarious Life: The Powers of Mourning and Violence*. London: Verso

Danielson V, 1997. *The Voice of Egypt*. Chicago: Chicago University Press

Elliott A, 2002. *Psychoanalytic Theory: An Introduction*. London: Palgrave

Fanon F, 1992. The Fact of Blackness. In J Donald and A Rattansi, eds, *'Race', Culture and Difference*. London: Sage/Open University

Ghoussoub M and Sinclair-Webb E, 2000. *Imagined Masculinities: Male Identity & Culture in the Modern Middle East*. London: Saqi Books

Gordon A, 1997. *Ghostly Matters: Haunting and the Sociological Imagination*. Minneapolis: University of Minnesota Press

Kaufman G, 1992. *Shame: the power of caring*. Vermont: Schenkman Books

Kristeva J, 1989. *Black Sun: Depression and Melancholia*. New York: Columbia University Press

Lambek M, 2002. *Nuriaty, the Saint, and the Sultan: Virtuous Subject and Subjective Virtuoso of the Postmodern Colony in Postcolonial Subjectivities in Africa*. London: Zed Books

Nandy A, 1983. *The Intimate Enemy: Loss and Recovery of Self under Colonialism*. Delhi Oxford: Oxford University Press

Passerini L, 2003. Memories between silence and oblivion. In K Hodgkin and S Radstone, eds, *Contested Pasts: The Politics of Memory*. London: Routledge, 238–54

Phillips A, 1994. *On Flirtation*. London: Faber and Faber

Rose J, 1998. *States of Fantasy*. Oxford: Clarendon Press

Rose J, 2003a. Response to Edward Said in E Said. *Freud and the Non-European*. London: Verso

Rose J, 2003. *On Not Being Able To Sleep: Psychoanalysis and the Modern World*. London: Chatto & Windus

Said EW, 2000. *Out of Place: A Memoir.* London: Granta Books

Said EW, 2003. *Freud and the Non-European.* London: Verso

West-Newman CL, 2004. Anger in Legacies of Empire, Indigenous Peoples and Settler States. *European Journal of Social Theory,* 7, 2, 189–208

Index